OUR STREET

OUR STREET

*A Chronicle Written in the
Heart of Fascist Germany*

by

JAN PETERSEN

Translated by
Betty Rensen

faber and faber

This edition first published in 2009
by Faber and Faber Ltd
Bloomsbury House, 74–77 Great Russell Street
London WC1B 3DA

Printed by Books on Demand GmbH, Norderstedt

All rights reserved
© Jan Petersen, 1938
Translation © Betty Rensen, 1938

The right of Jan Petersen to be identified as author of this work
has been asserted in accordance with Section 77 of the
Copyright, Designs and Patents Act 1988

The right of Betty Rensen to be identified as translator of this work
has been asserted in accordance with Section 77 of the
Copyright, Designs and Patents Act 1988

This book is sold subject to the condition that it shall not, by way of
trade or otherwise, be lent, resold, hired out or otherwise circulated
without the publisher's prior consent in any form of binding or cover other than
that in which it is published and without a similar condition including this
condition being imposed on the subsequent purchaser

A CIP record for this book is available from the British Library

ISBN 978–0–571–25420–0

Our authorised representative in the EU for product safety is
Easy Access System Europe, Mustamäe tee 50, 10621 Tallinn, Estonia
gpsr.requests@easproject.com

AUTHOR'S PREFACE

THIS BOOK, written with great difficulty in Germany, is intended as a chronicle of the events that took place in the "red" Wallstrasse in Berlin-Charlottenburg. But, despite the local character of the narrative, it is not the history of just *one* working-class street in Fascist Germany. Fascism has resulted in similar scenes in all the towns in Germany. The list on the next page contains the names of Charlottenburg's murdered anti-Fascists. It is authentic, but certainly not complete, and yet these are the victims of this *one* district of West Berlin.

This book is dedicated to the Dead of Charlottenburg, to commemorate all the victims of Fascism. It is meant to describe the courage of thousands, of tens of thousands, of nameless proletarian heroes. Threatened by the axe, by brutal imprisonment, they fearlessly continue their fight—the great fight for the deliverance of the German people! For Socialism !

JAN PETERSEN.

THE CHARLOTTENBURG DEATH LIST

Before January 30th, 1933

Oskar Owege	20 years old	Shot by the Schupos
Erich Frischmann	26	,, ,, ,, ,, ,, ,,
Hans Klaffert	19	,, ,, Murdered by S.A. Storm 33
Erich Ziemke	22	,, ,, ,, ,, ,, ,, ,,
Otto Grüneberg	20	,, ,, ,, ,, ,, ,, ,,
Max Schirmer	32	,, ,, ,, ,, ,, ,, ,,
Erich Lange	24	,, ,, ,, ,, ,, ,, ,,

After January 30th, 1933

Paul Schulz	20 years old	Murdered by S.A. Storm 33
Hans Schall	21	,, ,, ,, ,, ,, ,, ,,
Walter Harnecker	25	,, ,, ,, ,, ,, ,, ,,
Fritz Kolosche	24	,, ,, ,, ,, ,, ,, ,,
Martin Michallak	25	,, ,, ,, ,, ,, ,, ,,
Paul Voss	29	,, ,, ,, ,, ,, ,, ,,
Karl Malz	28	,, ,, ,, ,, ,, ,, ,,
Hans Mueller	46	,, ,, ,, ,, ,, ,, ,,
Walter Drescher	30	,, ,, ,, ,, ,, ,, ,,
Georg Stolt	43	,, ,, ,, ,, ,, ,, ,,
Richard Hüttig	26	,, ,, Beheaded in Berlin-Plötzensee on 14.6.34.

FOREWORD

by THE TRANSLATOR

IS THIS A NOVEL? The author had no intention, he says, of writing a novel when he started the book. He began by noting down the events as they occurred. But he soon realised that he must disguise some of the people concerned, and in certain cases transpose the events to different surroundings to prevent the Nazis suspecting himself and the comrades he was describing. It was therefore natural that this chronicle of the events that took place in Berlin-Charlottenburg between January 1933 and June 1934 should develop into a kind of novel. But it is no novel in the strict sense of the word. Everything the author has described is true, although Ede's name may not be Ede, and he has no " ugly raw cavity in place of one eye." The book is authentic in content but not always in form.

The names of the dead published by the author are all real names. The events leading to their death, as recorded in the book, are also all genuine. But many more murders and executions have taken place: they could not all be recounted here, because of the possible repercussions on relatives and friends. The author had, therefore, to be content with the names in the death-list. These names are all well known in Berlin-Charlottenburg, and in some cases the families have emigrated beyond the reach of Nazi " justice."

The author began writing this book because he and his comrades felt that, if the thinking men and women of the world could learn what Fascism really means, they would rally to the support of the German anti-Fascists. For the German anti-Fascists are not waging their great fight for liberty and justice for Germany alone; Germany and Spain are to-day the two main battle-fields on which the world-struggle for peace and democracy is being fought. Fascist Germany is one of the prime factors making for a disastrous world war: the very nature of Fascism makes war inevitable. And if the united anti-Fascist struggle is successful, then a great step forward for world peace, a first step toward liberty, equality, and fraternity, will have been taken.

But the German anti-Fascists cannot win " on their own "; they require aid. They have redoubled their efforts in the subterranean war against the National-Socialists since they have known that world opinion is on their side. The Reichstag counter-trial conducted in London, the questions in Parliament, and the anti-Fascist demonstrations everywhere, fired their enthusiasm. All this even penetrated the prisons and Concentration Camps in Germany, strengthening the resolve of the imprisoned anti-Fascists to remain firm, heightening their courage in the face of death.

It is difficult for anyone who has not lived in Germany to realise the conditions. But living in the country does not mean a four or six weeks' tour of inspection. The horrors and oppression described by some of these visitors is but a fraction of the whole. Only a few of the foreign journalists who still manage to keep up some of their old connections have any idea of what is going on. The official denials, which do not contain one grain of truth, unfortunately command more attention than authentic reports.

It has already been mentioned that the author noted down events as they occurred. The actual writing of the book took place in circumstances hardly less difficult. He was working on part of it at a quiet seaside resort. The other guests were very anxious to know what he was doing, and kept on asking the landlord why the young man never came down to the beach and what he was writing all the time. They were referred to the author, who produced a very thrilling love story with sufficient villains, blackmailers, innocent young girls, and exotic vamps, to satisfy the most exacting demands. It was not the first time that this manuscript had done duty. One has to be equipped for every possible situation in illegal work, even to the extent of putting oneself into the appropriate mental state by means of auto-suggestion. It was on

FOREWORD

this that the success of smuggling the book out of Germany depended.

The author was to all appearance crossing the frontier to go for a few days' ski-ing. But though he was wearing full ski costume, with a rucksack on his back, and carrying a small case with just one change of clothes, the customs examination was very strict. The official asked where he was going, made him open his case, felt all the pockets of the only jacket and inside the two pairs of socks, and even squeezed the tie to feel if there were any papers hidden in the lining. Having passed everything, he asked him what he had in the rucksack.

" Oh, nothing much." The author was quite obviously embarrassed as he slipped the haversack off his shoulders. Then, in a burst of confidence: " Well, you know what women are, don't you ? I told my wife I was only going away for three days, but she would go and bake me two whopping big cakes. It'll take me a week to eat one. Just look at the size of them."

The official took a quick glance at the two golden brown cakes and smiled understandingly.

" That's all right. Why, my wife's just the same," he said, and started telling him all about his own wife.

The manuscript had been baked in the cakes. The trick is a very old one and has often been used. In the ordinary way the official would have broken the cakes in half to see whether there was anything in them. But the talk about wives, and the author's obvious embarrassment, had seemed so genuine that the man had been deceived. The author had rehearsed the scene at least twenty times. His fate, had he been discovered, does not bear thinking of.

BETTY RENSEN.

SATURDAY, January 21st, 1933. I walk through the Wallstrasse in the evening with my comrades Richard Hüttig and Franz Zander. We stop at the corner of the Berlinerstrasse. Glaring arc-lamps above us. An unceasing stream of cars and trams. " There comes another batch," says Richard, nudging me. Three dusty open lorries come from the left. They rumble slowly through the circle of light cast by the lamps. Brown uniforms stand packed together in the lorry. The rays of light from the lamps show up a few boyish faces for the space of a second. They glance at us with curiosity, astonishment at the big town written on their faces. Richard reads the registration number of the last lorry.

" All of them from the country, called up to the last man," he says.

Franz Zander nods. " They're all farm workers."

He leans against the lamp-post.

" I once worked for farmers. It used to be the Stahlhelm[1] that got the jobs; now it's the S.A.[2] Otherwise there's no work."

An open car drives past; six brown uniforms sit on the collapsible seats.

" S.A. patrol cars ! " says Richard.

The Nazi[3] headquarters, the Hohenzollern banqueting-rooms, are only a few streets further on. More of their cars patrol the streets at regular intervals. The police never examine *them* for weapons.

" Let's go," says Franz curtly, and turns on his heel.

The Wallstrasse, with its crowded rows of houses, dimly lit by a few gas-lamps, lies before us like a long grey defile. Three Schupos[4] stand in a doorway. They have buckled their chin-straps under the chin. The barrels of their rifles show up above their shoulders.

[1] All notes will be found at the end of the book.

"They've been reinforced!"

People are standing in front of all the doors. They talk in whispers, as if they feared to wake someone. We nod to them. Richard raises two fingers to his cap, as if he were pacing down the lines of his Buildings Defence Groups. The street makes a sharp bend in the centre. There is a wide gap in the row of houses here. A building site, with rubbish-heaps and a dingy grey fence. Our political slogans, pasted over with the tattered posters of a wandering circus. Close by, the Charlottenburg Power Works, a large modern red-brick building. Low wooden houses stretch away to the left of the works. Lights still burn in all the windows. Temporary billets, run up in the years of the greatest housing scarcity, they have now become permanent dwellings. Nearly all the tenants are unemployed.

Suddenly Richard stops. He looks up at the solitary detached gable on the left that towers above the billets. It is quiet here, ominously quiet. Only the dull hum of the machines that run day and night comes from the huge windows of the Power Works.

"Our party slogans," says Richard.

High up on the gable in large painted letters:

ANTI-FASCISTS! VOTE FOR LIST THREE! COMMUNIST PARTY! RED FRONT!

Richard and Ede! Ede, the best climber in our district, lowered at night by a rope from the roof on to a swaying plank to paint our election slogans. The police don't dare to get up there even during the day, although the words burn their eyes like pepper. The illuminated row of windows in the gable seems to hang suspended in the night.

A gas explosion some years ago demolished the front of the house near the gable. Only the hall door was left, a miserable survival. The crumbling walls of the back yard now face the street. We see a few sticks of furniture behind the windows, the lines on which the washing is drying.

Werner's beer-house, near the gable, is our meeting-place. We cross the road. Our sentries stand outside.

" Red Front ! "

" Red Front ! "

There are small round holes in the window-panes. Revolver shots from the S.A. Stormtroop 33. Round brass plates are fixed in the upper half of the pane. The insurance company has had the window repaired several times already.

" Anything special ? "

" No, Comrade Hüttig, only the police cars. . . ." The sentry stops speaking, nodding his head towards the bend in the street. For a second, headlights blind us. Slowly the car drives past.

Glistening helmets. Rifles.

" They've been here twice already. Searching for arms . . . here . . . in our place ! " says the sentry mockingly.

Richard opens the door. A clamour of voices strikes us. The fat, white-bearded landlord nods to us from the bar. His red-faced wife is washing the glasses. Clouds of smoke float towards the ceiling. A feeling of suspense; my nerves react immediately. An excited group stands round the large centre table.

" . . . To-morrow is the Nazi's dress rehearsal. Will the Social Democrats[5] . . . . ? "

" I have spoken to a good many; they will be on the streets with us to-morrow," says Franz quietly.

" Since the 20th of July a lot realise . . ."

" From realising to fighting . . ." replies the other dubiously.

" Ready-made " draws a paper from his pocket. He is an assistant at Brennickmayer's Ready-to-Wear Tailoring Establishment, and has to dress like a " gentleman." He reads from the paper:

" . . . It is to be hoped that the Chief Commissioner of Police will even at this late hour realise the seriousness of the situation."

" As if the police would side with us."

"Even my Social-Democrat pals laughed at that. They are going to meet me to-morrow!"

I glance over his shoulder at the paper. A photo of the Karl Liebknecht[6] House, and above it in large letters:

S.A. PARADE TO THE BÜLOWPLATZ![7]

As if that were no provocation!

Behind us the door flies open. We turn round. A young comrade leans his bicycle against the shop-window and enters.

"For Comrade Franz," he says.

The latter nods. "Correct."

The youth searches in his pocket and hands over a folded slip of paper. The door immediately shuts noisily behind him. Conversation is silenced. All eyes watch the white slip of paper.

Franz nods to me and Richard. He passes in front of us, swaying his broad shoulders. "Strong Jim," we had once nicknamed him.

We go into the next room. Franz hands us the slip of paper.

"Instructions for to-morrow. You know already what to do with your Buildings Defence Groups, Richard."

"Yes, I must go now." Richard shakes hands firmly.

Franz calls in the comrades, one at a time. A circle of serious faces. He looks at them all in turn, as if he wanted once again to put each one to the test. He speaks with cool emphasis.

"I don't need to say much, comrades. We can't surrender Berlin to the Fascists without a fight. I shall inform the leaders later of the meeting-point for to-morrow. We shall start from various streets in scattered groups. See that they are all punctual and that no one fails. Sleep in your clothes to-night, three or five together. The workers expect our protection. Is that clear?"

A silent nod all round. The room empties.

We are the last to leave—Franz, Rothacker, "Ready-made," and myself. Our steps echo in the empty street.

The buildings warned; defence posts on the alert. If there is fighting to-morrow, the works must close down on Monday. Although the best have long since had the sack. Franz, Rothacker, and so many others.

We arrive at Rothacker's house. He goes upstairs. From the town hall clock come the hour strokes, and die away between the walls. The police car still patrols. Its headlights flood the street for a few seconds and disappear. A car hoots drowsily; now and then lorries rattle past. The Brown Shirts[8] are still rolling into the city!

Rothacker has returned. He is standing near Franz. The little clerk seems even smaller in the twilight, and his nickel glasses to have grown larger. We listen to him talking quietly and haltingly.

" Franz, if anything should happen to me to-morrow, I'm not frightened. . . ."

He breathes deeply.

". . . You'll see to Edith and the boy, won't you ? "

" Don't get upset, Erich. It won't be so bad."

Franz says that, but he doesn't believe it himself.

". . . Well, in any case, you can rest assured ! "

Rothacker grips his hand.

. . . .

We walk slowly through the streets. Käthe, my girl, hangs on my arm. She is wearing her new navy blue dress. Franz, her brother, goes on in front of us. He has Hilde on his arm. Nearly all of us are wearing our Sunday clothes.

Berlin has become an armed camp overnight. Police patrols, six and eight strong, pass us, rifles over their shoulders, chin-straps of the shakos buckled under their chins. Double sentries stand in front of every third house.

" Fifteen thousand police have been called up," says Rothacker in a low voice.

We come to Moabit. The *kleine Tiergarten* is the assembling-point of the S.A. The square is surrounded by a double cordon of Schupos; behind them stand S.A. Groups. From the neighbouring streets come troops of Brown Shirts, flanked by police. Mounted police occupy the park entrance. Police lorries drive past us with the side-flaps down, ready for jumping down into the crowd. The pavements are black with people. We mingle with the stream of passers-by, and are slowly pushed forward. We mustn't lose contact! But there are the others. Franz, Ernst, Paul, and " Fuzzy."

A volley of voices from across the square: " Down with the Brown Shirt murderers! Down! Down! Down!"

The mounted police pull their horses round; the police charge the crowd on the pavement. The faces under the shakos stand out hard and set; the rifles are reversed.

" Move on! Break up! Break up!"

Sounds of blows and cries of " Shame! Shame!"

I glance at Käthe. Her face is small and pale in her fur collar. The police break into the crowd. Two Schupos on our left rush a young worker to a waiting lorry. He runs bent double; they have twisted his arms behind his back. And they are still hitting him!

" The dirty dogs! Let's stop them!" snorts Rothacker.

I grab his arm. " Stay here! That's what they're waiting for!"

From the other side of the street a song is heard. The " Internationale."[9] The song wavers, ends in wild cries. The Brown Shirt column begins its march. A double cordon of police runs along with it. I am struck by the S.A. flank guards, without exception well-built fellows. Their trouser pockets bulge, with well-defined edges. Revolvers!

They sing:

" *Die rote Front, schlagt sie zu Brei,*
S.A. marschiert, Achtung die Strasse frei! "[10]

Cries drown the song. " Red Front! Down with the Brown Shirts!"

A signal whistle. The police cordon again rushes at us. Now they're hitting with their rifle-butts. We are pressed

against the wall of a house; many escape into the doorways. There, on the right! In the confusion a working woman runs through the police cordon. She stands a moment in front of the brown column, throws her arms in the air, and shrieks:
" A procession of cowards! Send the police home! You heroes!"

A Schupo drags her away.

Slowly the procession approaches the centre of the town, the people on the pavements continually increasing in number. From the windows they cry: " Murderers! Murderers!" A flower-pot flies through the air, right into the brown procession. Three Schupos rush into the house and others turn the barrels of their rifles on the windows.

" Close the windows! Close the windows!" Shrill whistling from the house, but most of the windows close with a snap. Suddenly our procession on the pavement comes to a stop. Advances a few times, like a car with a throttled motor, and then finally stops. In front they are waving their hands. Back! Back! I climb on to a low railing. Fifty yards in front of us the street is filled from one side to the other with black shakos, through which the brown procession pushes. Finished! Cut off! The crowd on the pavement wavers. The police clear the streets! Rothacker waves his arms excitedly about, his cheeks flushing.

" What now? What now?"

" First get back, and then ahead through the side-streets. We must get to the Bülowplatz. Pass the word on!"

Rothacker works his way forwards to Franz and his group.

" Round by the side-streets!" is whispered from mouth to mouth.

The police have halted opposite us. They point their rifles at the pavement. Behind them the Brown Shirts draw away.

" Käthe!"

She looks at me. Small light-sparks burn in her eyes. " If they stop us, we want to get to the Underground. Are you afraid?"

Käthe shakes her head. We come to a street-crossing. The police are holding up the demonstration and letting the traffic through. We run across the road, turn into a small side-street in scattered groups. Where are Franz, Rothacker, the others? Damn, the traffic has been signalled on: they have arrived at the crossing too late. We must carry on! The street is strangely quiet here. People lean out of the windows. Groups stand in front of the house doors, talking in whispers. Feeble singing comes from the side-street on the right, further on. Suddenly a Schupo column comes running round the corner, shouting: " Shut the windows ! Shut the front doors ! "

The people have disappeared. Windows rattle down, doors slam to. The hasty catching of their locks is heard.

" Keep calm ! Carry on ! " I whisper to Käthe.

She squeezes my hand. The walls of the houses re-echo the tramping of the heavy boots. Suddenly a rubber baton is thrust in our faces.

" Get back ! Go on, and quick ! "

I answer quite calmly :

" We want to get to the Underground ! "

The Schupo looks at us wildly. His face is red and perspiring. Käthe's forced nonchalance just turns the scales.

" To the right—but quickly—to the trams. The Underground is closed ! "

Then he runs on. The trams ! Why hadn't I thought of that? By tram to the demonstration point. The tram is packed. The conductor stands wedged in the middle of the car, and, like the others, peers through the panes. The men on the platform shout directions.

" There's still room in front ! Squeeze up a bit ! "

" Get out now ! " someone cries.

The conductor rings the bell twice. The car is empty in a second. We walk slowly up the street. Hundreds with us. Surprisingly few shakos are to be seen here. " Ernst Machnow: Bicycles " I read over a shop on the other side of the street. The name sticks in my head. The street seems quite deserted. Not a soul at the windows. The shutters are let down in front of the shop windows. A chorus of voices: " Down with Fascism ! " And then three times: " Up with the Red Front!" I shout and shout. Käthe drags at my arm.

"There! There!"

I hear the shop window-panes near us rattle behind the sliding shutters. From the end of the street a grey monster comes rumbling towards us. An armoured car! I look at the faces around me. They hold no new expression; quiet indifference. A man with a bristly moustache is standing in the gutter and laughing. His hands are in his trouser pockets. The others around him begin to laugh also. Shrill signal whistles pierce the air; the tank drives past. In the tower, the barrel of the machine gun moves from side to side! Pale strips of faces show behind the loopholes.

Those in front suddenly start running. A police charge? Where? No! They are forming up on the road. We run. In a second the crowd lines up four rows deep, swells, fills the whole street. We sing the "Internationale!" The narrow street reverberates. Next to Käthe marches a man with a grey beard, his mouth wide open, his body jerking to the beat of the song. On the lapel of his coat something gleams bright and metallic. Three arrows![11] Our glances meet. We still sing. The old comrade nods his head back and forwards. Then I see! More arrows gleam in the row! My pulse quickens; I glow with enthusiasm. I nudge Käthe. She understands, smiles.

How long have we been marching along—minutes? It seems to have been half an hour already. In front they turn into the Gormanstrasse. Wrong! A blind alley. Screams and whipcracks from the head of the procession. They are shooting too! We are pushed back. Everybody rushes into the doorways. Back, back at all costs. Käthe hangs heavily on my arm, her mouth twitching nervously. I shake her.

"Käthe! Käthe! No panic!"

We force ourselves to walk composedly to a doorway. The cordon of Schupos is only five yards away. The pistol barrels are levelled at the crowd. The shots crack out ceaselessly. The dull gleam of the metal, the small blue puffs of smoke, are within grasping reach. At our side, a man in a blue jacket suddenly throws up his arms. He turns slowly on his heels, then falls flat on the asphalt. We reach a front door, and are pushed in. Käthe rushes to the stairs.

"Stay here!"

If they come after us, we are properly bottled in upstairs. We wait, and wait. From behind the front door pane we see the police running past. Next to us a woman stands with a little girl hanging on to her hand. She tries to shut out the sounds with her other hand, her face working.

"Oh, God! Oh, God! What will happen—will happen?" she keeps on repeating.

The shots sound further away. I step out. The street is empty. We leave.

An army of Schupos, with armoured cars with nests of machine guns on the roofs, hold the streets around the Bülowplatz clear for the Brown Shirts' demonstration.

. . . .

The next evening. We are sitting in the parlour at Franz Zander's. Hilde is talking.

"My mother says Felix was running around the whole day. In the afternoon he came home and lay down on the sofa. Then an S.A. man came to fetch him with orders that he was to report at the Stormtroop[12] centre at once. New instructions had come in and the group leader was waiting. They fancy themselves since yesterday, I can tell you."

Franz plays with the tassels of the tablecloth. Hilde has told us all about her family, including her brother Felix. "Lamp-post," Stormtroop No. 33 calls him, because he is so tall. He is troop leader. The Trettins have a doorkeeper's job quite near us, in the Berlinerstrasse. Hilde's father has been unemployed for years. He is an unskilled worker, and has never bothered about politics. "You've got to earn your grub, that's all," is his maxim. The doorkeeper's job does not even guarantee him that. He rides out on his bicycle twice a week, to poach rabbits and fish. Mrs. Trettin looks after the job and Inge, their five-year-old daughter. Hilde is a typist—the only one in the family who earns any money. For Felix, the locksmith, is also out of work. He entered the S.A. just a year ago. " Because I don't always want to spend my life on the dole, and to be treated like dirt ! " he once explained to Hilde. " And I've had just about enough of being put up with here at home. I can sleep at our billets and there's always some grub going. I usen't to count for anything before, but in uniform I am somebody, whatever comes of it."

It's all the same to old Trettin " what that scamp does." But he always growls at him, because " the bloody lot of uniforms can't do anything else but trample all over me 'ouse." Hilde has been with us for six months. Käthe had got to know her at a commercial night-school. Hilde is very attached to Franz. They have become comrades, but Felix knows nothing about all that.

Mother Zander comes in from the kitchen with a pot of coffee. She even places a dish of cakes on the table. She moves her chair under the gas-lamp, starts knitting. I would very much like to say something pleasant to her, but nothing occurs to me. She has warm brown eyes, deep folds round the mouth, on her forehead. They are the imprints of life's ups and downs, hard and true. Käthe had told me what Mother Zander had said when Franz got the sack because he had organised a strike in the factory. She had been quiet for a second; after a moment's thought she had commented: " We'll manage. Father would have done the same."

Father was a Social-Democrat. Had fallen in France.

" It's a job, sometimes, to keep quiet," Hilde continues. " Only this evening Felix was bragging. ' Yesterday we showed Berlin something ! Our movement marches on; they can't stop it now. We saw yesterday that the Communists are down and out ! They jeered from the side-streets, that was all.' "

Franz stirs his cup. His fair eyebrows are contracted.

Then Hilde continues: " They must have thought that we . . ."

Franz glances at her sharply. We say nothing. Nobody

seems able to talk; the depressed atmosphere remains until the end.

. . . .

Three days have passed since the Brown Shirt demonstration.

To-day it is *we* who are marching. We are marching to the Bülowplatz. It is icy cold. The windows of the houses, of the trams, are frosted over. Our breath comes white from our mouths. The sudden bitter frost bores its way into the thin worn-out clothes. Faces, hands, are numbed.

The procession turns a corner. I glance back. Endless rows of four, and above them the red banners, as far as the eye can see.

" The district has never turned out so well before ! " says Rothacker. His nose is a bluish-red; his coat-collar is turned up; he appears slighter and shorter than ever. In front they start singing.

" *Im Januar um Mitternacht, ein Spartakist stand auf der Wacht. . . .*"[13]

The song is taken up along the procession, leaps past us. Left—left, tramp the feet.

The faces are serious and hard. Look, this is how *we* march ! Without tanks. Without machine guns. *We* are Berlin, working Berlin.

In the row in front of me, Heinz Preuss, a young comrade, carries our flag. He has no overcoat; his shoes are burst on one side, his lips one thin blue stripe. Heinz has been unemployed for years. Next to him marches Paul Teichert, a turner at Siemens'. He has his mess-tin with him; the blue coffee-can sticks out under his arm. On our left a police lorry drives slowly. They are wearing heavy coats, but sit crouched together like hens. Others run alongside the procession at short intervals. They have protectors over their ears. We are singing:

" *. . . und donnernd dröhnt die Art'llerie, Spartakus hat nur Infantrie. . . .*"[14]

A Schupo suddenly comes running along the length of the procession. He has a notebook in his hand. He halts, turns the pages, raises his head. " Stop ! Verboten ! " he yells. The song breaks off, but they are still singing in front.

" Stay at home ! We don't need you ! " someone from behind us cries across to the police lorry.

" On Sunday the S.A. sang about smashing us up. You didn't stop them ! " another calls.

" New song ! New song ! "

I see the officer on the lorry giving an order. The Schupos jump down.

" Ow ! Ow ! "

" . . . *wir kreisen wachsam über'm Sowjetstaate, die erste rote Luftarmee der Welt. . . .*"[15]

The Schupo with the notebook is again here. We are in the middle of the town already. On the pavement stand dense rows of people; they wave and raise their fists in the Communist salute: " Red Front ! Red Front ! "

People stand in the shop doors. Faces peer through the half-melted frost on the windows.

" . . . *und höher, und höher, und höher, wir steigen trotz Hass und Hohn. . . .*"[16]

The Schupo must at last have recognised the song by the refrain and found it in his book.

" Stop ! Verboten ! Verboten ! " His voice ends in a screech.

We obey. But in front the song is not cut short. They could not have heard the order. A file of police run past us, their rubber truncheons ready in their hands. A shrill whistle.

" . . . *ein jeder Propeller singt surrend . . .*"[17]

The song in front is hastily stopped short. Confusion and shrieks:

" Shame ! Shame ! "

They are using their truncheons on the procession! Yet from the very front the thin tones still come:

"... *wir schützen die Sowjetunion!* "[18]

A little further on we see five arrested men sitting on the lorry. As we near our goal, we pass masses of people packed on the pavements. All wave and call out: " Up the Red Front ! " to us. Three days ago, rage and disgust. To-day, open solidarity !

" *Die S.A. hat gold'ne Tressen—und das Volk hat nichts zu fressen!* "[19]

A clear voice rings out above the noise of the procession, then counts: " Two ! Three ! " Caught up by the many voices, the sentences re-echo from the walls of the houses Suddenly the marching steps cease, the ranks waver.

" They are arresting him ! "
" Who ? "
" Don't know ! "
" Fuzzy ! Fuzzy ! "

The procession moves on. Two Schupos hurry past us, Fuzzy, so called because of his thick shock of hair, between them. I see them pushing him on to the lorry along with the others already arrested.

Endless streets. We sing the " Internationale," " Bruder zur Sonne, zur Freiheit "[20]—ten, twenty times over. They are the only songs which are not accompanied by the cry: " Verboten ! "

" Halt ! Halt ! Stand still ! "
" What's the matter ? "
" Another district is turning in ahead of us. The street is full ! "

We wait, and wait. An icy wind comes from the Spree, and sends cold shivers down my back. I see Preuss's teeth chattering. He is still holding the flag. He won't give it up. In front, on our right, the other procession pushes its way round the corner. We stamp our feet, beat our arms about.

I rub Käthe's hands. Her face is small and frozen. Our procession turns into the Kaiser Wilhelmstrasse. We are quite near the Bülowplatz. Two processions stand side by side in the wide street. Eight abreast. They wait. We on the left move slowly forward.

" What are you standing still for ? "

" Don't talk too soon, you'll be standing before long too," laughs someone from the other side. " All the streets are full. They've been marching past the Karl Liebknecht House for hours, my lad ! "

Another ten yards. We stand still. Twelve abreast now. The whole width of the street is a densely packed mass of heads. All are singing. The sky is already reflecting the glare from the lights of the town. From the houses, the shops, women come running with steaming saucepans and cups in their hands.

" There, drink ; you must be frozen ! "

Hands pass slices of bread across.

" For the unemployed ! They'll be hungry ! "

In front of me, Preuss is munching bread and warming his hands on the cup.

" A change from last Sunday, when the Brown Shirts were here ! " says Käthe.

Where are the police ? Nowhere to be seen. The procession moves on. There ! The Bülowplatz—the Party House !

Red banners are drawn across the full length of the housefronts. Our fists fly up in salute ; the song is silenced. On the platform stands Thälmann ![21] A few others near him.

Behind me someone whispers : " The central committee."

Thälmann's fist, his face under the peaked cap, is left behind. " He's been standing there for hours in the icy cold," says Rothacker. His eyes shine behind the nickel glasses. Gone !

Clap, clap, go our boots. We march away without speaking.

. . . .

Two days later I am walking aimlessly down the Wallstrasse. It is early forenoon. Suddenly someone touches me on the shoulder from behind.

" Hello, Ede."

Ede turns his head round so that his right eye can see me. In place of the left one he has a glistening fleshy cavity. A red scar, the breadth of two fingers, runs from it to his ear. The lobe of that ear is a small lump of flesh rolled together. A wad of cotton wool is stuck in the middle. On his left arm he wears the yellow ribbon with the three black spots of the blind.

" Catchin' flies, eh ? Time to spare ? "

" Yes. Why ? "

" I'm goin' to the Relief Centre. No tin as per usual. Goin' to 'ave a go at the director. Got the 'ole bunch o' tricks wiv me ! "

" O.K. I'll come along."

Ede talks all the time. He has had a row with the landlord over the rent. He was two months in arrears. Stomachs come first ! Had I seen Franz to-day ? He must settle up his collecting list. Erich Hoffman—" Three-spotted Ede," as we call him—had taken part in a raiding-party during the war. His eye, and half an ear, had been torn away by a handgrenade. He has the Iron Cross, First Class, and the golden badge for the wounded. I was sure he had " the bag o' tricks "—his war medals—with him from the moment I saw the blind man's ribbon. He wears it only when he has to go to the authorities—or when he is " working " with us. Ede's speciality is painting our slogans on the dock walls and house gables while standing on a board swaying at the end of a rope. But he can also leave marks from his fists—when the Nazis attack us. He can see all right with his one eye. Ede has appeared before the courts dozens of times. When the Nazi witnesses had to identify him, they would become doubtful, and that saved him. The man with the ribbon of the war-blinded and the one eye had not been present ! Before the judge lay his military papers, all in order. This difficulty at recognising Ede is not surprising. He always wears his glass eye unless there is trouble ahead, when it wanders into his pocket and out comes the blind ribbon.

I sit in the waiting-room of the Relief Centre. Ede has just been called in to the director. The benches ranged against the dirty grey walls are closely packed, and the rest of the room is crowded. All have patched clothes and haggard faces. On my right two women are talking.

" Meat ? I've never bin able ter cook meat with my greens ! "

" But then you've only got to steam the cabbage, and not boil it, or all the goodness gets lost."

" Steamin' ? That's just as dear. That only uses up more fat."

The air is thick, dry waves of heat that burn the throat come from the stove in the corner. But they all press towards it, for they need warmth. A small pale woman sits on my left. She is rocking a baby on her arm. It cries softly and hiccups.

" Buh—buh—buh——" she quietens it.

" ' They'll still do. We can't give you any new ones. At the most, we can 'ave 'em mended,' 'e sez ter me a week ago ! "

A man with thinning grey hair shows his boots to his neighbour. The leather has split across the instep and along the sides; the grey socks can be seen.

" But I'll bloody well 'ang on to 'em ! They finks 'as 'ow they can bloody well do what they pleases wiv the likes of us, do they ? " he continues.

His neighbour, a young fellow, laughs contemptuously.

" Adolf'll give yer a new pair. 'E's talkin' bizniss already with the Dusseldorf banks, at Schröder's[22] 'ouse ! Don't yer fink it'll be abaht yer boots an' orl ? " he asks with biting scorn.

" The b—— ! " says another. " Goebbels used ter write aginst 'em in the *Angriff!*[23] The fine people as lays 'emselves in the beds we make, and Papen,[24] the arf dotty b—— ! "

The door of the office flies open. I can hear Ede's voice:

" Expec' me ter go 'ungry, eh ? But you could let me leave me 'ealth in the trenches. I tells yer once more: at your expense I'm goin' ter eat right now. At Aschinger's.[25] At your bloody hexpense!"

"I warn you!" comes an angry voice from the other room.

Ede closes the door with a bang, and comes across to us.

"Which of yer blokes is 'ungry?"

Silence! They stare at him, puzzled.

"What d'yer mean 'ungry? We've all got the gripes from 'aving empty stomiks," says the young fellow.

"Come on! Five of yer. A good feed. I'm payin'," says Ede.

No one moves.

But a few minutes later we are on our way. Five of us. The young fellow, a stranger to me, and two other comrades, whom I had not noticed in the room.

"Pick what yer wants!" urges Ede, as we sit in Aschinger's restaurant. "What yer fancies. Pr'tend it's Sunday to-day."

I order a cutlet. But the two are suddenly quite shy. For them, Ede tells the waiter: "Knuckle o' 'am with *sauerkraut*. But big 'uns!"

We eat. Ede does the talking. We nod, and smile nervously. I don't feel too pleased with the affair.

"Now a good 'arf-pint an' a cigar, eh?" asks Ede as we finish. We shrug our shoulders. But Ede gives the order. He himself has eaten two portions. We had quietly, but firmly, declined a second helping. The mugs are empty, the cigars smoked to the end.

"Now vamoose. I'll stay on," explains Ede.

We don't wait to be told twice. The waiter looks after us. I can feel his glance in the back of my neck. Outside, I look back through a corner of the window. Ede beckons to the waiter, who gasps and rushes off to fetch the manager. The latter waves his arms; his broad face reddens. Heads are turned from all the tables. Why should I . . . as well? I walk to the next corner and wait. Soon after, two Schupos run across the street. They come out of the restaurant a few seconds later with Ede between them. They are taking him

to the police station in the next street. I follow them at a distance, wait at the corner. Twenty minutes pass, half an hour. I shiver. There's Ede now, coming out of the building. Alone! He signals to me, grins. At the next corner I join him.
" Man alive! "
" What's the trouble? " laughs Ede. " I jus' laid the bag o' tricks on the table before that there sergeant.' 'Ave I got ter starve, me a soldier from the front line? ' I sez to 'im."
" And at Aschinger's? "
" The waiter chap's only one of us," says Ede. " I hexplained to that there manager; it ain't 'is fault. ' Ring up the Relief Centre; the director knows all abaht it.' "
" They'll make you pay for that."
Ede nudges me. " What can they do? Eight, p'r'aps fourteen days. I can sit through that on 'arf my backside! "

. . . .

At noon on January 30th a rumour spreads to all the apartments in the Wallstrasse: Hitler is Reichs Chancellor. Hitler is—I must read that myself! The midday editions are snatched from the hands of the newspaper sellers at the corner. The headlines of the paper stare back at me from the houses, from the stairs, and now lie in front of me on the table:

ADOLF HITLER: REICHS CHANCELLOR!

I read the lines underneath, read them again. Franz! I must see Franz! A knock at the door. Franz! I let him in. He shakes hands; walks slowly along the corridor, as if seeking my room, as if it was the first time he had come here. Then he takes off his cap. His fair hair is damp with sweat, his lips a thin line. He looks old. It seems to me that years have passed since I last saw him.

" You go with Ernst Schwiebus and inform your groups of five," he says. " The demonstration is at seven. The old gathering-place. See that everything goes quickly! "

His grey eyes gleam, and he speaks curtly, as though he

were only repeating something that had been arranged long before. He has already finished with the newspaper report; by now he is thinking one step ahead.

" See to it—I must get on ! "

I want to talk, want to tell him everything that surges up in me. But Franz is already at the door, nods to me, goes down the stairs in large strides.

Demonstrate—again ? ! As if we wanted to fill ourselves with demonstrating once more ! What remains for our private lives ? The day after to-morrow is February 1st. I wanted to move into the Zanders' then. We wanted to get married, Käthe and I, but last week they took in Willi. He is on the run. Has fled from Central Germany. They are searching for him. He had smuggled pamphlets into a Reichswehr[26] barracks. So everything remains as before. Five of us can't live in two rooms.

Evening comes. We walk down our street in small groups. It is like an ants' nest which someone has disturbed. People stand gossiping excitedly outside all the front doors. The meeting-ground is one swarming mass of people, which begins to line up into rows of four. There is a tense feeling. I can't see a flag anywhere. Then I realise the reason : they would immediately be confiscated ! The demonstration hasn't even been notified. Foolish idea ! How could it be ? Where are the police ? None to be seen.

There is our section.

" 'Evening," I say hastily.

Käthe gives me her hand. She is pleased.

" Is Willi here as well ? "

She looks at me in astonishment.

" No. He has to be careful."

" I'll march with the Buildings Defence Groups," I say quickly. I am annoyed. To think that I had asked that silly question about Willi !

" They're in front. I'll stay here," replies Käthe.

Only a few seconds have passed. In front, the procession is already starting to move. I run. A red flag suddenly rises above the marchers, on the left—there—another one ! Here come the police! In small groups they run alongside the procession, chin-straps under the chin. A police lorry drives up, closely packed with blue uniforms. How long the procession is! Rows of sturdy young fellows now come marching along—the Buildings Defence Groups, Richard Hüttig and Franz Zander at their head. They glance quickly at me as I walk up to them.

" They won't allow any more of our demonstrations after this one! " I hear Franz say.

His voice sounds bitter.

Hüttig's face works.

" Yes—then the Party will be suppressed! "

"... *reinen Tisch macht mit dem Bedränger-Heer der Sklaven wache auf* ..."[27]

We sing. It suddenly seems like a new song to us, as if we were singing it for the first time. It makes me glow; my heart beats faster.

"... *Erkämpft das Menschenrecht.* ..."[28]

The song ends. Only the tramp of our feet is heard. Few police, they hold back. They know that they haven't got only demonstrators before them, but also an extremely excited crowd, determined and filled with hate. The narrow, badly lit streets, the dense rows of people on the pavements; they'll think twice before ...

Franz looks at Richard Hüttig.

" Some turn-out to-day! The side-streets are packed. They're all here; many Social-Democrats as well."

" If only it weren't too late! "

A clear, strong voice suddenly calls out:

" Down with the Hitler Government! Down with Fascism! "

" Down! Down! Down! " cry thousands of voices.

On the police lorry the headlights, that have been keeping watch on the windows, are turned to the spot where the cry came from. Groups of Schupos hurry past. I see them ready to pounce on the procession over there. But they soon separate; some come to us at the head, others run to the back, where the procession, like a black serpent, is just turning the corner. Now cries are coming from all along the lines. The Schupos run up every time. But I have the feeling that they only want to intimidate us, that they are worried themselves. On other occasions they have always used force with less provocation. The lorry comes driving slowly past the procession. The headlights grope from row to row. They are taking care to safeguard themselves against surprises.

We pass a factory. The uniformed porter stands at the entrance-gate. The windows of the workshops are lit up.

" Franz ! "

He looks at me.

" We must be at all the factories to-morrow morning. If they should carry on working . . ."

" You're to come with me afterwards, but not too openly. It's already arranged," he says curtly.

. . . .

An hour later. Richard Hüttig and Franz Zander are walking ten yards in front of me. The streets are empty, sleepy. They enter a pub. I follow them. They are already standing at the bar, drinking their beer. They can drink beer calmly, at a moment like this ! Why, whatever . . . ? There, they're leaving already. The streets never seem to end. Why, we're not in our district any more ! They again disappear into a pub, and again I find them standing at the bar. What's the meaning of this nonsense ? I want to go up to Franz, tell him what I think of him, but there, they have already gone out. They don't even look at me as they pass. Their expressions are so forbidding that the words remain stuck in my throat. They act as if they don't know me from Adam ! Again I run along behind them. It is all so bloody stupid. They are crazy—completely crazy ! A third pub appears. By this time I am quite determined not to let myself be dragged along behind like an idiot. The two of them again order beer. There are scarcely any people inside except for a group playing pontoon at one table. The cards flap down onto the wood. I see Franz and Richard putting down their empty glasses. If they pass me now ! But no, they slowly walk through the room, disappear behind a door. This room is very full. I sit down quietly in a corner. The faces all around are unknown to me. Franz and Richard sit over on the other side. A tall, red-haired man stands in front at an obliquely placed table. He glances at every one in turn, throws a single word at each.

" You ? "

This is a complete question for everyone. The answers are just as briefly returned.

" Rote Hilfe "[29]—" Cell 217 "—" Internationale Arbeiter Hilfe "[30]—" Cell 274."

Franz gives our cell number.

" Buildings Defence Groups," says Hüttig.

" You ? "

The red-haired man looks at me with narrowed eyes. His glance disconcerts me.

" ... I ... I ..."

" Who knows him ? " I hear him asking sharply.

" I do—it's all right ! " says Franz on the other side. Next to him Richard raises his forefinger. " I know him too," that means. Richard knows me all right ! All of a sudden I am glad that he knows me; yes, I am even proud. Actually, how long have I known him ? Three years. Look at him as he sits there, bent over. His squat figure seems even shorter now. He always has such a serious expression on his face, as if he were continually worrying over difficult questions. The folds round the mouth, above the bushy eyebrows on the forehead, are deeper than ever. The thick hair hangs down untidily. How will he talk here ? As always, curt sentences. Roughly. He has always half barked. Richard !

I was the last to be asked. The red-haired man in front is talking.

" Comrades ! We are concerned with the following factories: the Aron Works, Zwietusch, the Werner Works and the Power Works at Siemensstadt. The pamphlets will be printed to-night in the places you know of in the hut settlements. Fetch them very early to-morrow morning!"

He pauses; his glance goes round the row.

" Until then be prepared for emergencies. You have already told your comrades. It will be . . ."

The door opens. A young comrade goes up to the speaker. His face is flushed; he looks worn out. They talk quietly, then the young comrade leaves. The leader continues:

" At the moment the entire S.A. of Berlin is holding a torchlight procession round the government offices. They'll come back full of fight—another reason for being especially alert. All clear? Or has anyone a question to ask?"

Silence.

We leave one at a time. The streets are deserted. The uncanny quietness sets my nerves on edge. My head aches.

. . . .

Quarter past eleven strikes from the town hall clock. We stand in the hall at Rothacker's. The front door bangs. Paul Teichert.

" Anything new?"

" No. The torchlight procession won't have ended yet!"

" Maybe we're only imagining that the Thirty-threes are going to try something to-night. They're sure to have enough celebrating their 'victory'!"

" I'll be surprised if they don't give us a taste of that 'victory.' What's going to stop them now? The police? They'll think twice before coming up against the political gangsters of the new State. It is scarcely twelve hours old—but it's their bread and butter! Who's going to put his job or his pension in danger?"

Franz speaks into the corner where Rothacker's nickel glasses shine.

" I didn't see a single helmet when I made my rounds just now. They're thinking of it already—as a rule a group of them comes by every second!"

Paul Teichert has turned his coat-collar right up to his ears. He says in an undertone: " That's right. If we don't protect ourselves, it's all up. We saw that at Braunschweig [31] and Altona.[32] The boys of Altona were all right."

" Has Stani been warned ? " asks Rothacker.

Stani is the abbreviated name of the pub in which our Workers' Defence Groups have their headquarters.

" Of course. They've even got bicycle patrols."

Franz clears his throat.

Not a word is spoken for a long time. Then Rothacker's voice—it seems to come from a long way off:

" I've often thought it all over, Franz. What have so many of us gone through already ? Me too. Four years of dirt and blood in the war. Spartacus[33] in nineteen,[34] then in twenty-three . . ."[35]

A car drives past outside. We peer out. It's only a taxi.

" . . . twenty-three. Then we also sat and waited—for the start. To-day our very lives are in danger again ! "

" The revolution has its ups and downs," answers Franz quietly.

Teichert stretches himself. He yawns. Then he says:

" Sometimes it makes me feel it's all so hopeless. Thousands of dead, dead. Hard labour sentences, persecution all these years. The Nazis are always chattering about their ' old guard.' The b——s ! They always had their revolvers in their pockets and got off—the courts on their side. Fine ' old guard ' ! "

The front door flies open. We jerk round. Ernst Schwiebus ! He waves his arms, struggles for breath.

" The Nazis—a cyclist is here. They're coming ! "

We rush out.

" They'll be here directly, the whole Storm," reports the cyclist hastily. He is a young fellow, wears a peaked cap.

" Inform Richard and the Defence Groups ! " orders Franz.

The cyclist races off. Franz turns round.

" Alarm the tenants. Each to go with a few comrades. Rothacker's to stay with me ! "

Comrades are already dashing out of our pub, the Werner. The blinds rattle down.

We fling open the front doors of the buildings, run into the courtyards, shout in a chorus at the black walls:

" Hello, there ! Wake up ! The Nazis are storming the Wallstrasse ! "

Lights flash on in all the windows. People come rushing down the stairs. The bolts of the windows opening on to the street snap. A man wearing a dressing-gown runs past me; he has only a nightshirt underneath. Our street is awake ! From the bend of the street a song comes suddenly !

" . . . *Die Strasse frei den braunen Bataillonen !*
Die Strasse frei dem Sturmabteilungsmann ! . . ."[36]

They don't sing. They yell. The next words are drowned in deafening whistles and cries.

" Down ! Down ! Red Front ! Red Front ! "

I see the dark mass rapidly approaching.

That's not marching ! They hurry, push forward in dense crowds. Suddenly a dull crash right in the middle of the mass. Flower-pots ! A wild roar rises from the crowd, then a shrill voice ! " Close the windows ! Clear the street ! " They want to play policeman ! They come closer. I see the buckles of their shoulder-straps shining in the lamplight, the clasps on their belts.

I grab Franz by the arm.

" There ! There ! A Schupo ! "

" Yes ! "

A single Schupo runs in front of the procession, his helmet gleaming. A Brown Shirt runs beside him. I see the Schupo talking excitedly to the Brown Shirt. But the latter turns round and yells, yells above the pandemonium:

" Extended lines ! Fire at the windows ! "

Rothacker grabs Franz by the lapels. His face is white.

" The swine ! The swine ! The swine ! "

The uniformed crowd draws up in loose formation. A ceaseless crackle against the walls of the houses; the dark street shows up the flashes from the revolvers. The firing-range slides slowly round to us. From the windows missiles still crash down to sound above the shots, cries still come from all the houses in the street: " Bloody swine ! Murderers !" A lump comes in my throat. I tremble; can't control myself. Suddenly I see that the Schupo in front of the procession stops running. He throws his arms forward, turns in a circle, and tumbles down. The lonely S.A. man near him jumps round; he evidently wants to call out something to the others. His arms jerk in the air—suddenly flop down—his knees sag.

Whatever has happened—whatever ? I can't think clearly. Single figures now run out of the near-by side-streets. They jump into niches formed by the houses. Sporadic shots flash out.

" Now . . . now . . . " yells Rothacker.

Now the S.A. clatter past us. The heavy knee-boots sound from round the corner. They've disappeared into thin air. Two dark bodies lie on the asphalt.

A few minutes later the siren of a police car pierces the air. The car races along. Its headlights slide over the roadway. The brakes shriek. Now the lights shine on the dark bodies on the pavement. Two of the Stanis go towards the Schupos, who are carrying their pistols in their hands.

I hear the steady voice of one of the comrades.

" The Nazis attacked the Wallstrasse ! "

He points to the bodies.

" They've got that on their conscience, sergeant ! "

They are helping to lift the two in the car.

" To the West End Hospital ! As quick as you can ! "

. . . .

The same night. In the Siemensstadt hut settlement. We have come here directly after the Nazi attack. Franz snaps the spring lid of the cyclostyle down and yawns. I wipe my ink-stained hands on a rag.

" What's the time ? "

"Nearly four," replies Strubbel. He holds his pocket watch close to the oil lamp.

I straighten my aching back. How cold it is! Sleep! If only I could sleep! I have a faint metallic taste in my mouth that turns the weariness to nausea.

"You're done in as well, eh?" asks Strubbel. His black hair hangs untidily over his face. It always makes me want to stroke it back into place.

"As if we're all not!" answers Rothacker for me. He lies half stretched out on the shaky sofa of the hut. His face is pale, his eyes behind the glasses red and inflamed.

"Never mind, it's already fifteen hundred sheets!" consoles Franz.

And to Strubbel, "Couldn't have rolled it on your own?"

"Nope!"

The leaflets lie piled up all over the table. They are still wet.

"If the others 'ave done as much, then Siemens'll be flooded!" rejoices Strubbel.

No one answers. I am sitting in the battered cane chair, dozing. Franz sits next to Rothacker. Now that the body is still, the desire for sleep becomes even more urgent. It is only with difficulty that I can keep my eyes open.

Stuffed rabbit-skins hang on the wooden walls round us. A camp bed with a ragged red eiderdown stands in the left corner. Behind the narrow door next to it, Strubbel's wife and the three-year-old Heini sleep. Strubbel had formerly lived in our street. He has been unemployed for three years. The landlord turned him out by piling the furniture on the pavement. Strubbel had then been taken in by comrades. Later, we had helped him to build the hut. Now he is the political leader of our cells in the Siemensstadt hut settlement. Siemensstadt, the Nazi stronghold! All middle class. At election time eight out of ten windows show swastika flags.

Someone shakes me by the shoulder. I have nodded off after all.

"Come on, it's time!"

Strubbel throws back the potato sack that hangs in front of the doorway.

" Do your best ! Don't get caught ! "

The alleyways of the settlement smell of dung and decay. Somewhere a dog is barking. A bank of fog hangs over the huts. It is bitterly cold. We turn sharply to the right. The high railway embankment appears before us. A long goods train rattles across the bridge, the engine puffing thick white clouds into the air. The station clock points to a few minutes before five. The booking-office is empty. The ticket-collector sits sleepily in his cubby. He looks at us enquiringly.

" We'll wait outside," says Franz in an undertone.

The light from the arc lamp ripples in the canal water behind the station track. I lean against the railing.

" They're coming ! "

Ernst Schwiebus, " Ready-made," Heinz Preuss, and Ede are there. Ede is wearing his glass eye. We shake hands.

" The Wallstrasse was raided to-night ? " says Schwiebus. " They occupied the side-streets at two o'clock. Paul Teichert wasn't at the meeting-place. Won't be able to get out, eh ? "

This " eh " often occurs at the end of Schwiebus's sentences; a habit of his.

" Do you know the further details ? Arrests ? " asks Franz.

" No. But it's possible, eh ? "

" We must decide where we were all night ! " Franz nods to me and Rothacker.

We hastily share out the leaflets. Each one fills his pockets until they bulge. A brightly lit-up train rattles over the bridge in front of us. Franz wants us to hurry.

He says : " You talk to your group, Schwiebus. I'll see to ours. Start at the front of the train ; we'll take the carriages at the back. We'll ride backwards and forwards, coming back here in the empty trains. If anyone is missing, the others had better leave the station. Look out at the stations to see that everything's clear. Go on, quick ! "

" I can't stay after seven o'clock, eh ? My delivery bike's

waiting for me," says Schwiebus hurriedly. He is the delivery man at a perfumery store.

" We'll have finished well before then ! "

We separate. My nerves are on edge. The weariness has gone. Except for the dull ache in my head and the burning of my eyes. The station is full of people. The electric trains run in one after the other. The early shift of the Siemens' Works are already travelling to work. Thousands. On the first morning after Hitler has been made Chancellor !

The compartment smells of sweat and stale smoke. The workmen sit on the seats with sleepy faces. A few let their heads drop. They continue their sleep here, making use of the train journey. We press a pamphlet into each one's hand. I am giddy. It's all so different from what I had expected. No discussions, no excitement. They take the pamphlets dumbly from us. A few read them; the majority put them immediately in their pockets. Franz stands in the middle of the carriage. He begins loudly:

" Workers ! Hitler became Reichs Chancellor yesterday. German capitalism called him. It sees no other way out of the crisis than still greater exploitation of the working class. Hitler is to make an employment prison of Germany. All opposition is to be crushed by a reign of terror. Yesterday evening the S.A. already started attacking working-class districts. Comrades ! Workers all over the world are watching you at this hour. It depends on *you*, people in the factories, whether Fascism will be able to carry out its bloody purpose."

Through the carriage windows still only the bleak countryside and coloured signal lights.

Franz throws a quick glance sideways, speaks quicker: " We Communists, unemployed, and factory workers, come to you, offering to fight side by side. We say to you : Don't lay hands on a single switch to-day. Don't set even *one* machine working ! Discuss the situation. Elect your executive committees. There is only one answer to the Hitler dictatorship: mass political strikes all over Germany! Your lives and the future of your children are at stake, remember that ! "

Franz speaks passionately. I am looking at the faces. All eyes are fixed on him, but the compartment remains dumb even now. They *must* understand us, they *must* comprehend. Now, at this very moment!

"Start discussing!" Franz whispers to us.

The train turns a sharp curve, slopes a little on one side. I step into a row of seats. Two young workers, an older one, and a woman, are sitting here. The woman has folded the pamphlet into a small square, twists it between her fingers. The old worker reads it; the two others must have already stuck it in their pockets. So they haven't read it.

"Workers! We mustn't leave each other like this. You certainly feel as we do, that something has got to happen. And to-day! The workers *must* defend themselves. Talk to the others in your sheds at once."

I stand bent over; the swaying train shakes me. The woman looks at me with small, disturbed eyes. Her lips are pressed together. "Strike! You're a sly one, me lad!" her glance seems to say. The young worker shrugs his shoulders. "That's right—yes," he says slowly. The other next to him fidgets nervously with his mess-tin. Outside, a dirty grey layer of frost lies over the countryside.

"We can't do anything. We've got to wait and see what the unions decide," says the old one.

I look straight at him. His eyes are calm and brown.

"Don't wait, comrade. After all, a start has got to be made somehow. The others will follow us."

The old one shakes his head.

"Without orders from the unions? Without strike pay? Just start off wildly?"

The youth on the left nods in agreement. "Impossible!"

"We'd only lose our jobs through that!" the woman throws in snappily.

"They can't do anything to the whole working class."

The brakes hiss as the train slows down and then stops. All push towards the doors. In large letters on an enamel signboard outside: "Werner Works." An icy wind whistles through the open station. Right in front of us tower the factory buildings. The bright squares of the windows climb high into the sky. The wide staircases seem like skeletons through the glass panes. The small dots, people swarming. Rows of workers, closely packed together, move across the yards down there on the left. Thousands disappear in a few moments. If they all . . .

"Look over there! Outside the station, at the entrance to the works—the leaflet distributors!" says Rothacker.

"They're the hut settlement cells."

On the other platform an empty train arrives. Schwiebus and his group jump down.

"What's doing, eh?"

"Stay up here; we're going to Fürstenbrunn station," replies Franz.

We run through narrow streets formed only by factory buildings. Dirty grey walls, in front a patch of green, and iron railings. Ede has caught us up. "I wanter come too," he had insisted. Workers crowd towards us. Rothacker starts handing out. There are no police to be seen.

"Leave the rest for the bridge," orders Franz.

Pamphlets lie scattered all over the pavements. Just thrown away: by the nervy ones. We pass the last factory; the Fürstenbrunn bridge comes into sight, on our right. The works are supplied with water from the canal here. The Fürstenbrunn station, the second railway connection for the works, arches to a hump behind the bridge. It is quiet and deserted during the day. But now thousands are arriving here. The workers push their way across the narrow bridge, four abreast. We distribute the leaflets, mumbling a few hurried words. There is no time to start a discussion here; they are all in too much of a hurry. My stock of pamphlets is soon exhausted. Rothacker comes along empty-handed as well.

"And not even a sign of the police!"

Franz stares fixedly at the crowd hurrying by.

"There should have been more here, many more! The first morning of Hitler as Chancellor, in Berlin's largest industrial district! A guard of a hundred men, a party leader in their centre. A two or three minutes' talk. That would have been a signal for all Germany ! "

We stand until the stream of workers breaks off. A few stragglers run past. A siren tears the silence, rises songfully to a clear tone, and then dies down whimperingly. Franz nods.

" Let's go ! "

Our boots clatter. Not a word is spoken. I am overwhelmed with a feeling of helplessness. Towards the left, the broad square of the Siemens' tower rises clear-cut above the sea of houses. Thin spirals of smoke creep out of the top. It is both chimney and clock, the landmark of Siemensstadt. There are yard-long illuminated clock hands on all four sides of the tower; round them bright squares, the hour markings. The time can be read miles away. The hands seem to me to be winking mockingly. " You want to bring disorder in the regular trot ? Here ? They all came in exactly to the minute. Can you hear the buzzing in the shops ? Ha-ha-ha ! Everything runs as usual ! "

Franz says suddenly, roughly: " We're all on the spot. We're storming the fort of industry. From outside ! And what's the answer from inside ? "

His cheeks are drawn; he looks tired. His cap hangs down over the back of his neck. His broad shoulders drop helplessly. Ede's and Rothacker's faces are also bitter. The awful truth is revealed in Franz's words. My feet drag heavily. The physical strain on top of it all. Sleep ! If I could only sleep !

The hut settlements begin on the left. *Our* hut colonies. They are called " Little Moscow " here. Yellow lights burn in a few low windows. A thin wisp of smoke rises straight up from a tin chimney. A cock crows.

Rothacker says : " Nearly all of us are unemployed. Why ? Because the fighters have always been sacked from the factories. You were kicked out of here, weren't you ? Working from outside—that's not the same ! "

Franz turns his head. He looks at Rothacker absentmindedly.

"Our work in the trade unions..."

He takes a deep breath.

"You heard the answer to-day! Wait and see—union leaders."

Ede spits noisily, slaps his arms. "Bloody cold, what?" Then, as if Franz's voice had just reached him: "Wait 'n' see, wait 'n' see. I tells yer, some 'ides be'ind that. That Heini Ketzel next door to us, f'r example. Yer knows 'im, 'Pasty Heini.' 'E's another as works 'ere, in the moulding shop. Bloody sweated laber, 'e sez ter me, with that wet sand an' all. The pay's rotten—abaht thirty bob a week. But 'is 'e frightened of losing the lousy work? 'E is that! And then 'e's saving up fer his gal. She wants ter 'ave a cab'net gramyphone!" He laughs contemptuously. "The names I've called 'im! 'N sweetie, that gramyphone, Sunday the picshers wiv 'er—nofing else interests 'im. There's a lot o' that ruddy sort. That makes an 'ell of a difference."

We have arrived at Jungfernheide station. Closely packed trams drive past, one after the other. Trains rumble across the railway bridge, their lights still on, although it is already broad daylight. The clerks are riding to Siemens' offices.

Franz stops.

"Let's separate. Careful in the Wallstrasse."

. . . .

Long articles appear in the papers about what had taken place in our street on the night Hitler became Chancellor. The Schupo who had collapsed in front of the S.A. during the shooting was called Zauritz, while the S.A. man was the Stormleader Maikowski of the 33rd Storm. They are both dead.

The Thirty-threes had killed a policeman, and in their stupid fright they had even shot their Stormleader. We saw it with our own eyes—and now we read in the papers, they were both victims of the Communists! There isn't a word in the papers to say that the Thirty-threes had paraded along our street, that they wanted to start trouble in our street that night. The Nazi newspapers write brutal taunting articles.

They describe Maikowski as the latest to be martyred by the Communists. It appears that Maikowski's death is to be the excuse for an increased wave of terrorism against our " red " street, so hated by them; for such baiting by the Press produced its desired effect last night. The entire West Standard detachments of the Berlin S.A. have marched through our street. It was a demonstration in revenge for the " murder " of Maikowski. Quite a time before the start, the police came to our pub, the Werner, and ordered the landlord to close. They then occupied all the corners and closed the street to traffic. A police car drove continually up and down, and lit up the windows of the houses with its searchlights. Even the roofs were searched by the police for possible hidden " defences." Not a light burnt in the windows overlooking the road. As if it were a street of the dead. Then the Browns filed past in long rows carrying burning torches. Their cries of vengeance, their brawling songs, were met with the silence of the grave.

But yet our silence emerged triumphant.

. . . .

The nervous tension of the last days has worked up in me a passionate desire for life and relaxation. I have never felt this so much before. I must go to Käthe. I want to see her, want to hear her voice.

Frau Zander sits at her sewing-machine in the kitchen.

" Is Franz here ? "

I am suddenly too shy to ask for Käthe straight away.

" No. But do ye go in. Käthe is there."

She is sitting on the sofa. A pile of stockings lies near her. She had not heard me coming.

" Evening, Käthe."

" Jan ! " Her eyes sparkle. " Sit down."

She is wearing the wine-coloured dress with the plaited leather belt to-day. It fits tightly. Looks very nice. A strand of fair hair falls over her face as she bends over the stocking. She blows it back.

" Why are you so quiet ? " She looks at me enquiringly.

"One can't always talk."

The sewing-machine hums in the kitchen. Stops, and then starts off again.

"I came to fetch you. Let's go for a walk."

She nods. "Only one more hole."

The street lamps are already lit. The weather is cool and dry. I take deep breaths. The air is so fresh this time of the year, not like the usual town air. Käthe's hand is in my coat pocket. It is so small that mine folds right over it. I take small steps, like Käthe. What a bright checked scarf she has round her neck. It's so vivid and jolly. All this is so pleasant. No thinking for once, just walking, walking along. We don't want to talk.

The café is tiny and almost empty. Käthe leans against me. We are both happy. The cups of hot coffee bring back warmth to us. Käthe's face is flushed; her eyes shine. I reach for the illustrated paper on the next table. On the second page, a picture of marching Schupos.

POLICE WITH SWASTIKA FLAGS ON THE
RHINE BRIDGE!

So it's official! I put the paper down.

"Willi has gone now," says Käthe.

She has also seen the picture.

"Yes?"

"It was too risky for him, after the raid."

Suddenly, all that comes back. Of course. I would have seen him in the apartment otherwise.

"Come on, Käthe, let's go to my place."

. . . .

I unlock the front door. Käthe is at my side. We grope our way up the dark stairs in silence.

"Quietly—the landlady!"

. . . .

The announcement appeared in the paper a few days ago that Maikowski, the shot leader of the S.A. Storm 33 and the policeman Zauritz were to receive an official funeral. They were both carried to the Berlin Dom on biers to-day, where a memorial service took place in the presence of Hitler, his Cabinet, and prominent S.A. and S.S. officials. Storm 33 and a detachment of police marched past the Dom. The evening papers have printed long reports with photographs on the front page. The lie is again repeated that they were both murdered by the Communists.

Franz told me that the service was broadcast from all the radio stations. He had visited a comrade at the time and had heard the wireless announcer (a photo shows him standing on the steps of the Dom in front of the microphone) greet the S.A. with the words: " Here comes the greatly feared ' Murder ' Storm Thirty-three."

" They praise the Thirty-threes in public for their years of terrorism," said Franz gloomily. " That's only meant to encourage them to further violence in our street. This Maikowski affair is sure to end badly for us; the Nazi Government doesn't make such a fuss about all that for nothing. We've got to impress on our comrades the need for being extra careful now."

Franz had never seemed so worried before.

" Germany isn't Italy," many comrades had maintained.

Our first attempt to bring about a general strike directed against the Hitler Government had failed.

Is Franz right? Are we really standing on the threshold of a terroristic German Fascism?

. . . .

The street climbs a low hill.

" Röntgenstrasse. Their hunting-ground ! " Franz indicates the pub on the other side of the street which serves as the premises of the Thirty-threes. Not a uniform to be seen. What are they up to ?

We have reached the highest point of the street. A wide bridge crosses the Spree. To the left, arc lamps sway from the dock walls. A large crane swings silently backwards and forwards, sticking its claws deep into the cargo-boats.

Behind it, long rows of illuminated workshops. From their centre a huge chimney climbs into the evening sky. The travelling cages of coal on the overhead railway rattle. They belong to the Charlottenburg Power Works on the banks of the Spree.

Franz stops suddenly. Loud reports are carried by the wind across the Spree. We listen. Now, again, three, four, five times!

" Sounds like shots! "

I relax from the strained listening attitude.

" Yes. Hope it's not at Willman's."

Willman's is the pub where our Defence Groups meet. It lies in a side-street near the Spree.

" The Storm premises looked so deserted," says Franz slowly.

He expresses my thoughts.

We walk past garage walls, then turn leftwards. Franz rings a bell at the gate three times. I haven't been here before. In the hall the porter looks out of his peephole. A small grey-haired man with glasses.

" We'd like to have a look at the empty two-roomed flat."

" Certainly. The first door on the right," says the little man in a thin voice.

A long corridor, then a large, sparsely lit room. Three men shake hands with us. I know only one; he's from the neighbouring district. The others are a large bald-headed man with an energetic face, and a short thick-set man wearing a beard. The tiny porter leaves the door ajar. His slippers shuffle back along the corridor.

" We can't start yet," says the bald-headed man to Franz. " The Defence Group leaders aren't here yet."

" All right."

A grandfather clock ticks. A bird-cage hangs above the sofa. It is covered with a dark cloth. We sit on heavy carved chairs. Outside, the bell peals out. The slippers of the old man slide along. We look towards the door. A deep voice.

" We'd like to have a look at the empty two-roomed flat."

The thin voice of the old man answers. Then heavy boots

tramp along the corridor. Richard Hüttig. Who is the other one? I don't know him. Hüttig's face seems depressed. Deep lines round his mouth.

"We've been held up. The Thirty-threes made an armed attack on the Willman half an hour ago."

Dead silence. Hüttig looks right past us.

"... One comrade was shot in the stomach—the other in the shoulder."

His face twitches. His heavy hands fidget with his belt. Silence again. The bald man speaks at last. "That can wait till afterwards. First of all ..."

He passes his hand over his forehead.

"You know that a few comrades have been arrested for what happened on the night of January 30th. Most of them belong to the Stani defences. The whole Press has made a big fuss about that night—on instructions from official quarters. It seems that another Horst Wessel [37] is to be made out of the shot Stormleader Maikowski. We must show up the real murderers to the public, comrades. By means of papers and pamphlets!"

For a moment only the ticking of the clock is heard.

"We must ask the following questions: What did the heavily armed Storm want in the Wallstrasse that night? Their way back lay in the opposite direction. Why wasn't a proper examination of the bodies made? Because it would prove that the shots had been fired from a short distance. Because it would prove that Maikowski and the policeman Zauritz had been shot by the Storm marching behind them."

The bald-headed man looks at us all in turn.

"Above all, remember: from what we have heard, this Schupo was not hostile towards us. His wife is now being forced to take part in the campaigns stirred up against us. Otherwise she'll lose her pension, and she has a child. The Nazi papers write that they want to rename the street Maikowskistrasse. A bronze tablet is to be set up at the spot where they died. You see, they will do everything to label us as the 'murdering Communists.'"

Richard Hüttig raises his head; he wants to speak.

"Just a second. One thing more: we are going to lay a wreath with a red ribbon on the spot where the policeman Zauritz was murdered. As a sign of our sympathy, and to show that we weren't the cause of his death. Above all, not a word about this. Not to anyone!"

Richard Hüttig places his large hands on the table. He looks at them, then says: "We of the Buildings Defence Groups will support you, as usual. For we are responsible for the lives of the proletarians of Charlottenburg. You know how many dead we already have...." He lowers his voice. "Perhaps it's one more now."

He clenches his hands, raises his head.

"But I must tell you, on behalf of my men, that we're not going to let ourselves be wiped out without defending ourselves any longer. No violence by individuals, of course. But we must be able to defend our lives. The S.A. have made a start to-day! We've been made outlaws!"

Hüttig is silent. I feel terribly excited. Then the comrade next to him says: "That's right. We can't do anything else."

The bald-headed man regards them steadily. "There's nothing to be said against defending yourselves. But no provocation, mind. We'll badly need chaps like you later."

He stands up.

"Once more! The cyclostyles must be kept working."

. . . .

I call for Franz and the girls. We want to go to the pictures. Hilde and Käthe go on in front of us, arm in arm.

The thought flashes through my head, "Franz is my friend and comrade. We are both in love. Our girls are also good friends."

The girls stop at the corner, in front of the advertising pillar.

"Love, espionage—the usual stuff," says Hilde.

"Here's a René Clair film," remarks Käthe.

"That's more like it."

Franz has gone round the pillar.

"Hey, look here!"

"His voice sounds excited. What's the matter?"

The advertising pillar is covered from top to bottom with Nazi posters for the Reichstag[38] elections on March 5th. A procession of starving figures, men, women, and children, is shown on one. Underneath in large letters:

OUR LAST HOPE
HITLER

A poster with Hitler's face is pasted at the top.

GERMAN PEOPLE, GIVE ME FOUR YEARS!
THEN JUDGE!

"Only theirs! The advertising contractors have been ordered not to stick up any other posters," says Franz.

"That's on the wireless all day long. They keep on repeating, 'Vote for Hitler. Vote for Hitler,'" adds Hilde.

"But they've already threatened to carry on the government with or without the majority, and to shut out our members."

We walk on slowly.

"Our boss, the old lady clerk who's been there for years," remarks Käthe, "has always voted German Nationalist,[39] Hugenberg,[40] first and last. 'Now we need a man with a strong hand,' she explains. 'And God has sent us Adolf Hitler!'"

As usual, closely packed crowds at the Zoo station. Franz nudges me suddenly. The headlines of the newspapers cry out from the stalls:

THE KARL LIEBKNECHT HOUSE AGAIN RANSACKED!
HIDDEN CELLARS!
INSTRUCTIONS FOR THE ARMED REVOLT!

We look at each other in silence. They had occupied the Party House a week ago, already searched it over dozens of times during the past few years. Now "hidden cellars," "instructions for the armed revolt" are found.

The people in front of us turn their heads. A Schupo, chin-strap buckled under his chin, and an S.A. man with the brown cap flat on his head, come towards us. Over his brown uniform the S.A. man wears a blue Schupo-coat, at his belt a rubber truncheon and revolver.

"S.A. special constable," says Franz softly.

We stand outside the cinema. I've lost all interest in the picture. But I don't want to disappoint the girls. Franz seems to feel much the same. He doesn't say a word; his eyebrows are contracted.

The canned music, the whispering people in the place; it is all suddenly unbearable. I can't force my attention on the screen. The newspaper headlines and the S.A. special constable flicker before my eyes.

We are on the way home. Newspaper boys cry out the headlines of the final editions of the *Nachtausgabe*:

NEW FINDS IN THE KARL LIEBKNECHT HOUSE!
SECRET TRAPDOORS: SUBTERRANEAN CORRIDORS!

"They've gone one better," says Franz. "They're preparing the ground for the elections. It looks that way. Mussolini ran the same racket. Wasn't an attempt made on his life, too? Pah!"

Loudspeaker music comes booming from a side-street. A Reichs broadcasting company's car. It is stuck over with glaring Nazi posters. The music breaks off.

"On March 5th. Vote for Hitler!" bellows the loudspeaker. It makes me wild.

We stop at the entrance to the Wallstrasse. We have covered the whole distance without a word. Hilde looks at Bill, the sausage-seller, at the corner. He sits covered in blankets under his mushroom-shaped tent. The nickel dixie steams in front of him.

"I'll stand you all a sausage. To finish up," says Hilde.

Sausage Bill is pleased to see us. He knows us well. I know

that Franz sells him a newspaper now and again, and he has put his name on collecting-lists.
" Do you want any bread ? "
We decline with thanks.
" Dirty weather, wot ? "
" That's about it."
" Just gotter keep yer pecker up, boys ! "
" We'll see to that," answers Franz. " Good night."
" 'Night. Best o' luck."

. . . .

Two days later. Franz had told me to go to Hinrich. He does the drawings for our paper.
I climb the steps. " August Hinrich, Teacher " is written on the brass shield. I ring. A second later the flap of the peephole is raised, then Hinrich stands before me—a tall man with a round face. His black hair is brushed straight back. The oil shines.
" You, Jan ? "
He motions stiffly with his hand. " If you please."
Whatever's the matter with him ? Looks so worried; behaves so strangely.
Clear, bright wallpaper in the hall; red lacquered coat-hooks; a small table of the same colour; above it a mirror. I hang my coat on one of the hooks.
" You must excuse everywhere being so untidy; let's go into the sitting-room."
Shirts, ties, and rolled-up socks lie thrown in a confused heap on the leather-covered steel chairs. Two suits on the couch in the corner. Hinrich clears a chair.
" Sit down."
He goes to the table in the centre of the room, rolls a stiff sheet of drawing-paper together. Is he going away ? As a rule the brand-new apartment always looks so spick and span. Hinrich unrolls the sheet, holds it out in front of me.
" You must have seen it already—I did it myself," he says slowly, with, I fancy, considerable embarrassment. It is a pen-and-ink drawing of a coal-mine. Pipes and steel girders

in tangled confusion. A red flag with the hammer and sickle flutters from the pithead derrick.

" It used to hang in the next room, didn't it ? "

Hinrich nods. He rolls the sheet together, ties a string round it.

" My reason for coming. You're to draw a new heading for our paper. I've got the wax plate here."

Hinrich raises his head sharply; his face trembles. Why, what's the matter now ? He's behaving as if I had asked him for heaven knows what !

". . . I can't. I'm leaving the flat to-day—disappearing from the district."

" That's news to me."

He throws the rolled-up picture on to the table.

" Why, don't you know what's up ? " he screams hysterically. Is he mad ? I get angry too.

" What should have happened ? " I control myself with an effort. Hinrich comes close up to me; a strand of hair has fallen over his face.

" The Reichstag's burning—the Reichstag's been set on fire ! "

I stare at him with wide-open eyes.

" The Reichstag ! " he repeats. " It was announced on the wireless. They keep on giving the latest news about it."

Now at last I gather what he is saying. The Reichstag— they have set the Reichstag . . .

" That's their star turn ! " I shout at him. " It's aimed at us ! It's their catch for the Reichstag elections ! "

Hinrich strides nervously up and down, twists the roll of paper in his hands.

" I've got to leave—I'm too well known—they're going all out against us now . . ." he stammers. He avoids my glance.

" In any case—I can't join in any more."

I stand up. Everything here sickens me. The clothes scattered about; Hinrich's face.

" Then good-bye," I say mockingly.

· · · · · · · ·

It is late by now, but people are everywhere standing and talking. The newspapers are snatched from the hands of the sellers.

THE REICHSTAG IN FLAMES!

I jump on to a bus. Back—to Franz.
Groups of people stand and argue outside the doorways of the Wallstrasse. They stand under the gas-lamps reading the first newspaper reports. There is Franz, outside his house. A crowd of people around him. I recognise Rothacker, Teichert, Schwiebus, Ede. I start running.
" Franz! Franz!"
He draws me apart. Ernst Teichert comes with him.
" Damn big splash," he says, without my having said a word about the fire. " They're letting this Communist baiting cost them a hell of a lot of public property."
He stands in front of me, just as usual. He speaks calmly, as always, while I am all worked up. He looks at me with clear eyes, his hands in his trouser pockets.
" How can we now . . . but we must . . ."
" We'll get to know details in the next few days," Franz interrupts me, " then we'll react to it. Short pamphlets, summarising facts."
He is right. I am ashamed of my previous excitement. Rushing blindly at things won't help now, either.
Ernst Teichert spits thoughtfully.
" Their way of doing it is new, but the idea's old," he remarks. " Just think of Spartacus Nineteen. They made up the report of the fifty shot detectives in Lichtenberg[41] then."
I get wild again.
" But to-day they're inventing facts! And they've got hold of all the means of propaganda—wireless, cinema, Press. How are we to stand up against their lying propaganda?"
" It always was hard for us," says Franz shortly. We return to the others. I had almost forgotten Hinrich!
" Hinrich has turned yellow; won't join in any more."
Franz raises his eyebrows.

"Won't be the only one," he replies, as if he had not expected anything else.

We remain with the others quite a while.

"I'm going up," says Franz.

I accompany him and Teichert as far as the back yard.

"If anything's wrong, knock on the window," Franz says to Teichert. They live on the same floor: Franz in the side wing, Teichert in the main building. Their windows face in the corner, where the walls meet.

I walk slowly through the Wallstrasse. Lights burn brightly behind the tall windows of the Power Works. The machines hum. Our latest posters are stuck on the wooden fence of the building site. There's Ede's patent! The dark streak on the detached gable. The isolated one- and two-storeyed houses seem even tinier and more crooked in the lantern light, amongst the tall tenements. They are left over from Charlottenburg's early days; have outlived generations. The tiles on the roofs are weatherbeaten and moss-grown. Heavy wooden shutters hang in front of the windows on the ground floor. Wallstrasse. The town wall used to be here. A meadow must once have been behind it, with rustling trees. Now there is not the smallest green twig in the street. But I am glad, nevertheless. It is our street, my street; I belong here.

My eyes burn. I am tired and worn out.

. . . .

The next day. Teichert rang at my door before the house was up, so that I had difficulty in calming my landlady. He had to leave at once, for work. Franz had fled during the night. Teichert warned me against going to his lodgings.

I made careful enquiries. Police and S.A. had raided the Wallstrasse in the night. I must warn Hilde.

The sausage-seller told me how it began. He was sitting under his mushroom tent at the time. Two open lorries drove into the street with dimmed lights and quietly running engines. Police and S.A. uniforms sat on the rows of seats. The cars stopped at the bend in the road. The uniforms sprang down. An S.A. man with stars on his uniform collar gave instructions in an undertone.

"Third floor on the right—Zander."

A small group went off.

"House eighty-eight—Fischer. Eighty-five—Katoreck!"

"Yessir!"

I got to know the rest from Zander and Teichert. Frau Zander sleeps so lightly that she hears the slightest sound in the house. Heavy feet came up the stairs. She ran to the door of the next room.

"Franz!"

He jumped up. Käthe was also wakened; she sat straight up in her bed.

"There's someone coming up the stairs!"

Franz jumped into his trousers and boots, threw his jacket on. He could hear them himself now; they must have been on his landing by that time. Käthe pressed her purse into her brother's hand. Then she ran to his bed, smoothed it tidy. Franz tore the window open, looked out at the yard. There was no one there as yet! He climbed out on to the window-ledge and knocked at Teichert's pane. Behind him, they were already thundering at the door of the flat.

"Open the door! Police! Open the door!"

Käthe made her voice sound sleepy: "Just a moment, please. We must put something on."

Teichert appeared behind the pane on the other side, wearing only his nightshirt. He tore the window open, silently stretched his hand out. For a second Franz hung across the courtyard, then he stood beside Teichert. The latter closed the window; Franz saw Käthe doing the same on the other side.

At the Zanders' they were already kicking against the door with their boots. The crashes woke the whole house up. They were listening everywhere.

Käthe opened the door. Her mother stood behind her. They had slipped on their coats. They both jumped back from the blinding glare of the electric torches. Pistol barrels flashed. The first man pushed the door wide open with his foot; it flew against Käthe's arm. They came into the kitchen: four special police and two Schupos. An S.A. man, a broad-shouldered giant, levelled a pistol at the old woman's breast.

"Are you Frau Zander?"

Käthe saw how her mother's hands, that were holding her coat together, suddenly stopped trembling.

"Yes. What do you want?" she asked quite firmly.

The broad-shouldered man gave no answer. He let the lamp's rays sweep round the kitchen, pushed the door of the room open. The rest jostled in behind him.

The empty room enraged the S.A. man. He turned round with a jerk, let the light rest on the women standing in the doorway.

"Where is your son Franz?" he shouted.

"I don't know," said the mother.

"You don't know?"

Now it was Käthe's turn.

"And you? You don't know, either, what?"

"No!"

The men all turned their lamps on Käthe. She pulled her coat closer, turned up the collar in front.

"Turn on the light!" was yelled at the mother.

She went into the kitchen, an S.A. man with her. As she was fumbling about under the curtain in the corner, he asked her suspiciously: "What are you doing there?"

"Turning on the gas-tap."

"Oh!"

"Search the rooms!"

The huge S.A. man was apparently in command, or just behaved as if this were so; in any case, the two Schupos obeyed his orders immediately. The men threw the bedclothes on the floor, lifted the mattresses high and let them drop with a thud. Two S.A. men went into the kitchen. The women heard crockery clattering. They were moving the kitchen dresser. An S.A. man stood at the bookcase. He examined every book carefully; threw some on to the floor, and laid others on the table near him. Käthe saw that those volumes by Gorki and Lenin were among them. The broad-shouldered man had flung the wardrobe open. He rummaged in all the suit pockets, even felt the hems of the dresses. He threw all the things already examined on to Käthe's bed. Then he took the pictures down and tapped the walls. He smashed a Lenin portrait on the edge of the table. Käthe noticed that the Schupos only searched under compulsion. They merely glanced under the beds, and passed their hands over the upholstering of the sofa. The big man climbed up on to the table so as to look at the top of the stove.

" You're only ruining my table. The most you'll find up there is dust," said the mother calmly.

The S.A. man jumped down.

" Just you mind your own business, will you? We came here chiefly because of your perfect son. But, of course, you don't know where he is ! "

He suddenly went right up to the mother. " Was he here at all to-day ? "

The old woman was silent for a moment, looked at Käthe.

" No ! " she said firmly.

The S.A. man looked right through her, and the other turned round.

" He hasn't been here—really ! " said Käthe, breaking the silence.

The leader turned on her.

" Then we'll wait for him here ! "

" Do we need the lights ? " one of the others asked.

" No. We're not going to give him a warning as well. The torches will do later on ! "

He turned to the women with an affected gesture.

" If you please, ladies ! You may continue your so roughly disturbed sleep—in the next room, of course."

. . . .

Teichert had provided Franz with hat and coat.

" Monday, after the elections, at three. Jan knows the spot," Franz had just stopped to say. Then he ran down the stairs of the main building, climbed over the wall in the yard, and fled past the Power Works.

. . . .

Perhaps they're shadowing me as well? They've got hold of a list of names. Yesterday's raid is sure to have been organised a long time ago. Why did they go to Franz? How is it possible, otherwise, for just Fischer and Katoreck to have been arrested, both leaders of the Buildings Defence Groups. The round of the pubs with Richard Hüttig and Franz on the evening of the Chancellor's nomination occurs to me. At the time I had inwardly cursed at the silly air of conspiracy. How the few weeks have changed us all. Richard Hüttig. Is he safe? I have been trying to get in touch with him all to-day. Without success.

I come to a lonely car stop, wait until the tram is in motion, then jump on. The tram is densely packed. Most of the faces are buried behind newspapers. Here in the car there is a feeling of suspense; everyone is busy with the Reichstag fire. I glance over my neighbour's shoulder at his newspaper.

THE REICH PRESIDENT'S DECREE!

One of the latest editions. At a car stop I beckon from the platform to a newspaper boy.

" . . . Death sentence for high treason, arson, and plotting against the Government, restriction of personal freedom, abolition of the secrecy of the post, legalisation of house searches any time of the day and night . . ."

Hilde is already standing at the car stop. I had made the appointment by telephone. She looks at me anxiously.

" You talked so strangely. Has anything happened? To Franz? "

I take her arm.

" Yes, to Franz. He had to fly during the night."

Hilde grabs hold of my arm. She stops.

"Come on! Keep calm. Otherwise we'll attract attention."

"Yes—yes," she chokes. "Fled—but why?"

She hangs heavily on my arm.

"They raided our street last night. Everywhere the same. He fled at the last moment, through Teichert's window."

She still looks at me, bewildered. I squeeze her hand.

"Do you know—where he is now?"

"I'm meeting him next Monday."

"Can't I... just to-day...?"

"You must be reasonable, Hilde. I'll tell you later how to get in touch with him. We must be careful; the rest of us are probably being watched as well. That's why I met you here!"

Hilde stares straight ahead for some time.

"Yes... yes..."

Poor girl. I look at her. I have never walked arm in arm with her like this before; she is a trifle taller than Käthe.

"It's just the same for me, with Käthe. We've had to drop her as a safety measure. Anyway, Franz is not lost."

Hilde is silent for a while.

"Yes, you are right, Jan. I was so upset for the moment."

It sounds like an apology.

"That's all right. I'll keep you posted. We'll meet again here."

Hilde nods.

"When you see Käthe or me in our district, you mustn't recognise us. We don't know each other!"

"Yes, I understand," she says quietly.

We walk a few steps in silence.

"So that's why my fine brother wasn't at home all night!" she bursts out. "He only came in in the morning. He must have been giving a hand!"

I don't answer. It's doubly hard for her, poor girl.

"Come along, I'll see you to the tram. We'll travel separately."

At the stop Hilde feels for her purse in her handbag. She gives me five marks.

"For Franz. He'll need it. I haven't any more."
By this time she has pulled herself together.

· · · · · · · ·

I had just got home when Rothacker arrived.
"We must try and get into touch with Franz, at once!"
A heavy weight seems to press on my chest.
"Why, what's up?"
"I've just come from the Unemployment Exchange—went to collect my money. They can arrest him!"
Rothacker keeps a tight hold on the lapels of my jacket. His hands tremble; he gasps excitedly. His glasses are misty. I can't see how his words can refer to Franz. I push a chair towards him.
"Sit down, Erich. Tell me all about it. I don't quite understand!"
His excitement has gripped me as well. Something unexpected must have happened. Rothacker sinks down limply, like someone dulled by a shock. He removes his glasses, wipes them with his handkerchief, his short-sighted eyes blinking nervously.
"Well, what's wrong?" I urge.
Rothacker puts his glasses on, takes a deep breath.
"It was my day for the dole to-day. We were standing in a long queue, moving forward a few steps at a time. The heads in front were suddenly poked forward. There was a hold-up at the cash desk. 'Mr. Neumann?' I hear the cashier ask sharply...."
"You mean the one from the Stanis?" I can guess what's coming.
Rothacker nods. "Yes, Neumann. I recognised him at once. 'Wait a minute,' said the cashier to him, and we saw two men jump up together. They had been sitting on one side. One of them sprang over the wooden railing, grabbed Neumann by the arm." Rothacker lowers his voice. "He didn't even have time to defend himself, he was taken so much by surprise." He wipes his glasses nervously with one

finger. "Then they went out with him in between them; they both had one hand in their pockets."

Rothacker is silent. I go hot all over. To-day is Saturday. I can't see Franz before Monday. We're to meet in a street in another district. We had arranged the spot a long time beforehand in case something unforeseen should separate us. I ponder moodily, but can find no way out. I am only half listening to Rothacker's further description. The unemployed had argued heatedly. They had been searching for him; why did he still come here, when he knew they were after him? How else could he live?

"Do you know when Franz goes for the dole?"

Rothacker thinks for a second.

"He has his card stamped on Thursday—gets the dole on Wednesday," he says.

"So he won't go there again until Wednesday? Are you sure?"

He nods emphatically. "Quite certain!"

"I can't see him before Monday, Erich. That will do, won't it?"

"Yes, that's all right, Jan!"

We are silent. I think things over. My landlady's vacuum cleaner starts humming loudly outside in the corridor.

"It's best if you come along, Erich. He wanted to rent a separate room in his new district, to provide a centre for us which would not be under suspicion. Then you'll know where it is . . . in case . . ."

Rothacker nods. "All right."

"Don't forget: Monday, three o'clock. Franz will be standing looking into the shop window of the K.D.W. in the Tauentzienstrasse. Follow us at a distance. I won't speak to him either; I'll just follow him too. Is that all right?"

"Yes. I'll be there."

. . . .

Yesterday Ede came to me with an evening paper.

ERNST THÄLMANN, THE COMMUNIST LEADER, ARRESTED!

I stared and stared at the print, couldn't say a word. Thälmann—arrested!

" Heavens, Jan! It can't be true! Why don't you say something? "

Ede talked and talked, shaking my shoulder.

So I had reassured him. That was sure to be a false report. Just a Nazi trick, trying in every way to unnerve us, I told him. Only yesterday evening I had reassured Ede, to-day we know that the newspaper report was correct. Thälmann, the leader of the Party, has been arrested. In Charlottenburg, in our district. Rothacker has confirmed the fact to-day. He did not say how and where he had learnt further details. He merely mentioned that he had known the apartment where Thälmann was arrested for a long time.

The comrades come to me, depressed and moody. They all ask the same. How could it have happened? Hadn't a safe place been found for Teddy? But I know no more about it than they do.

. . . .

I walk slowly past Franz and stop at the next window of the shop. I see him turn his head. He has seen me. He pushes his way through the crowds, winks. I give him a few yards' start, then follow on slowly. At the corner I bend, as if tying my shoelace, and give a quick glance backwards. It's all right! Rothacker is behind us. Franz soon turns into a small side-street. I let the distance between us increase; there are only a few people here. Franz! I could pick him out of thousands, even with his back turned towards me, as now. I could always recognise him by the broad shoulders with their peculiar roll. By the jerky movements of his arms, by the thick shock of fair hair. He walks with the ungainliness of a bear, as if testing every step. Seamen who always have to contend with decks swaying under their feet must walk like that. Nonsense! Franz was never at sea. I know all about his past life. He has knocked about a lot. Especially during the last years of the war, when he had worked in different towns and provinces. Always in order to have " working capital " for a few months without a job. He got stuck in Hamburg in the first months after the war. Then he joined the newly organised Volkswehren,[42] and helped to keep "law and order." He had often told me about those times. What did he know about politics then? There was good food and high wages. He was eighteen at the time. I also know how he turned to politics. That was in 1923. He was a mechanic in a tool factory. Then the inflation came. The workers didn't know whether they would be able to buy a pound of fat for their weekly wage. One strike followed the other. Franz was arrested for the first time. He was already a member of a trade union, but was still very far from being a politically conscious and active worker. He was sentenced to four months in prison. These four months changed Franz's whole outlook on the world at large. Brennert, his cell comrade, an old Spartacus fighter, saw to that. Franz read a lot afterwards and attended Marxist study-circles. He gradually became a class-conscious worker and fighter.

I start. Franz stops outside a house. He pretends to look for the number and then goes in. I meet him on the first landing. We shake hands. His grey eyes brighten.

" Hello, old man ! " he says.

" Rothacker's coming as well, he ought to know this place; sure to be of use later," I say hastily.

" Yes." He sounds rather surprised. " Second floor on the right, Mahlke. You can both come."

Franz opens the door. We pass along a landing. A baby is crying behind a closed door on the left. Another door is half open. The kitchen. But there is no one here. Then we are in a tiny room. A couch, a small table, two garden chairs. A solitary gable is seen through the window. We sit down without a word. I feel terribly dejected. We've only got bad news.

" You don't look well, Erich. Are you ill ? " asks Franz.

Rothacker smiles. Dark shadows under his eyes show behind his glasses. His face seems thinner than ever.

" We haven't slept much the last few days; besides, it's all been bad news," he replies.

Franz looks at me.

"Have they arrested someone at home—Käthe?"

"No, but . . ."

"You're going for the dole on Monday, aren't you?" interrupts Rothacker.

"Yes, why?" asks Franz.

"They arrested a Staniman at the Exchange on Saturday," says Rothacker in a heavy tone.

Silence. Franz twists the corner of the tablecloth thoughtfully.

"Just got to manage without," he answers. "I'll report it to the others. In any case, they only make use of me in this district."

Outside, crockery clatters. A whistling kettle boils.

"You must all stick together now," says Franz again. "Let Teichert and Schwiebus help; they're both reliable." And, after a pause: "You must also make arrangements for carrying on the groups; we'll suffer more losses. I'm thinking of Heinz Preuss and Ede."

Rothacker nods dumbly.

Franz's only thought is that the Party work must be carried on. He does not say a word about his own difficulties.

"Keep in contact with Strubbel. You know that he's our only link with factories apart from Teichert."

Strubbel. I look away at the gable outside.

"Strubbel isn't in the hut settlements any more," says Rothacker slowly, as if weighing every word.

"Strubbel isn't . . . has he been arrested?"

Rothacker leans his arms heavily on the table. "He would most likely have had worse than that. He's fled too. We've put him up at comrades'. His wife and the boy with others."

"How did it happen? Police?"

"No. S.A. They obviously wanted to do him in properly. You know that they quartered twenty S.A. men in the settlement during the last few weeks. The comrades who were known to be Communists couldn't move a finger without being watched."

"Yes, and . . ."

"They came on the night of the fire, about the same time as the others came to you. Strubbel woke with a start. Shots were bursting out. He saw a dark mass of people on the path to the settlement; they were kicking his fence over. He woke his wife and snatched his son from the bed. Wearing only their night things, they climbed over their neighbour's wire fence and hid in his earth-closet."

Franz rests his head between his hands, looks at the table.

"They sat there shivering in the cold. Strubbel had the child on his lap; he soothed it quietly. Two yards away, the S.A. were searching for him in the hut and sheds with electric torches. Enraged because they didn't find him, they broke everything they could lay hands on. There are a couple of dozen bullet-holes in the walls of the hut."

A knock on the door. A tall, fair woman brings in a tray of coffee. She nods to us.

"Have some coffee," she says in a friendly tone.

Franz takes the tray. "Thanks, Edith."

As soon as the woman is outside, I say softly: "That's not all . . . Richard Hüttig has been arrested."

Franz, who had been stirring his coffee, lets the spoon drop. He presses his lips together, and looks past us. The silence in the room is oppressive.

Then Rothacker remarks: "They're writing in the *Angriff*, 'The Terror of Charlottenburg Arrested.'"

Franz remains silent.

"They'll drag him into the Maikowski affair as well. They're already holding him responsible for the fight with the S.S. on February 17th. An S.S. man died the next day from a revolver shot. Our men were unarmed, of course. The conflict started with our chaps and the S.S. The S.A. came along and immediately started shooting. They were armed, as usual."

My thoughts turn to Paul Schulz. He was twenty years old. How gratefully he used to look at me when I explained his difficulties. The Thirty-threes had stabbed him in the street a few weeks ago.

Franz had stood up and is staring out at the gable.

My friend Otto Grüneberg. I will never forget the morning when we left the late night meeting of the I.A.H.[30] It was about two o'clock. " I've had more threatening letters from the Thirty-threes," he told me. " How can I defend myself when I haven't a gun ? " I had wanted to see him home, but he would not hear of it. " You live in the opposite direction, Jan," he said. " These two comrades are going my way."

Half an hour later, Otto Grüneberg was riddled with shots. The Thirty-three Stormleader, nicknamed Carrot Hahn because of his hair, had posted men at all the street corners where Otto lived. They let him go as far as the middle of the brightly lit street-crossing, then shot at him from all sides. With seven bullet wounds Otto still managed to reach his door, and then fell down, dead. He was one of our best and bravest comrades. Leader of the Charlottenburg Red Youth Front. Sixty thousand Berlin workers attended his funeral.

Franz had turned round.

" Where did you print the pamphlets on the Reichstag fire ? "

" At ' Ready-made's,' as usual."

Franz walks up and down.

" You're all in the greatest danger now. We've got quite a few safe places for cyclostyling here, you can make use of one now and again."

" That'll be fine," says Rothacker.

" Then I'll arrange it with Jan. You understand, Erich, only one of you is to come along. It's the rule now. The safest comrade mustn't be allowed to know anything that isn't absolutely essential for his own particular work."

Rothacker nods.

" One thing more," says Franz. " You must all look around for somewhere to sleep for a few nights in case of need. Where you can hide to begin with, if you have to disappear." He nods to me. " I can arrange that for you here, because of our work. You must stay in the district for one or two nights beforehand so that it won't look suspicious."

Rothacker goes. I give Franz the five marks from Hilde.

He is pleased. He mentions a meeting-place which I am to pass on to her.

I go home by a roundabout way. Outside the branch office of a newspaper stands a crowd of people. I join them. The night edition, with the final results of the Reichstag elections, have just been put up. Those who have finished reading step aside and leave. No remarks are made. The readers' faces are expressionless. The new Government closes their mouths, and puts masks on their faces. How excited they used to be here at previous elections.

I walk on slowly. The Nazis have started unheard-of persecution of opinion. For weeks now they have been using all the resources of the State for their propaganda. Yet Labour parties have received eleven million votes. Five million people have even declared themselves as " murdering incendiaries." Have voted Communist. In this way they had all given their verdict on the true incendiaries.

Here and there a street attracts my attention. The black, white, and red flags and the swastika flags hang close to one another. In other streets again, only a few. But the restaurants are all beflagged without exception. Also many other businesses. The race for showing " loyalty " has begun.

. . . .

The pub Werner, where we used to meet, has been closed by the police. But to-day the S.A. came and painted our slogans over with black paint, on the wooden fence of the building site, on the walls near the Power Works. Ede's slogan in red paint on the detached gable has also been painted over. They have even taken the trouble to scratch off the remains of our posters.

The next day. New arrests have taken place in connection with the Maikowski affair. Gloomy depression affects all of us. Who else will they fetch ? Who will be the next ? Mutual distrust and suspicion have suddenly sprung up to add to our troubles. Now I only talk with comrades whom I have known for years, and even then only by hinting at things. Even Rothacker thinks that these arrests are not random strokes. The first ones arrested must have betrayed names, or there must be a few informers in the street. It is difficult for us to see things impersonally. Nearly every day fresh arrests are made and all are closely questioned. We have suspended all propaganda for the time being, keep contact only amongst ourselves.

Our Wallstrasse is unrecognisable. No one stands outside the doors to talk any more. As soon as it becomes dark, the street is deserted. Persons walking in groups of two or three immediately place themselves under suspicion.

Two days later. The S.A. Stormtroop Thirty-three have quartered themselves near the Wallstrasse. They have occupied the Charlottenburg People's Centre. This is only a little more than a hundred yards from our houses, the fourth in the Rosinenstrasse. Rothacker warned me not to go past there. It seemed as if an invisible signboard had suddenly been hung over the street: " Beware ! Area closed ! " Pedestrians avoided the Rosinenstrasse. In the evening the houses round about seemed empty. Hardly a light burns. The S.A. would have stopped passers-by, who would then have had to prove that they lived there. But I intend to go through to-morrow morning nevertheless. One's ordinary business occupations must surely make that possible during the day.

I walk slowly round the bend in the Wallstrasse. The machines hum in the Power Works across the way. No one is to be seen outside Franz Zander's house. A few children play with tops on the pavement. Käthe ! It is a beautiful day; the sun burns. In a few weeks we will be able to get out into the open, will be able to meet and talk without danger. Certainly Käthe has let me know that, in spite of watching for it all the time, she has so far not noticed any signs of being kept under observation. Spending a day on the river will provide us with new possibilities. No one will recognise a meeting of Party officials in a group of people in bathing-suits.

A few seconds later I am at the Berlinerstrasse. It serves a broad stream of traffic crossing the Wall and Rosinenstrasse, at right angles. The latter is a continuation of the Wallstrasse, on the other side of the Berlinerstrasse. I stood here at this very corner as the S.A. lorries rolled into the town on January 21st. With Richard Hüttig and Franz. Richard has been arrested; Franz has fled. Our street has changed. It seems to me that it is years since then.

I glance round carefully, walk slowly across the road and along the Rosinenstrasse. Only a few steps. There, on the other side, the People's Centre. An S.A. double sentry stands in front of the broad entrance-gate. They have their chin-straps buckled under the chin.

On the left, in front of me, is a cigar shop.

" A packet of Juno," I say.

I pretend to be looking in the shop window, but I glance quickly across the road. Cars and motor-bicycles stand in front of the building in a long row. The nickel and the paintwork reflect the sunlight. Brand new. They've got hold of the State funds now. I can see part of the courtyard through the entrance. Cars are there as well. Next door, on the left, is a co-operative store. Not a customer to be seen. I light a cigarette clumsily.

The long rows of windows of the large grey house are closed. Heavy curtains hang in front of a few. There, on the first floor, were the offices of the Social-Democrat Youth Organisations. One always used to see the red lettering on the wall. That has gone now. A large car drives up. A standard banner protected in stiff gauze is fixed on the nickel radiator cap. A highly decorated uniform jumps out of the car. The S.A. sentries click their heels together, stand at attention.

I leave the shop. Outside I puff nervously at the cigarette. If they should stop me ? Rubbish. Only the sentries are to be seen. The People's Centre is built on a corner, on the far side of a short *cul-de-sac*. The rooms of the District Health Insurance Committee are on the ground floor, otherwise only Social-Democrat comrades live in the whole house. The slogans on the house gable on the left, fronting on to the alley, have been painted over by the S.A.

I walk slowly. The Charlottenburg People's Centre—S.A. barracks! "This Marxist pigsty will be the first to be cleaned out," the Nazis had always said. They have renamed it Maikowski House. The barred cellars in the courtyard are said to be filled with prisoners. What changes the People's Centre has seen in its time! Long before the war Social-Democrat meetings were held there. In 1918 the homecoming troops were quartered there. In the revolutionary days arms of the Republican People's Defence Forces stood piled up in the courtyards—against the Spartacus.

Now the People's Centre is the barracks of the Thirty-threes, the "Murder Storm."

The People's Centre—Maikowski Barracks!

To-day all our lives are threatened!

. . . .

Rothacker was almost arrested to-day.

"Maybe you want to write that down, Jan," he said. He knows that I make notes on all the happenings.

Rothacker cycled to Jungfernheide station. He had to meet the new man who keeps us in touch with the Siemensstadt hut settlement in place of Strubbel. We had chosen the knocking-off hour of the Siemens Works for the meeting. There are crowds of people all round the station at that time.

Trams drove past. They were all densely packed. "Perhaps Teichert's in one," he thought. Teichert is a turner at Siemens. A short way before the station Rothacker felt in his vest pocket. All in order. The piece of newspaper cut with irregular edges was there. The other man had a similar piece; they had to fit when laid together. Rothacker recalls once more the signs by which to recognise the comrade. A round bowler, a fresh face with a small black beard, the *Deutsche Allgemeine Zeitung* in the left hand.

"Can you please tell me the shortest way to Tegel?" he would ask him.

"I'm sorry. I'm a stranger to Berlin," the answer had to be.

Rothacker then leant his bicycle against the station wall and kept the tram stop in view. The station clock pointed to two minutes to the hour. The comrade was not there yet. The trams brought a ceaseless flow of people along, who crowded into the station. The big hand of the clock was exactly on the hour mark. Wherever was the comrade? It was impossible that he could have missed him!

Five minutes past. Still no sign. Rothacker walked up and down. "Another five minutes, and then I'll go." He glanced round carefully. On the other side, near the cab ranks, stood two cars. The chauffeurs were talking. A newspaper stand mounted on wheels stood at the corner. The owner was looking out of the tiny peephole. Rothacker became restless because he was the only one who stood about for any length of time. Behind the last taxi he suddenly saw a motor-cycle, beside which two S.A. men were standing and talking. Were they only pretending? Rubbish! "You're seeing things. You'll be making the first mistake if you have a 'guilty conscience,' and imagine yourself watched. If you behave in an unusual way, you're sure to attract the attention of the police—an old tale."

Ten minutes past the hour. Rothacker pushed his bicycle into the gutter and rode off. He was annoyed. The comrade had not kept the appointment. As if one could afford such carelessness these days! One had to be dead or arrested; no other excuse could be allowed. He would jolly well give him a piece of his mind, unless something really serious had hindered him. He turned past the railway embankment on the left into a quiet side-street. At the crossing further on he heard the spluttering of an engine behind him. The motor-bicycle with the two S.A. men drove past. The driver slowed down suddenly, the tyres skidding on the asphalt. The machine turned, then stood at right angles to the street. So he hadn't been mistaken! The pillion rider jumped down.

"Stop!" he shouted.

The other one rested the machine on its stand. He was tall and broad-shouldered, the pillion rider short and very young. Rothacker looked calmly at both. "33" was pinned in bright metal figures on their shiny uniform collars. " Damn ! ' Our ' Storm. Hope they don't recognise me."

" Search him ! " ordered the tall one.

" Hands up ! " growled the younger one.

Rothacker laid his bicycle on the asphalt and obeyed. The street was empty except for a man, with a woman holding his arm, a short way further on. They glanced nervously across. " I'm properly at their mercy here," thought Rothacker.

The younger S.A. man began feeling the outside of his pockets. As he came to the back trouser pocket he drew back with a jerk.

" What's in this pocket ? "

" A leather wallet with keys ! "

" Take it out yourself ! "

The heroes ! It could be a revolver with the safety catch unfastened. He pulled the wallet out and opened the zip fastener.

" Here you are ! "

" None of your lip ! " shouted the S.A. man.

" Have you your identification papers ? "

" Yes. My military papers."

The two exchanged glances.

" You were at the front ? "

" Yes."

" That's given you a jolt," he thought.

" Hand them over ! "

Rothacker pulled out another wallet, and selected the required papers. The S.A. men turned their backs to the light cast by the street lamps and read. Rothacker saw the tall one nudging the younger one.

" You were wounded ? "

" Yes. Three times, once severely."

The tall one returned the papers. A pause.

" Who were you waiting for, then, at the station ? "

" For an old work-mate. From Siemens. He was going to try and find me work."

The two exchanged glances again. The tall one nodded.

" No harm meant. Things are just like that nowadays, so

that the innocent must expect these things." He shrugged his shoulders. " In any case, we're only doing our duty ! "
" Heil Hitler ! "
" Heil Hitler ! "

. . . .

The next day. Strubbel is at my place. He keeps on pushing his hair back from his face, even more fervently than usual.
" Did Rothacker tell you all about it ? "
" Yes."
Strubbel is silent for a long while, rests his head in his hands. The strands of black hair fall forward. They always hang over his brow. Doesn't he ever use a comb ? I wait, can see by looking at him that he wants to say something and is struggling with himself.
" It'll soon be evening. I'm goin' to the settlemen'; we've gotter keep in touch." The words come from his lips with difficulty. " Edith and the boy also need clothes. The typewriter and cyclostyle are still there. Coming along ? "
The S.A. has an " alarm regiment " stationed in the hut settlement. He had just managed to escape their bullet a fortnight ago. Now he wants to . . . Madness !
" Give us the name of another comrade. We'll try to get in touch with him. You can have clothes by to-morrow. We'll fetch the machines later. We, not you, Strubbel ! "
Strubbel shakes his head. He pushes his fingers again and again through his hair. Talks for a long time. For some time he has regretted " deserting his post." Whatever would the settlers think of him, after years of . . . ? Is he, perhaps, a special case ? Any other comrade would have remained. In any event, he must continue to look after the work there. Yes, of course. As for the machines, he had told a settler to hide them. A short, lame cripple. He was regarded there as a harmless fool. Had never had anything to do with him before. He wanted to go to him; he lived close to the edge of the wood. But he would only give Strubbel the things; trusted no one else.
I try once more to dissuade him. He is acting contrary to

the first rules of underground work. I even threaten to report his lack of discipline.

Strubbel stands up.

" I'm goin'." He cuts my words short.

I waver. Can I let him go alone ? What I said applies to me as well. I'm a Party official and am not allowed to do anything rash. But he will think I am a coward. I take my hat down from the hook.

. . . We cut across a muddy field path. Our feet sink in deeply at every step. We keep ten yards apart. Strubbel often stops to listen. We reach the wood. I find difficulty in keeping him in sight amongst the trees and undergrowth. Strubbel suddenly falls flat. I throw myself down behind a clump of blackberry bushes. Two S.A. men ride past the edge of the wood on bicycles. Rifles hang slantingly over their shoulders.

" . . . and then, orl at once, she . . ."

By now they have passed us ; only their laughter still drifts back.

Then we are in narrow paths bordered by decrepit fences. Low, box-like huts stand behind them. Strubbel glances round, takes a few long strides. The hinge of a door squeaks.

The petrol lamp throws a yellow patch of light on to the table, leaving the rest of the room in semi-darkness. There is a smell of dung and something acid. The " half-witted " cripple sits opposite me. His head is sunk deep between his shoulders; the ears stand out like large flappers. His arms lie on the table. They are unnaturally long. The backs of his hands are very hairy.

" It's all here," he says. " I've waited two days already."

He has a thin, shrill voice like a child's.

" We wanted to meet someone from the settlement yesterday, but 'e didn't turn up," says Strubbel.

" Who ? "

" Dunke."

" Arrested three days ago."

Silence.

" Are the S.A. . . . ? "

" Still at Schwenke's. Twenty men. The dirty swine went

with them from hut to hut. They fetched Eber. He was back again two days later. Knocked to bits. The comrades say that they're leaving him here as a bait. Want to see who's got anything to do with 'im."

" Anything else ? "

" Haven't seen anything special. They've been asking for you all over the place."

Steps outside. The tiny window is only half open. We listen. We can't see anything except that there are three of them. They go by. The cripple rummages in a corner. Comes back to the table.

" Collected it for you."

A twenty-mark note lies in front of Strubbel. He takes the money hesitatingly, wants to say something . . . glaring light thrown from a headlight suddenly fills the room—disappears. Outside a motor-cycle rattles past.

" There isn't one in the settlement," says the cripple.

The S.A. !

" Can you keep in touch with us in the meanwhile ? "

" Yes."

I name a spot, and arrange the time.

" Come on, now ! "

We grope our way round the hut, then stand in the shed. Hens sit on long poles and shake themselves. The beams of our flashlights startle a goat. She stares at us, bleating softly, her taut udder swaying to and fro. The cripple opens a battered case. It is half filled with yellow feeding-corn. He digs his hands deep into it, and brings out two large packets: the typewriter and the cyclostyle. We stuff them in our rucksacks, the clothes on top.

We return past gooseberry-bushes, past the tiny lavatory shed, and finally the fence. Behind that the wood. The cripple lifts up the wire railing for us.

.   .   .   .

Two weeks later Strubbel and his wife moved into the Königswusterhausen district. He has got a job with a farmer. He couldn't earn anything in our district.

During the first few weeks after the Reichstag fire we had no communication with the central Party offices. The whole organisation seemed to have fallen to pieces. Added to this, the wave of terrorism and arrests has been specially concentrated in our district. We could issue no paper, only the leaflet on the Reichstag fire. As neither information nor instructions came from above, we had confined ourselves to keeping together the most reliable comrades. We had also managed to maintain our two factory connections, through Strubbel's hut settlement and Teichert.

But a Party committee was formed in our district a week ago. We were supplied with newspapers and the *Rote Fahne*[43] for the first time. Franz's suggestion that we print the next issue of our own paper in his district was approved of by our committee, on account of the special danger in our neighbourhood. Our new Party committee has even asked us to-day whether we have a reliable comrade who could take supplies to the provinces on a motor-bicycle. Ernst Schwiebus carries his firm's express orders on a motor-cycle instead of the tricycle. But that's out of the question because of his work. What about Ede? Rothacker suggests that although he has no driving licence he can ride well. He had once gone for a ride with him. It hadn't been Ede's bike; the devil only knows where he got hold of it. Ede was just Ede.

I meet Ede in the afternoon. He has followed Rothacker's advice; is wearing his Sunday clothes, a blue suit and a soft hat. The glass eye is in position. He shakes hands briskly.

" That Erich did make a fuss. I've 'ad to get all dressed up in me Sunday clo'es for the doings."

I have to laugh. " Why, you look almost respectable."

" I feels like it, too, Jan," he assures me.

We walk down an avenue flanked by trees.

" What kinderva bus is it ? "

Ede turns his head round until his right eye is looking at me. He seems excited; is sure to be delighted at the prospect of the motor-cycle ride.

" They didn't say. The place is fifty miles away; you ought to be back in three hours at the most."

He pulls a wry mouth, shaking his head.

" It'll 'ave ter be a five hundred c.cm. one at least." He laughs. " Three hours—an' what if a tyre busts ? "

Five hundred c.cm. I don't quite follow. I pull at his arm.

" Are you a careful driver ? It's no joy-ride. You'll have a risky load with you, old man."

" Jan, you're barmy. Yer knows me long enough." Ede shakes his head reprovingly. " Does I drive carefully ? I was motor-bike driver for more'n a year in the Army."

Of course, and he's a mechanic as well. But when he manages to get hold of a job, it's only for a short time. He can't do the tricky bits up to standard any more, because of his eyes.

We walk back slowly.

" What I wanted ter tell yer—Kurgel was at my place."

" Well, and . . . ? "

Kurgel is the comrade from the R.F.B.[44] who keeps touch with us.

" 'E wants ter see Franz. 'Ow is it 'e don't know where Franz is ? "

" No one is to know that; you're not to either. Arrange a meeting for me with Kurgel and then let me know where."

" O.K.," says Ede, and, after a pause, " 'e also asked me whether we knew anyfing abaht Dammert."

" Nothing certain. He's supposed to be in Maikowski House."

Dammert was arrested two weeks ago—we believe in connection with the Maikowski affair.

We walk for a while without speaking. Ede chuckles suddenly. I look at him enquiringly.

" Kurgel, 'e told me a tale, 'e did. The fife-player Rudi—but yer knows 'im, don't yer ? "

I nod. He also belongs to the R.F.B. Used to play the fife in Spielman's Group.

" Wasn't he sent with other comrades into the Stahlhelm Youth Organisation, so as not to be known? "

"That's what it's all abaht. Well, 'e goes 'ome with a Stahlhelm from that there recruitin' pub abaht a week ago. They was both wearing their blue shirts with the swastika ribbon round the arm. That Steelhelmet jaws a mouthful at Rudi all the way 'ome. Wouldn't 'e jes like ter get 'old of a real flesh-and-blood Communist. 'E would jest abaht give 'im wot for. 'E'd knock 'is block off, 'e would, and more of that kinder talk. 'E jaws and jaws. Rudi starts to get mad. Orl at once 'e lashes out an' gives that there ' comrade ' a juicy one, and then a lot more. 'E finished 'im off jest nicely."

Ede roars with laughter, holding his sides.

" And you think that clever ? "

Ede is good comrade, but he's just Ede. And he would behave in exactly the same way himself on a similar occasion. And I had just arranged the motor-cycle journey with him ! Can I accept responsibility for that ?

" Of course it was crazy," he answers. " 'E was arrested, as was only ter be expected."

He tapped his chest melodramatically. " But I can understand the chap's feelings. I'd 'a' seen red meself ! "

He pauses, shaking his head thoughtfully.

" I can't even salute the bloody flag," he starts off again. " I goes into a 'ouse when I sees one o' them there proceshuns comin' along."

I look at him. Even the glass eye seems to express his loathing.

A decree has been in force for some weeks that the swastika flags carried in the marching processions must be saluted by all the Volksgenossen[45] or otherwise they will be charged with being Marxists.

" The other day I couldn't get to a 'ouse in time," Ede continues, " so I turns me backside on 'em ! "

" You're mad ! You really touched toes ? "

" Bosh. You don't think I'm agoin' to let meself be catched, do yer ? I just turned round, tha's what I did."

But now it's my turn to laugh.

" What's up ? What's up ? " demands Ede.

"Do you think they knew what that meant?"
"I knew; tha's enuff for me," says Ede in offended tones.

. . . .

Many rumours circulated about the Maikowski House the last few weeks. It was said that the comrades arrested were brutally tortured. But we never heard details. Didn't even know for certain which of the arrested comrades were there.

But I had a talk with X yesterday. He had begged Ernst Schwiebus to arrange a meeting with me. I had hesitated for some time whether I should meet him but went in the end. Schwiebus had assured me that he had the impression that X was reliable. X used to belong to one of our mass organisations. After the Reichstag elections on March 5th we saw him running around in S.A. uniform. We then avoided him and warned all the other comrades.

He told me yesterday that he was forced by his employer to enter the S.A. His chief had explained that he could only employ S.A. men in the future. X is a baker. He has worked for many years in this particular bakery, and felt he couldn't let his family down. His wife is often ill, and he has two children.

"I'm not in the Storm Thirty-three, only belong to the West Standard," he explained. (He also wears a different Storm number on his brown shirt, and to prove his words he showed me his S.A. certificate.) "I am on the S.A. reserves, am over thirty-five. I don't usually go to the Maikowski barracks, but they had ordered me to be there that evening. I was to take over the cashier's job." X paused. I did not press him, as it was obvious that he spoke with difficulty. "We sat at the tables; a lot played cards, a few read newspapers. Suddenly the door flew open.

"'The Stormleader,' someone cried.

"Then everyone jumped up. A few Thirty-threes were with him, with two civilians in between. An S.A. man cried, 'The one on the left is Karl, the fife-player from the R.F.B.' I saw that the mouth of one of the arrested men twitched."

X broke off here. He was twitching nervously himself.

He started again: "The whole crowd pushed forward to the centre of the room. The Stormleader sat down on a table, propped his knee-boots on a chair. 'Now we'll have a nice little talk,' he said to the fellow they had called Karl. Kind of black-haired chap. He then pointed to the other one.

"'Stand him in the corner. We caught him right now, outside the front door. He can take a look at the business: he won't need more than a few pairs of dry trousers. At the same time he'll lose the habit of sniffing around.'

"All the S.A. laughed. The other man, short and fat, was trembling pitifully. He had a kind of stiff bowler which he turned round and round in his hands. It seemed as if he would soon burst into tears.

"'Herr Stormleader . . . Herr . . . I only wanted to go home. . . . I . . .' he stuttered.

"'Shut up!' shouted the Stormleader.

"An S.A. man pulled the fat man to one side. Then they tackled the black-haired chap again. The Stormleader cried: 'You're one of the cowardly murderers who did our Hanne in—you belong to the red gangster's club! Look alive; out with your name.' The latter answered calmly: 'Kurgel.' He then said: 'It's true I was once in the R.F.B., but I had nothing to do with the Maikowski affair. I wasn't even in Berlin at the time.'"

(I am startled to hear the name, but suppress any show of feeling. X need not realise that I know Kurgel. We already knew that Kurgel was arrested. Ede had not been able to get in touch with him after our talk. The other tenants had told him that the S.A. had fetched him late at night. But we did not know where he was. The reason for the arrest was still a riddle to us.)

"All the S.A.s had moved closer to Kurgel at the name 'Maikowski.' But the Stormleader went right up to him.

"'Where is Zander? Franz Zander?' he asked suddenly."

(So they had arrested him on account of Franz. I hid my excitement.)

"Kurgel looked at him. but remained silent. The Stormleader threatened him: 'Are you going to answer? Or must we help you?' Kurgel's only reply was 'I don't know any Franz Zander.' But he spoke quite differently now, in a kind of dull voice. I could see that he had come to a decision in the few seconds. The Stormleader's face went purple with rage. He raised his arm and hit Kurgel in the face with his fist. The blood came in thick drops from his nose, ran down on to his shirt.

"The Stormleader now lost his temper properly: 'You don't know any Zander? You're lying, you b——.'

"'No!' said Kurgel once more.

"'He's got guts,' someone behind me whispered.

"'Fetch Dammert from the cellar!' ordered the Stormleader."

(I interrupted X here: "Are you sure you heard properly —Dammert?")

"Yes. Dammert!"

(So Dammert had denounced him! And two days before this Kurgel had still asked Ede whether he knew where Dammert was.)

"Two S.A.s ran off. The Stormleader paced excitedly up and down. Then the S.A. men came back with Dammert. They half pulled him. He looked awful. His whole face was swollen and covered with dried blood. His clothes were dirtied and torn. The Stormleader yelled: 'Put them face to face!' They dragged Dammert into the centre of the room. The Stormleader stood in front of the two of them. He gave Dammert a blow on the chin. 'Heh! Wake up! Is this Kurgel here? Zander's partner?' he asked.

"Dammert raised his head with an effort. His glance seemed to say: 'Forgive me—I can't stand any more.' Dammert nodded his head wearily. The Stormleader laughed. 'The cure seems to have done him good, what?' He turned to Kurgel. 'Do you still refuse to answer, you swine? Out with it. Where is Zander hiding?'"

(X asked me whether I knew Zander. Of course I said no.)

"'Yes, I know Zander, but don't know where he is,'

Kurgel said defiantly. He knew quite well that, after once pretending not to know him, they would not believe him any more. The Stormleader waved his arms about wildly in front of Kurgel's face, mad with rage. The other S.A.s were excited as well. ' Put him through it—use the whip on him,' a few cried. ' Hell ! The chap's got nerve,' said the one behind me. He was very tall, with bushy eyebrows. They called him ' Lamp-post.' But Kurgel kept on staring straight ahead. He was still bleeding.

" The Stormleader said : ' So you know him all right, but you still don't know where he is ? ' He slowly unbuttoned his revolver holster and took the pistol out. He pulled the safety-catch back, and pointed the revolver at Kurgel. He shrieked at him : ' You've got two minutes to recover your memory ! '

" Kurgel stood quite still, not uttering a sound."

(I had to clench my teeth so as not to let X notice that I knew all these comrades. Kurgel—he really did not know where Franz was.)

" ' Stand him against the wall ! ' the Stormleader roared.

" They dragged Kurgel round. He stood there quite calmly, and looked at the wall. The Stormleader shot twice. The plaster spurted. I had stepped back with the other S.A. He had fired wide on purpose. They dragged Kurgel round again. The Stormleader raved at him : ' Have you changed your mind yet ? You'll be sorry if you haven't ! Where's Zander hiding ? ' Kurgel looked him straight in the face, that was all. The Stormleader called out to the man behind me, ' Fetch the rawhide strap, " Lamp-post." '

" ' Are you ready for the fun ? ' he then asked. The others all laughed at that.

" But the S.A. man ' Lamp-post ' did not laugh. He said, ' Better let 'em play with each other.' The leader agreed to this.

" I believe that ' Lamp-post ' did not want to knock them about," said X. " He just didn't want to. There are a few like that among them who don't fancy the job of putting prisoners with guts through the mill.

" Two S.A.s came up with strong leather whips. Dammert was laid over a bench, his shirt pulled up to his head. His back was one mass of raw weals. The Stormleader gave Kurgel one of the straps and said: ' So you won't talk? Here, you can tickle your " comrade " now. Until you've changed your mind! ' He threatened him with a clenched fist."

X stood up from his chair and demonstrated the clenched fist.

" ' If you don't hit him, it'll be your turn to be hit. Get on with it ! ' " he continued. " They shoved Kurgel to the bench. He stood there without moving.

" Sudden silence in the room.

" The Stormleader went for him. ' What about it ? '

" And I," said X, " I was so afraid all the time that the others were sure to hear how loudly my heart was beating. But Kurgel made no movement. The others watched in dead silence. It was Dammert who broke the silence with a groan. ' Hit me . . . you must hit me. . . .' Kurgel dropped his head on his breast at that. Then he suddenly jumped round and threw the whip at the Stormleader's feet. Then they grabbed hold of him and threw him on to the bench. The Stormleader started on him. Kurgel shrieked so that I had to bite my lips to keep quiet. Then a bubbling sound came from his lips, and he was still. He had fainted. . . ."

We sat quite a while without a word. X then begged me not to make any use of what he had told me; he was afraid the worst would happen to him. He refused to keep in constant touch with us. He was only in the S.A. reserves, didn't have much chance of getting to know things. But I managed to persuade him to report to Schwiebus in the perfumery at irregular intervals.

I know what will happen to me if the Nazis get hold of what I've written. I did not write a word all last week. I was even very near to burning it all. The obstacles seemed too great. I have tried to obtain another room for writing. But that could only be among comrades. And they're all just as much up to their necks in the illegal work as I am.

A sudden raid at night is quite likely to take place in their houses. And then they would be certain to be compromised through me.

The spot where I am hiding the manuscript isn't safe either. But I was terribly restless during the week when I did not write. There seems to be a heavy weight on my mind forcing me to carry on. I *must* write all that down! We *must* succeed in getting this manuscript out of the country. We *must* try to rouse the conscience of humanity.

· · · · · · · ·

I met Franz in his new district yesterday and told him at once about X's report. He listened in silence.

He then took me to the comrades with whom I was to spend the night. We wanted to meet toward the morning to print our paper.

The idea of ringing up Käthe at her office occurred to me yesterday. Dare I arrange to meet her in this district? I felt I must see her again after such a long separation. She had kept on sending messages that she had not noticed the slightest signs of being followed. But dare I ask her to come? To an apartment that was to be my operating base for political work? I hesitated for a long time, invented a whole string of plausible reasons for doing so: it is sure to be all right, just for once; she says that she has not noticed any signs of being under observation. But my political scruples would not let themselves be allayed. However I rang her up to-day after all.

I saunter along the streets. It is warm, the sun is reflected from the windows in the row of houses. The days are lengthening. In the Tauenzienstrasse there are crowds of pedestrians as usual. The women are wearing new spring outfits. The restaurants are packed, there are many S.S. officers among the guests. Behind the shop windows are posters:

GERMAN FIRM!
GERMAN GOODS: GERMAN MANUFACTURE ONLY!

Pictures of Hitler mounted in heavy silver and gold frames, some entwined with green garlands, are set above the posters. Many shop proprietors defend themselves against the sudden " vulgar competition." Their posters are larger:

OLD NATIONAL-SOCIALIST CONCERN SINCE . . .

In one window Hitler looks ponderously, with crossed arms, at the rare and costly flowers arranged around him. Behind him, a large glass bowl, in which tropical fish and goldfish swim about, illuminated by red lights. This shop also declares on its poster that its flowers and fish have always been patriotically German.

Käthe is already in the café. Her face lightens up. She flushes with joy.

" It was a job to keep a seat for you." She says that just in order to say something. I can't get any further than a formal greeting myself. We hadn't seen each other for so long, and now I can't utter a word. I just take her hand. The shrill ring from the cash desk is heard. Waitresses wearing white caps rush to and fro. I am content. If only our time were not so short ! A newspaper boy passes along between the tables.

" Paper."

NEW LAW AFFECTING CIVIL SERVANTS !

I just have to start reading. Even let go of Käthe's hand.

" The new regime is doling out the jobs," I comment.

We leave. Käthe hangs on my arm. She is wearing a light spring costume, a coloured triangular scarf round her neck. I feel happy.

" Do look where you're going, Jan. We're knocking into all the people."

" It can't be helped to-day—I hardly know you any more."

" Where are we going, anyway ? "

" Wait and see."

We walk for a while in silence. I turn into a small side-street.

"Jan?"

I start. My misgivings have returned. Nonsense! We have not been followed. I had been watching carefully, especially the last few minutes.

The steps are broad and badly worn. The plaster has fallen off in large pieces. It smells of fried onions here. Four doors are ranged in a semicircle in the hall on each floor. I ring. Comrade Lamprecht, a short dark woman, opens.

"Here we are."

"Come right in," she says in friendly tones, opening the door wide.

We walk down the long corridor always to be found in the old Berlin houses. In the open doorway of the living-room stands her little girl, the light from the lamp shining brightly on her fair hair.

"Uncle Karl—Uncle Karl."

"That's my name here," I whisper to Käthe.

The Lamprechts are having their supper. The husband sits at the table in a blue checked shirt, with the sleeves rolled up. He is tall and well built, looks very young. We shake hands.

"Here is Käthe."

"Kurt—Erna," they answer. Erna has soft, flabby hands.

"I was out washing to-day," she remarks.

"And I carry coal," laughs Kurt, "so that there's enough washing to do for me as well."

We sit down.

"Won't you have a cup of coffee with us?"

"No, thanks, really not."

The little girl stands beside her mother but looks at Käthe.

"What's your name?" asks Käthe.

She approaches shyly. Käthe takes her on her lap.

We want to have a house of our own one day. A cheerful room like this in which to have our meals.

"What's the news, Kurt?"

"At the yard? None. Rudi was here just before you came in, he brought the rucksack and the suit. You should be punctual; three o'clock."

"Nothing else?"

"No."

"Then that'll be all right. A smart lot, your fellows."

Kurt speaks about the yard after all. He supplies most of his mates with papers. The drivers then pass them on to the barges on the Spree. We talk for a long time. I ask Kurt about this and that, but hardly hear his answers.

"I'll show you my den," I say to Käthe at length. It is further back along the corridor. I unbolt the door, and light the oil lamp. A washbowl on a chest of drawers, a small table, a chair. Near the door, on the right, a camp bed. Faded pictures cut from the illustrated papers are pinned over the bed. I lie half across the camp-bed, with my arms crossed under my head. Käthe goes quickly to the window, looks out.

"Tiny, isn't it?"

Käthe nods, sits down near me. I put my arm round her. She points to the chair on which a pair of blue overalls is lying, together with a rucksack.

"What do you need that for?"

I take hold of her neck in my two hands, pull her towards me. Her hair hangs over both our faces, our breath mingling.

Try how I will, I cannot get rid of the thought that she should not be here in this room.

. . . .

Not a soul in the streets. In the early dawn the lamps hang from their tall iron posts like glowing balls of fire. I shiver, and take longer strides. Long ranks of taxis stand at the street corners. The drivers have their coat-collars turned up; most of them lean back asleep. They are waiting for late fares. There are a number of dancing-halls and bars here in the West End of Berlin. Their coloured neon signs are still shining. Their entrances are built in a heavy style, some made of small thick bull's-eye glass panes. Posters hang outside: " So-and-so's band to-night."

Franz is already waiting with Rudi and Bruno at the corner. They are wearing their blue overalls. Rudi carries a large leather tool-bag over his shoulder. The others have rucksacks. We shake hands.

" Mornin', Karl."

" Come on," says Bruno, " we haven't got a single moment to lose."

Two Schupos stand at the corner. They watch us go.

" If they only knew what we were up to—strewth ! " whispers Rudi.

Bruno laughs. His pug-nose broadens. He used to do a lot of boxing, that's where he got that nose, Franz told me once.

Rudi comes nearer to me.

" We're mechanics from the firm of Scheidler & Co., No. 3 Bülowstrasse. We've a locksmith's job to do for the stage decorations. Got that ? "

" Yes."

" 'Ow many 'ave we this time ? "

" Six hundred."

" The charwomen come in later. Will we have finished by then ? "

" Sure; easy."

Silence. A metallic clink from Rudi's tool-bag.

" There's the brothel," says Bruno.

" The Spanish Rose " in blue illuminated letters above the entrance. A small iron door on the left of the entrance, with a brass button at the side—the " Night " bell.

" Now keep quiet," says Rudi. The door opens with a slight buzzing from the automatic release. We pass along a narrow hall. A dimly burning lamp hangs from the ceiling. There is a small window further on—open. Rudi puts his head in. " Heil Hitler." The room is small. A lamp with a green glass shade rests on the writing-table. A fat man stands in front of a wash-basin in his shirt-sleeves. He is wearing black trousers with heavy gold braid down the sides. The jacket, to match, hangs over a chair. He is holding a towel, and has red spots on his face. His nose has a bluish tinge.

" Heil Hitler," he replies in a deep voice. " Back already ? I'm just clearing out."

He wipes his bald head with the towel, his corporation wobbling.

" With an extra hand," answers Rudi. " We want to finish the job to-day."

" Good, good. You know the way," mumbles the fat man.

We pass through the kitchen. The white tiles are reflected in the brightly polished electric stoves; refrigerators and cupboards are built in the walls. We come through a frosted glass door to an oblong room which smells of stale smoke. Tiny cubicles are divided off round the walls. They are hidden behind heavy red velvet curtains. One of the curtains is not drawn to; it reveals two deep armchairs and a low round table. Half a cigar, with a broad band round it, lies on a gleaming ashtray. The tablecloth is badly stained with wine. The bar is further on. High stools are ranged against the curved bar. The nickel taps gleam. Bottles of wine and spirits in long rows are reflected in the mirror; some are still in their raffia baskets.

" For the . . . ! " says Bruno, stopping.

" Carry on, up to the cabaret rooms," urges Rudi. " We've got no time to waste."

There is a highly polished dance-floor in the centre of the room. A platform on the right, holding a grand piano and two rows of chairs with music-stands in front. Silver lacquered tables and curved chairs are ranged against the walls. Lamps, with crystal shades to match, are fitted into the walls. They contrast brightly with the navy blue cloth drapery.

Bruno moves a few tables together and places a cloth on a near-by chair.

" Come on, let's start putting the machine together. If anyone comes, chuck the cloth over the bloody lot."

" The fat fellow with the gold braid was the last one 'ere," remarks Rudi.

Bruno whistles through his teeth.

"The last one. That's what my ma said too—and I got born fer all that!"

Rudi points to the tiny stage near by.

"You kick up as much row as you want; we'll be making enough mechanics' noise."

He goes over there with Bruno. Franz and I unpack the cyclostyle and take the wax sheets out of the rucksack. We had put them between cardboard, and they have remained quite flat. The boys have got plenty of guts, for each of us would get any number of years' hard labour if we were found out.

Franz inks the gauze sheet with the tube of ink. Then we pin the wax sheets firmly on to the apparatus with drawing-pins.

"You put them down from the side, Karl. I'll roll across. Look, like this," says Franz. "It's the quickest way."

He places a sheet of paper in position; the rubber roller slides across. How well he remembers the different names. It seems quite natural that I should be called "Karl" here.

"It's got to be non-stop work. Paper in position, paper removed, paper in position, paper removed."

We examine the first sheet. *Die Rote Fahne.*

"Too greasy; it smudges," I point out.

"The next will be . . ." The words are deafened by the noise the other two are making, hammering away in front. I nod.

I am in swing after a dozen sheets have been printed. Paper in position—Franz moistens the rubber roller—rolls it across—raise the gauze lid—paper removed—paper in position. The printed sheets are piled up on the near-by table.

The red flag—the red—the red——

They are hammering at something made of iron on the stage. The hall reverberates.

Right hand removes sheet—new page in position with the left—straighten it out—lid down—Franz—right hand removes sheet—— My hands work backwards and forwards automatically. What had the local Berlin papers written recently? " Taken from a secret report of the Gestapo. ' We must be quicker and more precise in our observations and arrests. We have so far failed to catch up with the everchanging methods of the Communists. . . .' " A jazz band had played here two hours ago. High S.A. and S.S. officials had most likely sat in the screened-off cubicles in the other room. Now we're doing this work here. At the moment, dozens of cyclostyles are most likely working at top speed all over the city. Goering orders arrests and " shot while trying to escape." But pamphlets and papers like ours keep on reappearing.

Right hand—left hand——

Bruno jumps down from the stage. He stands near us, swinging his hammer. The rubber roller moves to and fro, my hands with it. Bruno's face is smeared with sweat. His boxer's nose broadens.

" It's doing well, eh? 'Bout a third now, I reckon." He nods at the printed pile, goes back to Rudi. We work silently. The pile of clean sheets is getting smaller. The hammers clang. Now and again the two call out to each other. But I can't make out the words. Perhaps it's only a bit of bluff. They're fine workers ! As we finish off the last sheet I glance at my watch. A few minutes past seven. My eyes ache, my arms are stiff. Every movement starts a shooting-pain in the shoulder-blades.

" That's the lot," says Franz. He wipes his brow, smearing himself with ink. He straightens his back.

" You'd better cut it now, Karl."

" Yes."

We pack up. A loud knocking outside. We jerk round. The hammering in front continues; they have not heard anything. Franz looks at me, petrified. He ducks, as if ready for a jump. I throw the cloth over the tables. We look at the door on the right as if frozen. They are still hammering away in front ! The door flies open. A woman carrying a scrubbingbrush and pail stands in the doorway.

"Mornin'," she says, and nods to us.

Franz takes a deep breath of relief. His back relaxes as if a heavy load had just slipped off.

"Mornin'," he answers, relieved. I can only nod. The fright has set my nerves quivering.

The charwoman goes out. I tie up my rucksack.

"Hey, there! Hey, there!" calls Franz.

The hammering ceases; the other two come running down from the stage, making a noise with their boots.

"Karl's going."

"Cheerio, 'assistant fitter,'" says Rudi. His red hair is moist, and there are beads of sweat on his freckled face.

"Wish the others luck," says Franz.

"Thanks."

I avoid looking him in the face. Busy myself with the straps of the rucksack. I have not told him about the meeting with Käthe. He'll hear about it from the Lamprechts in any case; by then it will be too late for him to be angry.

I go by bus. Scrutinise carefully the other passengers who get in with me. A tall man, wearing gold-rimmed glasses, and a young girl. The narrow seat in the front of the bus, with its back to the driver, is free. I sit down there. Have the whole length of the bus in front of me from here; can keep the two in sight. How natural all these little dodges seem by this time. "To watch while travelling, that you are not being shadowed, is most important, Jan." An S.A. man sits in front of me on the right. Why is he staring at me like that? Nonsense. He is only taking his forty winks. He is almost asleep; has very small eyes. The tall man with the glasses soon gets out. The girl a few stops further on. Walking along the streets, I feel very bucked that the "roly-poly" job was so successful. The others will be as pleased as I am.

  · · · · · · ·

We have none of us been able to form a proper link with the Social-Democrat comrades. Two of our group, Teichert and Schwiebus, think that we can only pull together if these will realise that our opposition to the policy of always trying to choose the lesser evil had been right after all. I think that things are far too serious to be fighting over such differences. We must stress all the points on which we are agreed in the discussions. The Nazis were able to jump to power because the workers couldn't oppose them with a united front.

We know a few Social-Democrat comrades from former meetings. Some have been so intimidated that they are too scared even to *talk* politics. With others, again, we don't know whether they haven't been " converted." But they regard us in the same light. There have been traitors in both parties.

Our comrade, " Ready-made," the salesman at Brennickmayer's, again approached his two trade union mates. They told him that illegal underground work was now useless. The comrades who knew each other must keep together, that was all. He could only sell one of them a paper; the other one was too frightened.

I had to report to Joachim, of the district committee, two days ago on our unity work. He promised to arrange a meeting with Alex, and he told me that Alex had already made contact with a few Social-Democrat comrades in our district. I have never worked with Alex, but have known him a long time. He was the leader of one of our dramatic groups.

I met Alex to-day. Yes, he was in touch with the others, he said. But he had not been able to get further than talks. The Social-Democrat comrades were very suspicious. I would have to have patience; it might take weeks until he could introduce me to them. These comrades categorically refused to have anything to do with anyone whom they had not known for some time. Yes, he sold them papers, but nothing further. We then arranged a weekly meeting, always on the same day, but the time would vary from week to week. Alex then told me the following:

" I stood at the Unemployment Exchange, in a long row. A short, bald-headed man stood behind me. I noticed that he kept on looking at me, and wondered whether he knew me. Suddenly he whispered, ' Well, Herr Meyer, it's all over with the lectures and meetings now, isn't it? ' He grinned as he said this, but I didn't feel like grinning, you can be sure.

"'Lectures?' I queried, and laughed. 'You're thinking of someone else. I am a locksmith.'

"The man only grinned again, and even winked slyly. 'You can't leave now,' I decided. 'It will only arouse his suspicion.' A ticklish situation. Then he started off again. 'Don't you really recognise me?'

"'No,' I answered. 'I've never seen you before.'

"'Try to remember; it's not such a long time ago.'

"I could hardly think. My only thought was that he knew much too much about me. And yet, somehow, his face did seem familiar. He must have guessed my thoughts, for he then said in an undertone, 'You don't have to be scared of me.' I thought it better to keep quiet and let him do the talking. He bent forward and whispered in my ear, 'I used to be in the police force, Department 1A. You used to have to report your meetings to me there!' Of course. Now I recognised him. But I kept quiet. He must have been cleared out, to make room for the 'Nazi guard.' Then, barely above his breath, 'Your records aren't there any more. We let a whole lot disappear just before the election.'"

. . . .

Ernst Schwiebus is already waiting at the appointed corner with a woman. Hell, she's all done up! Quite a smart-looking piece. I am used to seeing Schwiebus in his best clothes in the evenings. No one would recognise him as the delivery man then. He looks just like a "better class" young man. He wears good suits and clean shirts, his wavy hair neatly brushed, and he is always well shaved.

"Good evening."

Schwiebus's companion lisps. Maybe because of the prominent teeth. She is a Jewess, and can't be much more than twenty. I would never have believed it of Schwiebus. She's so smart. He never has a word to say for himself.

"Go on in front," says Schwiebus. "I'll wait for Teichert, eh?"

"And Hilde?"

"I arranged to meet her later, at another corner. You start off. I'll bring her, eh?"

Always this "eh" at the end of his sentences. Funny habit. The street is in the fashionable West End. Glowing electric advertisement signs. We take short steps; have to push forward through the crowd of passers-by.

"My name's Ruth," the girl says suddenly.

A good guess, that one before. A Jewess. She's very plucky. Lets us use her room. She'd be treated twice as badly if anything were to go wrong.

Our greatest difficulty is always that we haven't enough of such unsuspected apartments. The rooms where we do our cyclostyling are all situated in the "red" district, which is closely watched. That was why Schwiebus had suggested this place when we were discussing the printing of the gummed posters. He had never told us about the girl before, and that's why I questioned him thoroughly. He has known her a long time—from the perfume department—and has slowly "educated" her politically. She was a fine girl, and it was all perfectly safe, otherwise he would not have made the suggestion. She had a room in a boarding-house in the West. But we had to fetch another woman along; so many men were too conspicuous.

If I had not known that Schwiebus was absolutely reliable —— Ruth looks as if she knew all about scents and nothing about politics.

"Pension Ritter" is illuminated on an electric sign over the entrance.

"We'll go up by the back stairs," says Ruth.

A dark courtyard and a narrow winding staircase.

"And when the others come along?"

"They won't be noticed. People go in and out here all day, and Ernst has a key."

Many doors led off from the long corridor. No one to be seen. Everything is red in the room. A couch, a bed, two chairs, a large wardrobe, and a toilet set. Ruth draws the curtains.

"Do sit down."

I can't think of anything to say to break the ice. How friendly she is. And yet she seems more out of place than ever in this room. The *décolleté* dress, the bracelets. Her nails are painted red; her eyebrows are two thin lines. The black shingled hair is set in well-groomed waves.

Ernst Schwiebus comes in with Paul Teichert and Hilde.

"We must sound as if we're enjoying ourselves," says Ruth. "I'm supposed to be holding a party." She rings a bell. "We'll order coffee."

We laugh and joke as the maid enters the room. Ruth plays the gramophone and dances with Schwiebus as the coffee comes in. She can at least act wonderfully. Teichert draws a small packet from his pocket.

"The stick-bills. Five hundred. Convenient and easily pasted up. Ready glued this time; only have to be moistened."

We examine them; they are satisfactory. Schwiebus unpacks the toy printing set.

"How's Franz?"

We know that Hilde often meets him.

"He sends his best wishes. I met him yesterday. He was pleased that there was no hitch with the paper."

"Who's got a snappy rhyme?"

"Not me," comes from Hilde.

We like Teichert's rhyme best.

"*Margarine wird teuerer, die Butter noch mehr,*
Volk ans Gewehr!" [46]

"You're always so surprised where the jokes and rhymes come from. That's what the workers are saying at the works," explains Teichert.

I take a glance at Teichert. He's very pleased with the success of his slogan, and passes his hand self-consciously over his unruly fair hair. What bad teeth he has! It looks so awful when he opens his mouth, with the wide gaps and the two black stumps in front. "Have 'em seen to? Too bloody expensive!" he had replied when I mentioned it to him.

" That's fine, eh ? Volk ans Gewehr ! It's well known since the wireless took that line from the song for their interval signal."

Ruth winds the gramophone. Hilde takes the required rubber letters from the toy printing set with the tweezers, fits them into the metal grooves of the die.

" I can't take any this time; have to wait a bit. Otherwise they'll be hunting out our factory cells," explains Teichert. He had taken some of our pamphlets with him to the factory the first time. Communist slogans were pasted on the Siemens machines, in the cloakrooms. Eight workers were then arrested. Their names were on an old collecting-list that the Nazis had somehow got hold of. But none of the comrades of the factory cell were among those arrested.

". . . *Ninon give me another smile* . . ." A tenor voice. Ruth had put a new record on.

" Of course, they're all afraid of opening their mouths," Teichert continues, " but those who know each other have plenty to say. ' They've been chucking us out for years, because we kept the First of May; now they're doing it if we won't celebrate it as a Nazi " day of rejoicing," ' the mates say."

The gramophone is filling the room with jazz music, and we draw our chairs close together.

" They know quite well what the workers think of the First of May."

Hilde has finished filling in the letters. We print a trial sheet.

" Not clear enough."

" The letters are too close together."

" Yes, that's much better."

Schwiebus starts printing. I pass him the papers. The girls sit opposite us; they suddenly laugh artificially.

" For next door's benefit," says Ruth. " So that they'll think we're having a good time."

" And the march on the First of May, eh ? " Teichert places the finished posters in piles.

He answers slowly, " Of course we had to go along. The

Nazi bosses called the roll to see if we were all there. But quite a number had got lost on the way. Some went to ' buy fags.' Others had to ' be excused,' and many more disappeared in the confusion in the Tempelhofer Feld. A good few of the remaining ones started grumbling there. Because we had to stand for hours in the heat and dust. And at the toffs on the grand stand: ' They're quite comfortable on their twenty-mark seats—a good chance to see a few parades, fancy uniforms, and shiny top 'ats, if yer interested that way,' they said. One of the workers told me next day how disappointed he was, and said: ' I thought Hitler was going to tell us his plans for conquering unemployment.' ' You heard him,' I answered. ' " Your duty, the duty of all of you, consists in buying, buying, buying. Don't wait; the more you buy, the more money in circulation, the better for all of you ! " ' "

We all laughed.

" What did he say to that ? "

" He seemed puzzled. ' Me ? ' he asked. ' What wiv ? ' "

Schwiebus lays the die down, rubs his hands. They are red and swollen.

We work for a while in silence. The girls wrap the finished adhesive labels in paper, thirty in each small packet. A tenor voice again comes from the gramophone: ". . . *you're my only ray of sunlight . . .*" Teichert continues, " But the next day was even more exciting. The Gleichschaltung [47] of the unions made the others all realise that the workers were being robbed of their last rights. The Social-Democrat comrades were struck dumb, I can tell you.

" ' The union leaders called on us to support the May Day demonstration, now you can see what the result of their funk is: the enemy are in control of the Union Buildings ! ' That's how the workers talk about things among themselves."

" We must make the most of this state of mind, bring them nearer to our way of thinking ! "

" Yes. But you can't imagine how difficult that is. The blow at the unions has confused so many. And we have to be so damned careful. Every comrade in work is worth two out of work to-day. We can't . . ."

Teichert breaks off. Voices are heard in the corridor outside. Steps. I put the die down, look at the door.

"It's all right," says Schwiebus; "people keep on coming and going here. It's almost a brothel here, eh?"

"That's why I live here. No one takes any notice of the others," explains Ruth. It sounds rather like an apology.

We drop the subject and carry on with our work, more conscious than ever of our danger.

What a longing I have these days for distraction—to get the most out of life. The thought never leaves me that it will be my turn, too, some day. It may be all over to-morrow—Sievert, Neumann, Ritter, and so many others. I knew them all so well. Pulled in in connection with the Maikowski case. Kurgel. Richard Hüttig! He knows all our names. The names of all of us sitting here in this room printing these gummed slips. How they must have tortured him! If he hadn't held out we couldn't be sitting here now, putting this stuff together.

She's a sailor's sweetheart . . .

This damned jazz suddenly gets on my nerves. Teichert takes the die from me.

"What do they think of the Maikowski affair?"

Teichert, who has already started printing, does not glance up.

"It's difficult to form an opinion, and you can't get at the families concerned. But the other day, when I was collecting for them, I did speak to some of the tenants in the houses. They think that someone must have split, either through torture or in order to save their own skins. We can't tell."

"Do you think that's the reason for the new arrests, eh?"

"Perhaps."

"They confiscated bikes in a few houses the day before yesterday."

"That's got nothing to do with the other affair. That's

only 'securing themselves against a Communist mobile column.' Do you know Paul Ritzhaupt?"

"Yes. What about him?"

"He was in the Fichte Motor-cycle Club. They confiscated all their vehicles. He went to the police station at Alexanderplatz. There were hundreds of complainants there. 'Policemen stand in pairs at both ends of all the corridors,' he said, 'and everyone who goes in is searched.' How they must have the wind up!"

"But it would be crazy to try anything there," puts in Hilde.

I notice that she has not said a word all the evening, except for an occasional whisper to Ruth. They've made friends quickly. What a contrast Hilde makes, in her simple jumper with the short sleeves, with Ruth! So much fresher and more natural. But Ruth! How appearances deceive!

Then Schwiebus remarks, "Of course it's crazy. One often comes across people who talk about assassinating Hitler. They don't seem to realise that just another Nazi boss would carry on in his place, eh? And what a revenge they would take on all the thousands in prison!"

Teichert soon has the last bill under the die.

"Where's the stuff going to be kept now?"

He looks at me.

"I'm going to take it to a house I know of. We'll fetch it from there to-morrow morning. It's got to be stuck up pretty soon."

"Does Ede really stick them up at the Nazi bosses' places, eh?"

"Of course."

We leave one at a time. But Schwiebus remains behind. So he and this Ruth are really thick? It's beyond me.

· · · · · · · ·

The posters have been divided among the comrades, all except for Heinz Preuss and his group. I go with the others to the prearranged place. There he is. He is standing in front of a newspaper kiosk, reading. I can recognise him a long way off. His black-and-white checked breeches ! His blue, short-sleeved tennis shirt ! His long fair hair ! Heinz Preuss is an old hiker. He can never be found at home at weekends; he always goes hiking then.

He looks so brown and healthy. We chaff him and call him " the Freeman with the long hair."

I stand near him for a second and then move on into a neighbouring tenement. Preuss comes in a few minutes later. We meet on the first-floor landing.

" How many do we get ? "

I loosen my plus-four trousers at the calf.

" Seventy. Here you are."

" That's a lot. There's only Emil and me to-day."

I straighten up my trousers. It's no use discussing that now; we've got to hurry.

" You take the side-streets near here ! "

A door bangs above our heads. We listen, but no one comes down the stairs.

" Be careful."

" You bet I will."

I leave, Preuss stays behind.

. . . .

" Fresh 'errings. . . . German 'errings. . . . What would you like, sir . . . ? "

The costermonger places her right hand on her hip; her other arm waves the fish-knife about in the air. Her apron is covered with scales and blood. Women carrying shopping-bags and baskets push their way between the stalls.

The sounds of costers crying their goods, the dull thud of a butcher's chopper, somewhere a horse's shrill whinny. The weekly market stretches from the Wallstrasse to the Wilhelmplatz, in front of the Charlottenburg town hall. A lane is suddenly formed in the crowd of women. Even the women examining the goods on the stalls turn their heads towards the centre of the street, where a man is walking along, feeling his way with a stick. He wears a yellow band on the sleeve of his jacket, on which three black spots **are** printed. He seems quite young and is well built. In place of his left eye he has an ugly red cavity. The right eye stares straight ahead.

The man steers away from the crowd and bustle with slow and uncertain steps, then feels his way along the row of houses towards the Wilhelmplatz. His stick taps against the walls of the houses at regular intervals, avoiding obstructions. Ede then taps at the massive stone blocks of the Charlottenburg town hall.

" It was there that I got mad," he told me later. " Ullstein's newspaper seller, the one who sits at that corner, kept on crying: ' The Government guarantees no interference with trade. All attempts to cause an economic crisis will be stopped ! ' They wants ter stop us striking, yer see. So that the bosses can get away with their profits in peace ! "

A fat man wearing a Nazi Party badge comes towards Ede.

" Can I be of any service ? "

" Tha's all right, I kin manage," Ede answers.

The fat man raises his arm in the Nazi salute and continues on his way.

" 'E didn't even know wever I seed that at all," grinned Ede. People are hurrying to and fro in the corridors that branch off on all sides on the ground floor. There are many doors on both sides of each corridor, with benches by a few on which the callers are sitting and waiting. They talk loudly, waving their arms to emphasise their words, each one describing his " case " to the others. Ede thinks he had better start higher up. He climbs the winding staircase. It is quieter upstairs. Except for the people who occasionally get out of the automatic lift. Officials, carrying piles of documents under their arms, hurry past. A few are in S.A. uniform.

Ede taps his way along the corridor. He stops in front of the third door. " Regierungsrat Lehman " is written on the white door-plate. He puts his hand in his pocket, moistens the stickbill, and quickly sticks it on, above the name.

Margarine wird teuerer, die Butter noch mehr,
Volk ans Gewehr !

He sticks the rhyme on all the doors and walls on this floor in less than ten minutes. He then takes the lift down to the next floor. Here everything goes smoothly, too. But it becomes a bit difficult on the next floor. Minor officials are frequently rushing backwards and forwards, so that he has to keep on waiting for the moment when the passages are empty. He is just turning a corner, after passing a group of waiting applicants, when he suddenly hears excited voices behind him.

" Look here ! And here too. . . . They must have been stuck up a moment ago. . . ."

" Baurat Lehman has just rung through. Labels have been stuck up on all the upper floors ! "

" Ring through to the porter at once . . . he's to inform the police . . . if we hurry we might catch some of them ! "

" Stormtroopers are to watch all the passages. No one is to be let out ! "

Doors bang; men keep running along the corridors. The people waiting jump up excitedly from their seats.

" What's wrong ? What's up ? " asks a man wearing an old-fashioned suit. He pulls nervously at his pointed white beard. A fat woman near him, who is wearing a silk blouse, answers tremulously :

" They've been sticking up seditious posters . . . a few seconds ago ! On the walls ! "

Ede sees some of them whispering together and exchanging knowing glances.

Then the woman who had spoken before starts off again.

" There you are ! They are closing the doors. . . . We shall all be suspected. . . . Oh, the robbers, the murderers ! "

The old man with the beard is asking questions again.

" What's wrong ? . . . Have robbers been sticking up posters ? "

" No. Communists ! Don't you understand ? We'll have enough trouble with all this ! " the woman screeches at him.

The old man's mouth drops, his tiny pointed beard quivering with fear.

" Time to clear out," thinks Ede. He feels his way along

the wall towards the staircase. An official stands by the lift.

" You can't leave now," he is telling the people whom he has stopped and who are standing in front of him, arguing.

" I've got to go home . . . my husband'll be coming home for dinner ! "

" I've had a summons to the court served on me . . . I shall make you responsible for my absence ! "

Ede taps his way through them all. They make way for him, even the official at the entrance to the lift. Ede goes slowly down the stairs, continuing unchallenged out into the open street. The regular tap, tap of his stick dies away in the distance.

. . . .

I am at Rothacker's. It is early evening. I want to tell him about Ede's latest prank.

" Come in," calls Rothacker.

His left hand is inside a child's shoe. He is wearing a blue apron. The four-year-old Inge clutches his trousers; her mop of fair hair peeps shyly round her father's legs. So he's mending shoes. His wife is cleaning the kitchen stove. She jerks her elbow in greeting. She looks worn. Inge is just the image of her. But the mother is painfully thin; her breasts seem shrivelled. The very fair hair makes her complexion appear even paler, yet gives her beautiful features an almost ethereal air. Rothacker searches about in his tool-bag, does not look at me. Have they been quarrelling ? I know that their money troubles are often the cause. I came to tell them about Ede's tricks, but I feel I can't. I haven't the slightest idea what to say.

" My life's been wasted. Always trouble and worry," Rothacker's wife had often complained to me. He is almost twice her age. She was not quite twenty when they married. The child was born soon after. They have been drifting apart since Rothacker lost his job. The woman is still young, she wants to " live." She has become very much aware of the difference in their ages.

" Didn't you meet Emil Schmidt ? " asks Rothacker.

"No!"

"He was here a moment ago. Said he'd be going to you."

Rothacker looks at me. He puts the child's shoe down. The movement is mechanical, as if he were entirely unaware of the action. The eyes behind the nickel-rimmed glasses hold such a vacant expression. . . . I am shocked.

"Has anything happened?"

Rothacker answers slowly, picking his words.

"Preuss did not meet Emil at the spot they had fixed, after sticking the bills up."

Silence. Frau Rothacker stops polishing, looks at me wide-eyed. The child plays with the rubber soles that are laid ready for sticking on.

"Emil then went to Preuss's place. No one at home."

The sinking feeling returns to my stomach.

"His mother will be coming home now . . . she works at the Underground."

Rothacker stares at the hammer in his hand. He seems to be speaking to himself.

"You mean someone should go to her? To make enquiries?"

"Yes. With some sort of excuse. It'll have to be straight away. They can't have been at her place yet."

I had said "someone." The woman had looked at me so strangely as I said it. I must go; can't expect it of him. He's probably right. But what if they are already at the mother's house?

"We would know then for certain. Could warn all the others," says Rothacker. He twists the cobbler's hammer about in his hand.

"When did you leave him?"

"This afternoon."

"Your flat is 'clean,' isn't it?"

"Yes."

So he won't take on the job in front of his wife. He's quite right. They have a child.

I am not tied like he is.

"Had you decided where you got to know each other?"

"Of course."

We know that the Gestapo usually cross-examine their victims separately. The first question is nearly always: "Where did you first meet?" It is of vital importance that the replies agree. We had, therefore, all arranged something beforehand. Heinz Preuss knows that he had "got to know" me while hiking in the Grünwald.

"I'll go. We've got to know what's the matter."

. . . .

Frau Preuss seems about to collapse. Her eyes, in the bony yellowed face, express all her anxiousness.

"I wanted to see Herr Preuss. It's about his collection of butterflies." I make use of one of his tramping hobbies as an excuse for being here.

Frau Preuss shuffles ahead of me in the narrow corridor. Once in the room, she pushes a hideously carved chair towards me. She would be more upset if she had already been "visited." So it's all right so far. I had often been to see Preuss during the day, but his mother does not know me. She had always been at work at such times. I know that we are sitting in the "best" room. A coloured print in a heavy gold frame hangs above the sideboard. "The Sermon on the Mount." A large wooden plate in the corner on the right, with the words: "Blessed are the poor in spirit, for theirs is the Kingdom of Heaven," burnt in round the edge. I sit down conventionally. Preuss has often told me of the continual differences of opinion and opposing outlooks on life which he and his mother hold.

"She comes from a parson's family, and she's old and can't be changed any more. I let her alone, only she won't do the same to me," he told me once.

I know also how he suffers because he, the young man, is unemployed, while his old mother has to work hard to keep the two of them. It was with great difficulty, and at the cost of depriving herself of things, that she managed to afford to let him learn tool-making. His father had been killed in the war.

Frau Preuss interrupts my thoughts. She is standing in front of me wringing her hands.

"You want to see Heinz.... Where can he be?... I've just come from work. Nothing's been done, nothing bought!"

I move uncomfortably about on my chair. She has found someone at last to whom she can unburden herself. But how can I tell her? I feel horribly depressed.

"Perhaps something has happened to him?" I suggest.

"What can have happened to him! He is no child."

She gesticulates with her hands, suddenly lets them fall slackly on to her lap.

"How do you come to know him? Are you another one of those...?"

"No." I cut her words short.

I must prevent the least semblance of suspicion. Who knows to what extent the woman will let herself go in her excitement? If she knew...

She wails: "What didn't I tell the boy? 'You are sinning against God.' I begged him every day, 'Leave all that alone; it's sure to end badly for you.'" She cries softly, rocking to and fro. I am so sorry for her. The two had never understood each other; they had lived in different worlds. She could never learn to understand her son. But she is a mother, his mother. Frau Preuss takes her hands away from her face.

"It was for his own good... I often wanted to take him with me to the Salvation Army.... He sings so beautifully...."

She looks at me with eyes wide open, as if she had discovered the culprit in me.

"Oh, my God, my God. He never thought of his old mother. He was mad with his 'politics.'"

"Why don't you go to the police, Frau Preuss?"

"To the police?"

She breaks out into more uncontrolled crying.

"To think I should have to suffer that as well in my old age.... I've never had anything to do with the police all my life, and now... oh, the shame of it all...!"

"You ought to make enquiries. You could even advertise for him as being missing, if that did not help!" I say forcefully. I must rouse her from her lethargy. Frau Preuss looks dully at the wall opposite her. I daren't persuade her any more, in the guise of a chance visitor. She might realise that I had only come to make enquiries. "Auf Wiedersehen, Frau Preuss."

She nods apathetically and offers her hand. The veins are hard and knotted.

I am thinking hard on the way home through the Wallstrasse. What can we do for her? Collect money? But she has a job. Heinz could not provide for her, either. We must be very careful about making further enquiries. Better to try the other tenants.

. . . .

Heinz Preuss was only able to tell us about the affair a long while after it all took place. He had entered a quiet street with Emil Schmidt and had looked at the wording of the posters and thought how suitable they were for this district. Minor civil servants and clerks lived here. They previously voted Nazi, but now they would be feeling dissatisfied with the Hitler regime owing to the increased cost of living, and the ever larger deductions from their salaries.

"Always start on the top floors, and don't forget the ground floors," he said to Emil Schmidt before they separated. Preuss stuck the bills on the windows, the letter-boxes, and the quiet porters' lodges on the ground floors. It all went well without anything special happening; he seldom met anyone on the stairs. His store of labels was getting low. "Another ten minutes," he thought. He had already finished the two upper storeys of a house when he heard someone coming hastily down the stairs above him. He put the moistened bill back in his pocket and sauntered down the stairs. A tall, pale man with black hair went past, giving him such a searching look that Preuss started. "Better leave the house at once," he thought. But his scruples fled when he was out in the street. The man was nowhere to be seen. "You must have made a mistake," he told himself. "Fancy giving up the job because of that! The last few bills must be stuck up." He went into the next block of flats. But on the stairs he started worrying again. The few remaining labels did not justify putting himself in the slightest danger. And, in any case, he should have gone on to the next street and not into the neighbouring house. He began to lose his nerve and ran down again. He looked round carefully as he left the house. A few children were playing in a group on the pavement. A vegetable cart was passing along the street. The coster had his hands to his mouth and was crying:

"Tomaters . . . tomaters . . . nice firm tomaters . . ."

A milk-cart stood on the other side of the street. The driver, wearing a blue cap and apron, was pouring out the milk. An electric shock seemed to dart through Preuss's body. Of all the . . .! There stood that fellow behind the cluster of women buying their milk! He could only see the black shock of hair and the upper half of his face. He had waited for his return, wanted to keep him in sight! "Mustn't get nervy and run," thought Preuss. He judged the distance to the next corner. Thirty yards. He forced himself to walk to the corner with normal steps.

Was he being followed? "It will only make you look more suspicious if you turn round," he warned himself. He tried to obtain a reflection of the other side of the road in a shop window on his left. But it was impossible. It seemed an eternity to Preuss until he reached the corner; his feet seemed to stick to the pavement stones. "It's like a nightmare," he thought. "When you are being followed and you can't . . . can't move a step forward?"

He reached the corner at last and glanced back quickly, but was petrified by what he saw. The dark man was about twenty yards away from him; must have been following him all the time. He now ran straight across the road, calling out and beckoning to the two S.A. men who were just coming out of one of the houses on the other side. The people in the street turned round in astonishment to look at him. Preuss was paralysed for a second, then he took great strides down the next side-street. What now? His start was of little value. The street in front of him turned in a small bend on the right. That might—but he had no time to get out of their sight. They would soon be at the corner, and would see where he was running to. His heart was palpitating wildly.

A dairy appeared just in front of him. The shop door was wide open. Through the window he saw a group of women standing in the shop. Preuss had stepped into the shop in a flash. Another woman came in after him. One of the saleswomen was patting a roll of butter in shape with the wooden butter patters, nodding her head in answer at the same time. The woman in front of her chattered away without stopping: "... especially here, on the right side ... just before a change of weather.... What did you say?... X-ray...?"

Preuss stood behind the women, between two barrels and the glass centre piece of the counter, on which various kinds of cheese were set out. He was thinking rapidly. He could keep the street in sight from here when they ran past, would then wait a few seconds, run out, and sprint back in the direction he had come from.

He shrank back. The S.A. men and the dark man were just passing. The latter was talking excitedly to the other two, drawing a circle in the air with his arm.

"He can't have got very far! We must..."

They disappeared from sight. What now? Stay here; above all, win a little time. Let the three outside get a bit further. He would run right into their arms if he left now. He was being spoken to.

"What can I serve you with, sir?"

Preuss looked round. The shop was not so full. The woman with the pains in her side had already been finished with, but still stood there. She seemed to be waiting for an opportunity to carry on with her tale. The second assistant was serving another woman, and near him stood the one who had come in after him.

"Oh—er—please serve this lady first.... I can wait..." he stammered.

"A quarter of Edamer—in thin slices," he heard the woman near him say.

How far would the three be? Should he risk it now? He took a step towards the shop window, looked out carefully. Blast! They were walking up and down on the other side, looking for him. If only they'd go into a house! Behind him the shop-girl repeated:

"And now, sir?"

"... er ... er ... let me have ... let me have ... a quarter Edamer cut in slices!"

Preuss stared at the slices falling from the knife. The woman next to him groped clumsily about in her market basket; the chatterbox over there had started off again.

Suddenly a male voice came from the shop door.

"Miss, have you seen ...?"

It broke off hastily, and then rose to a shrill cry.

"Quick!... Quick!... Here he is ... here he is!"

Preuss had started round. The black-haired man stood in the doorway. The fright seemed to affect his heart, and then he felt past caring. "Done for," he thought. "It's not worth while running away from this one; the other two would soon catch up." There they were! Preuss stood as if made of stone. The assistant's mouth opened. She stood there with wide, astonished eyes, the knife in her right hand, the cheese in the other. One of the S.A. grabbed Preuss by the arm. He was a huge broad-shouldered fellow. His eyes gleamed under the bushy eyebrows. The other one, short and fair, stood in front of Preuss with his hand in his revolver pocket. The black-haired man spluttered:

"That's him! He's easily recognised! Because of his long hair! That's the chap who stuck the bills up—I watched him doing it through the peephole in my door!"

"Bring him along!" ordered the smaller S.A. man.

The big one bent one of Preuss's arms behind his back. The pain went right through him.

The women pushed towards the doorway. The people in

the street stopped and turned their heads. A crowd of children ran alongside the group of men.

. . . .

I couldn't fall asleep for ages last night. The thought came to me that I must be very careful what I write. If the Gestapo should somehow get hold of this manuscript, it must on no account give away any of our secrets. I took everything I had already written from its hiding-place to-day and read it through carefully. A lot had to be crossed out, sometimes whole pages destroyed. That had taken precious time.

The time, or, rather, the lack of it!

I have to cut down the hours for writing as I have my political work to do. The comrades would soon notice my not having my " heart in things." None of them, except for Franz and Rothacker, know that I am writing a book.

But I *must* carry on with it now. Otherwise all the trouble and the dangerous situations will have been in vain.

. . . .

A memorial tablet for Maikowski is going to be inaugurated in the Wallstrasse to-day. I walk down the street with Rothacker. We have not spoken a word since I went to call for him. Rothacker's eyes behind the glasses are contracted, a deep fold between his eyebrows. His glance flies from window to window.

" Vogel friss oder stirb," [48] he says.

I don't answer—nod.

Swastika flags are hanging in the Wallstrasse!

Our street always had its flags, but red flags. Never flags that had stolen their red.

The concierges of some of the blocks of flats owned by the town council received the order yesterday to hang out the recently delivered flags. Then S.A.s came to the tenants whose rooms overlooked the street and offered flags for sale.

" But we can't afford it," many replied.

" Then keep the flags without paying for them; we'll call back for them later ! " the S.A. answered.

By the way they said " keep the flags without paying for

them," the tenants realised that they could either accept them, or . . . be kept under observation from that moment onwards. Others had even *bought* the flags. Over there—the Meyers—the Radlis—have hung them out. They had previously sympathised with us, or had at least stood on good terms with us. The months of terrorism, the many arrests in the street, had intimidated them. They are afraid of a concentration camp. But Matteck as well! He must be feeling anxious about his job. And the—and the—— They none of them want to become " known to the police " ! They explain their reasons shamefacedly to the neighbours for not wanting to " excite attention." They are valid in some cases, in others they have been made up to conform with a new political outlook.

We come to the bend in the street. The Power Works are on the other side. The machines hum. The paint on the solitary gable with which the S.A. had painted over Ede's slogans is already somewhat faded by the sun's rays. I can read the words underneath without difficulty; but, then, I know the text by heart.

" He would ! " says Rothacker softly, and nods towards a beerhouse near us.

" Afrikander " is written in large letters on the pane. A swastika flag hangs loosely across the door. On the other side of the street is the pub where we used to meet. The empty shop windows are like eyes. Eyes set in a face which is the street. We know how to read this face. . . . We are not deceived by the apparent indifference.

Swastika flags in the Wallstrasse !

We exchange glances, and nod to the people standing outside their houses. Not a word is said about the flags, although we greet and talk to each other. *We* are all friends, but neither knows if the other is still " active."

More faces are to be seen looking through the windows further on. The coming event seems to make the atmosphere tense. Rothacker looks at me in silence.

He stops at the crossing between the Wall and Krumstrasse; nods, and pulls a wry mouth.

MAIKOWSKISTRASSE
is written in blue Gothic letters at the corner.

Men with ladders have been there in the early hours of the morning. They have removed the old weatherbeaten " Wallstrasse " sign-plates and have put up this new " Maikowskistrasse " ! It seems as if the letters are taunting me: " Stop it if you can ! Bah, you can't alter things in the slightest ! "

Near a broad gateway on the other side of the street stand two S.A. sentries. In the bicycle-shop on its left, nickel parts flash in the sunlight; there is a chemist's on the other side. The S.A. men stand stiffly to attention, the chin-straps of their flat peaked caps under their chins. A large part of the wall behind them is covered with black cloth. Wreaths tied with bright bows lie on the pavement. A laurel-tree stands on each side of the sentries. Cars drive past. Traffic is still normal. But I notice that the pedestrians use the other side of the street, as we do. They take large strides; no one salutes.

The night of January 30th comes back to me. We stood in a doorway on the other side. The bawling mob came from the back there. Then Maikowski roared out his order to fire, the shots spat out red in the dark. Dozens of them. It was here that the Schupo ran in front of the crowd, Maikowski by his side. How the Schupo suddenly flung his arms out, and then fell. How Maikowski roared out an order that we could not hear in the noise, and then how his knees gave way. It was here that the two of them lay on the asphalt. The S.A. fled. It was only then that our comrades from the beerhouse Stani arrived on the scene. The Stanis did *not* shoot the two. Would they have gone up to the police car which arrived if they had ?

Murderers would not have helped the police lift the bodies into the car. They would have disappeared before the police came. But they remained, knowing that they were innocent. The chaps won't even have a lawyer to defend them. And then there's Hüttig's trial. I can picture him as he was the last time I saw him. He was sitting on the sofa, his heavy hands rested on his belt. How he told us about the attack on Willman's. In rough growling tones.

"He's been damned brave—he knows all our names," says Rothacker quietly.

We have come to the next turning and we stop there. The corner house has a long row of dull coloured windows. The entrance is in the side-street a few yards round the corner. The wooden door bangs continually. Haggard-looking men and women in their worn clothes are coming and going.

CONTINUATION SCHOOL!

It's a long time ago since a lecture on "Den Segen und Nutzen der Arbeit"[49] was given here. The Charlottenburg Welfare Centre is now housed in the building. When the door is opened we see a long queue waiting, stretching right across the untidy courtyard into the rooms on the ground floor. It ends at the Welfare Centre cashier's desk.

"We can wait here. It won't attract attention," says Rothacker.

The memorial tablet is less than fifty yards away.

Rothacker fidgets with his glasses.

"I was behind with my rent. They gave me the money in small doses. We used it up for food." He taps the ash thoughtfully from his cigarette. "What else could I do?"

I can't think of anything helpful to say. Wife and child? And he himself. He is so pitifully thin; his clothes hang as if on a pole. His face is pale and drawn. He does not know where to turn for worry—but he is always ready to put himself out for others. He has led the same life for so many years.

"If they find out and give me less money..."

But now a number of people are moving backwards and forwards. Groups stand by the memorial tablet.

"Let's go nearer!"

All the people are well dressed. They look as if they took care of themselves, and as if they could afford it, too. Quite a lot of women are among them.

". . . Pack of criminals . . . why haven't they all been exterminated . . . should be burnt at the stake . . ."

So they still believe that they are in " enemy country " here. I take a good look at the man who had made the last remark. He is tall and lanky. Most probably a schoolmaster. A heavy gold chain dangles from his waistcoat. " You don't look like one of the ' old guard ' who's going to do the burning, old man," is my secret thought. The woman standing near him nods energetically. The feather on her hat wags down over her face. A large Nazi Party badge gleams on her blouse. Rothacker nudges me. He says softly:

" If we stay here, we'll have to salute the swastika."

" Well, what about it ? " I whisper back.

" But we might be recognised from the windows."

" That's true. We'd better stand in the garage doorway."

S.A. and police come and close the street soon after. They push the crowd back to form a wide circle round the memorial tablet. Suddenly all heads are turned to the right. A song is heard. It comes nearer. We can hear the refrain now, repeated after every verse.

" . . . *Wir sind die Dreiundreiss'ger* . . ."[50]

The arms fly up. In the houses opposite only heads are to be seen, no arms. But yet ! A few here and there. But *they* only emphasise the silent protest at the other windows. A few workmen come clattering in their wooden clogs from the repair shop in the courtyard behind us. Two raise their oil-smeared arms. The third stands near them with his hands in his pockets. The regular sound of marching can be heard from outside. We can only see the brown caps bobbing up and down above the crowd of heads. A loud, shrill command suddenly stops the song.

" Division—halt ! Ri-i-ight turn ! "

Silence.

The owner of the bird-shop in the basement comes out with a chair, stands on it. He towers above the heads. Then someone starts speaking.

" Remember the blood sacrifice . . . land of honour and freedom . . . murdered by the reds . . . faithful to the *Führer* . . ."

The speaker seems to talk for ages. Then another one gets up.

Silence again.

Then they sing loudly:

" . . . *Kam'raden die . . . erschossen* . . ."[61]

Just let them march past, *our* comrades! Shot by you in the middle of the night, tortured to death in your prison cells. A long row of ashen-coloured men. But the living are everywhere, unseen by you. They are watching you all the time.

I grab Rothacker's arm, forget that there are people all round. We stare wide-eyed at each other. Rothacker's face is strained. It seems unbelievable, impossible—and yet, as the last resounding " Heil " of the crowd died away, a woman's shrill voice had cried: " Down with Fascism! Red Front! "

Now—another voice; it seems to come from the other side of the street.

" Down! Down! Red Front! "

We rush out of the garage entrance almost at the same second. We forget that we can be recognised in this dangerous situation. We are surrounded by faces distorted with anger, fists raised threateningly. Groups of people arguing—no shouting, at each other.

We see the S.A. running together, then forming two groups which storm into houses on both sides of the street. One group soon returns. They have a woman with them, hold her arms tightly. For the fraction of a second I can see a blue apron, a pale face, and dishevelled black hair. The crowds of people push forward. We press backwards and forwards between the excited people. My nerves are on edge. The others are almost falling out of the windows. They are as excited as we are. We can see it by their gestures, by their nervous faces. *Their* street had spoken. Orders ring out. The S.A. are on the march a few seconds later. Hard, soured faces, shaken with rage and impotence. The cry coming at such a moment, on an occasion like this, must have been a blow.

When the crowds leave, we go across to No. 52. A bronze plate hangs on the wall of the house. It is entwined with fresh green leaves, a swastika at the top. Underneath:

> Hier fiel am 30. Januar 1933
> am Tage der nationalen Erhebung
> der Sturm führer des SA Sturmes 33
> HANS EBERHARD MAIKOWSKI.
> Er fiel für Deutschland.[52]

A little further on Rothacker says quietly, "' Here fell ' is written on the plate, not ' Here was murdered by the Communists . . .' "

He looks at me.

"They usually write *that* on their memorial tablets. There's one like it near the canal. They don't even believe it themselves—that our lads shot him."

. . . .

When Heinz Preuss did not come home on the second day after his absence, his mother decided to follow my advice. She went to the police. A large signboard hung on the door of the police station: "The German Greeting Is: ' Heil Hitler ! ' "

Frau Preuss pushed the door open, stopped hesitatingly in the brightly lit corridor. There were doors everywhere. She walked down the corridor, read the names and numbers on each door. Where should she ask about Heinz? "They're sure to know all about it here; the police know everything," she thought.

Three officials were sitting in the room, bent over their pens. The one in the middle, a fat, good-natured-looking man, called out:

"Come along in, mother. What do you want?"

Frau Preuss walked slowly towards the wooden railing that divided the room.

"Good evening," she said timidly.
"You mean, ' Heil Hitler ' ! " said the fat man loudly.
"Well, what do you want ? "
"Heil Hitler ! " answered Frau Preuss, frightened. " I wanted to make enquiries. I'm looking for my son ! "
She seemed to shrink, become tinier. The men wearing the blue uniform were people in authority. The Bible said one should obey and respect them.
The fat Schupo laughed.
" Your son ? He must be quite a big boy. How old is he ? "
" Twenty-two," said Frau Preuss softly.
" Well, and . . . ? "
" He hasn't come home—since the day before yesterday," answered Frau Preuss anxiously.
" That often happens at his age." He grinned. " He'll be at his sweetheart's place."
" No. Something must have happened to him."
The worry in the old woman's voice must have moved the official.
" Yes ? Where do you live ? " he asked.
" Eighty-two Wallstrasse."
" Maikowskistrasse ! " the fat man corrected her loudly. He stood up.
" Come along with me. You're on the register here."
They went through a communicating door to the next room.
" Your name ? "
" Preuss—Alwine Preuss."
The fat man pulled out an index drawer from the desk. Fingered the cards.
" Alwine Preuss—Heinz Preuss—born on April 8th, 1911. Is that it ? "
" Yes," said Frau Preuss in a whisper, as if he had read out a list of previous misdeeds.
The fat man waved the green card about in the air.
" Well, and—what do you want now ? "
" I thought you knew—I'm so worried—he must have had an accident——" said Frau Preuss in troubled tones.

"But you can't expect us to know where everyone is! Do you want to report him missing? And it's closing time too!" he answered impatiently.

"Couldn't you make enquiries? I'm so upset——"

Frau Preuss wept. The fat man watched her for a second. "Now, now," he said. "Sit down now. I'll have a try!"

Frau Preuss heard him ringing up different official departments.

He mentioned her son's name and date of birth every time.

"No? Thanks. Heil Hitler," he repeated a few times.

He suddenly raised his voice.

"Preuss. Yes—Heinz Preuss. What? General Papestrasse? No, really? Thanks. Heil Hitler!"

He pushed his chair back noisily, stood up.

"Your son has been arrested!" he said sharply.

"Arrested? What for——?" Frau Preuss stammered.

The fat man put the card back in the index drawer.

"He'll know that best himself!" he answered harshly.

"Can't I see him—talk to him? Can't you——?" Frau Preuss started crying again.

"That's not our job. And we've no say in the matter either. The Feldpolizei have him under arrest!" he said curtly.

Frau Preuss then went home, crying.

. . . .

We had warned all the comrades the first day Preuss did not come home. He knew a few of the hiding-places where we kept our political material. These were changed at once. We know that Heinz Preuss is an honest and reliable comrade. But we have made it a working rule to bear in mind that every comrade arrested can give us away. Although we have explained to them all that statements made to the Gestapo only prove their own share in the illegal work, we cannot rely on each one standing firm against physical torture.

Dammert has been released from the Maikowski barracks in the meanwhile. We have informed all the others of his treachery. We are human enough to understand his naming Kurgel; he could not stand up against the torture. He might also have been thinking of his wife and two children. But our political verdict has to be hard and unequivocal. It would run the same for all of us.

. . . .

I walk slowly down the street. The sun is shining brightly. The people are all wearing light summer clothes. I am very fond of this mixture of colours.

I rang Hilde up yesterday.

" Coming to the Havel Sunday ? "

" Yes. I'm looking forward to it."

We change the questions each time. Her " Yes " means that Franz has told her of a new meeting-place for us. I then meet Hilde in the evening near her office. Franz has mentioned a flat this time. They've got better chances of working in their district.

" For the Auslandsdeutschen ! "[53]

One of the Hitlerjugend[54] boys rattles a collecting-box in front of me. The other one has a small basket in his hand. Blue and white flags are stuck on the inside. I shake my head. They have already run on. They're here in swarms ! Hitlerjugend, tiny little girls and boys from the Jungvolk,[55] schoolchildren, wearing ribbons round their arms authorising them to collect. Each and every passer-by is stopped. I see quite a number of people holding out their flags to the children a good way off. Why don't they wear them ? They have only sacrificed the ten pfennigs so as to get rid of the locust swarm of collectors, but don't want to take part in propaganda for the Nazis by wearing them. I watch the faces of those who are accosted. They don't express any pleasure at giving; some just walk past the proffered boxes without a word Their faces, devoid of all expression, seem to say more than " No ! "

How long is it all going to last ? Every week a new " contribution." The Ministry for Propaganda never comes to the end of its new ideas for squeezing. The N.S. women's organisation, the S.A., the Hitlerjugend, the Jungvolk, the Party. The boxes never stop rattling.

Those who only look at the surface of things are forced to the conclusion that Germany has gone National-Socialist. Black and brown uniforms all over the place. Flags, pictures of the *Führer*, in almost every shop window. Marching S.A., marching S.S., marching Hitlerjugend, marching Jungvolk, all booming chauvinistic songs. On motor-cycles, uniforms! In new cars, uniforms!

The people in front of me turn their heads. A man limps across the road. His temples are grey; he has a glass eye in his wrinkled face. He is wearing an old Hussar uniform; white cords dangle from his chest. Left over from Kaiser Wilhelm's days, now moth-eaten.

I begin to think of my two relatives, both S.A. men. They went through four years of war. Wear their medals proudly on their brown shirts now. One is a clerk, the other a barber. They always felt themselves to be cut out for "something better." The barrack drill and trench dirt days are over. But the uniform has come back. The uniform.

X, who told me about Kurgel, could only continue baking bread by being an S.A. man. Brown uniforms have even appeared in our street the last few days. One is chauffeur to some director. The boss insists on having an S.A. man at the driving-wheel, he told me. The other one works for a metal merchant, who only employs S.A. men, although the wages he pays are under the agreed minimum. That kind always have a thousand excuses why they mustn't risk their jobs. They wouldn't be able to take their girls to the pictures. They'd have to stop smoking. They don't want to have to eat meals provided by their mother's charity.

The third S.A. man in our street is out of work. He hopes to get a job through the S.A. Yet he always used to lend a hand in the past. He belonged to one of our defence organisations.

Here, out in the street, the less anxious can get rid of the collectors with a shake of their heads. But in their own four walls they are entirely at the mercy of the collectors and

Nazi group leaders. Each one has to play the Volksgenosse in his own home. Two weeks ago a neighbour had denounced an indifferent worker to the Gestapo[56] because she hated the man. He lives a few houses away from me. He comes home every evening carrying heavy sacks, the woman said. The house was searched. The man was under arrest for two days. It then came out that he had been fetching wood home from his job in the sacks. What had the woman who sells me vegetables said recently? She only knows that I am not a Nazi, nothing else. " What are we to do? You've got to join one of their organisations, if only for the sake of peace and quiet. We've chosen the one with the smallest subscription."

And our neighbour's daughter? She works in a factory in the city. The staff were provided with forms which they had to sign, for the second time. " It has been repeatedly proved that the Volksgenossen do not make use of the German salute in their private lives. . . . I am quite aware that failure to fulfil this order makes me unfit to continue working in this factory."

They have forced the " German salute " on the public with the threat " that every Volksgenosse who does not salute the swastika flag will be regarded as being a Marxist."

The Underground train comes hurtling from the tunnel, travels up the steep hill to the stop. Nollendorfplatz. There is the telephone box. It is empty. I open the directory. Albrecht—Krämer—Nathan—Here! On the first page of the letter " N " is a small pencilled cross. So the new flat is still all right. Franz must have made the cross, as arranged, less than half an hour ago. A good idea. It prevents us running into a flat that is no longer " safe." Rothacker is at the appointed corner. I slowly walk past him, glance into a shop window, and see that he is following me.

" Dr. W. Schönbeck," reads the door-plate. I ring. A slim young woman opens.

" We'd like to see Herr Stückert."

The woman nods.

" Come in, please," she says pleasantly.

A wide corridor, deer's antlers, a large hall-stand with a

bevelled glass mirror. We go past two white enamelled doors. " Waiting Room " is written on the one. The woman knocks on a door with an opaque glass pane.

" Come in," a man's voice calls. But that's not Franz !

A tall man with greying hair comes towards us. Is something wrong ? But the sign was there !

" Herr Karl ? "

The man looks at us questioningly.

" Yes, that's my name."

" Sit down for a moment, please. Franz will be here in a second."

The man leaves the room.

" Funny business," whispers Rothacker, and shakes his head.

Karl—he can only know the name from Franz. But I feel nervous all the same. We sit and wait for quite a while. Not a sound is heard. Rothacker's fingers play nervously on the table. Then Franz comes in at last.

" Franz, we thought that . . ."

" . . . you had been caught in a trap ! " laughs Franz.

His grey eyes gleam; he puts his arms on our shoulders.

" I was busy with someone else in the other room. It wasn't necessary for him to see you."

We sit round the table.

" And how are you both ? "

" *We're* all right," answers Rothacker.

" And at home, Jan ? "

" They send their regards. Everything's O.K. I saw Käthe the day before yesterday."

" Give her my love. And how's your shop going ? "

" Work is being carried on as usual. But——" Rothacker hesitates.

Franz rests his hands on the table. He does not look at us.

" Preuss has been arrested—Hilde told me——" he says softly.

Silence.

" While sticking up labels, Hilde said."

"Yes."

"He's in the Papestrasse—the Feldpolizei barracks," says Rothacker.

He looks at the floor. How tired his voice sounds! He needs a rest badly.

"They must still be looking for you as well," Rothacker remarks.

Franz shrugs the broad shoulders.

"It's possible. A good thing you didn't tell Hilde about Kurgel. She would only worry."

"They've released Dammert."

"Have they?"

"Of course, we've warned all the comrades. He doesn't have anything to do with the others; seems to be very depressed. They've knocked him about terribly. And he's lost his job, of course."

Silence again. Rothacker plays with the edge of the tablecloth.

"Do you look after the relatives of the men arrested?"

"We collected money for them twice."

"From the business people as well?"

"Yes. From the two we know well."

"No food?"

"Food? No."

"You must try that as well." Franz taps the table with his index finger. "We've collected quite a lot of food in this district."

Rothacker turns his head towards the door at the same moment as I do. Steps are heard in the corridor outside; the door of the flat is opened several times.

"It's nothing," says Franz. "The surgery has opened. It's our best alibi."

He scratches his head.

"Something else I wanted to ask you—the link for the hut settlement. Have you found someone to take Strubbel's place?"

The hut settlement. We are silent. Franz looks at me questioningly. Rothacker blurts out:

"You knew Herbert Ziemeck, didn't you?"

"From Strubbel's colony—the one the Nazis roped in over the Röntgenstrasse case?"

"Dead," says Rothacker dully. "Only twenty-one——"

It's quiet in the room now. Franz rests his head on his hands. Rothacker removes his glasses, passes his hand over his eyes. He looks haggard and worn.

"The S.A. surrounded the settlement with motor-bikes. Ziemeck fled from his hut, climbed over the fences, rushed along the paths mad with fright. It was early afternoon. The whole settlement watched the hunt, man chasing man——"

Franz sits there without showing any signs of having heard a word.

"They fired after him. The bullet hit him in the back. Then a motor-bike drove up, stopping with a jerk. They pushed him into the side-car. His mother ran behind them screaming wildly. He tried to defend himself near the Charlottenburg district court, in the open street. He pushed the driver's hands off the handle-bars. The machine overturned. The driver broke a few ribs; he's still in hospital."

Rothacker looks at the table; only his lips move.

"They knocked him to bits in the Maikowski barracks. He's the second dead out of the eight lads they had to release at the time of the S.A. cases. . . . His mother has gone out of her mind . . . she runs about telling everyone that her son has been murdered. . . ."

Franz still sits there without moving.

"The Hamburg member of the Reichstag, Georg Stolt, was buried a few days ago. . . . Another one from the Maikowski barracks. . . ."

A bell rings shrilly outside. We take no notice.

The Maikowski den—how many hells like that are there in Germany to-day?

Goering announced a new decree a few days ago.

"The death sentence will be enforced for attacks on the S.A., S.S., and the Stahlhelm."

For attacks? He who defends himself is the attacker!

Franz raises his head at last.

"It seems as if they——" He does not complete the sentence, but looks away from us.

I answer.

"It seems as if everything is working against us. They caught our newspaper distributor. It was even a comrade from another street, as a precautionary measure, because we are all too well known. We can't understand how he was arrested. That was the first time the thought occurred to us that there was a spy among us. We're going to test and watch all the other comrades now. He still had five papers on him. They arrested all five buyers. He told them the names; they had beaten him about until . . ."

"Do I know—?"

"Georg Krüpel. Three years' imprisonment. They said in the summing-up that, because he had once been an official of the Party, leniency was out of the question."

Franz stands up, paces up and down the room.

Rothacker says, "You wonder every time whether you should go home. And, once you're there, it's as if you're sitting on hot bricks. I had the same feeling in the trenches. You were surprised to be still alive."

He raises his arms, lets them fall helplessly.

"I've got a family—and no money"—his voice hardens—"but we don't want to leave! Not until it comes to the worst."

"The two women who called out during the inaugural ceremony——"

Franz turns round, looks at me enquiringly.

"—one got four weeks' imprisonment. They didn't arrest the other one; she's in her eighth month."

Silence.

Then Franz says:

"We've built something new. Come along, I'll show it to you."

We pass through a communicating door to the next room. Thick carpet on the floor, armchairs ranged round a smoking-table. A large oil-painting hangs above the grand piano. I've seen something like that at an exhibition once. Medea. Franz looks out in the passage. There is no one in sight. We turn a corner on the left. A door opens behind us. A woman's voice asks something in a low tone; a man's voice gives the answers. Franz takes us into a small room. Shelves are fitted on the walls. Glass bottles, tin boxes, and wooden pegs are scattered about on them. A small table stands in the left corner of the room.

" Here we are," says Franz.

A wooden board is placed on the table. A small tin pail is fixed on to one side with string, on the other side a sheet of cardboard folded to form a cone. Pieces of paper folded together lie in the cardboard cone. Franz fills his hands with something from the tin pail. The cardboard bowl sinks.

" Sand, just ordinary sand," he says, opening his hands and showing the contents. He points to the pail.

" There is a small hole in the bottom here. It's filled up with paper at the moment. The whole outfit is fitted on a roof which overlooks a busy street." He smiles. " Why, you're both as excited as school-kids."

" And how ! " answers Rothacker.

I'm delighted with the thing, and Rothacker looks years younger.

" The paper cork is removed at the last moment," explains Franz, " the sand runs slowly out of the pail, so that cone and pail are no longer balanced, the cone weighing more and dipping towards the street."

" Fine. Fine."

" We've tested it a couple of times already. It takes a few minutes until the pamphlets drop out of the bowl. And we use very thin paper into the bargain, so that they are tossed down slowly and sometimes carried on a bit by the wind. Of course, it must be well balanced at the start."

" We could try it too. When things quieten down a bit," I say.

Rothacker nods.

"It's simple and pretty safe. Let us know through Hilde how it works, will you?"

"Of course."

. . . .

I stop at an Ullstein newspaper kiosk on the way home. We left singly. Rothacker went first.

RESULT OF THE POLICE RAIDS!

"The search which was so suddenly carried out at 12 noon yesterday in all trains and cars has had concrete results. Seditious writings have been found. . . . Communist messengers . . ."

Six other people are reading the report. I glance secretly at their faces. They look so deliberately indifferent. If they were Nazis they would not be so expressionless. And they would be passing remarks of satisfaction.

. . . .

I was in a tight corner yesterday. I was cycling to a comrade who lives in a neighbouring district. I had to collect first-hand information about the S.A. for our paper from him. He was just having supper with his wife when I arrived. They overwhelmed me with persuasions until I joined them at the meal. We told each other of our experiences in the illegal work. Discussed the coming Reichstag fire trial for a long time. The comrade told me that they had organised regular radio evenings. They had a number of groups of five or six people, who listened in to the Moscow station for news about Germany, but especially about the coming trial. Strong feeling had been roused abroad. Well-known foreign lawyers had joined to form a committee which had decided to hold a counter-trial in England. A book containing documentary proofs was in preparation. The contents would prove quite clearly that the Nazis were the incendiaries. He also told me that two Social-Democrat comrades had offered the use of their flats and wireless sets. I told him that we were unable to organise listening-in evenings; we were surrounded by enough dangers as it was.

I learnt a lot of new facts from him, but when I finally looked at my watch it was already past ten. I hesitated. So late, and with the illegal material? But in the end I let the air out of the front wheel of the bicycle and removed the outer tyre, wrapped the material round the inner tyre, pumped up again, and drove off.

The summer night was quiet. I soon turned into a wide, lonely street. The bicycle seemed to roll along the concrete cyclists' track of its own accord. Still quite a way to go. Poor workers' hut settlements lay on both sides of the street. Coloured Chinese lanterns hung in front of a few of the huts; somewhere a mandoline was being played. In the centre of the street was a double row of trees, close by the bicycle track. Isolated benches in between. The pale green foliage seemed unreal in the light of the street lamps. How quiet it was there. In the heart of the city. I shall ride out with Käthe. We will bathe, and play about. It will be splendid. How quickly the wheels turned. My feet drove the pedals mechanically. A few lovers sat on the seats. A hasty glance revealed a dark group to the right, on the pavement. Otherwise it was like a desert. But one day things will have changed. Fright robs me of thought. Twice, three times, four times a sudden explosion. Has the tyre burst? That would be the last straw. My feet still worked the pedals. I glanced down at the tyre; it was quite all right! Something whistled past my head. Someone was calling over there. I turned round. Dark figures were running across the pavement behind me. Did they mean me? All at once I made out the words: "Stop! Stop! Stop!" I put on the brakes and jumped off the bicycle. "S.A.! They've caught you!" flashed through my brain. They were coming along now. Five, six, seven men, I counted. The shock paralysed my brain. The two in front pointed their revolvers at me. My hands gripped the handle-bar of the bike.

"Why don't you pull up as soon as you are called, you swine?" shouted one of the S.A. men at me.

He still pointed his pistol at me. The metal gleamed dully.

". . . I didn't know . . . that you meant me. . . ."

"When you are called by an S.A. man you're to stop, you swine!"

"Punch him on the jaw—punch him on the jaw!" shrieked the S.A. man nearest him. He thrust the barrel of his revolver at my chest.

"Examine him first," said the first one roughly. And to me, "Put the bike down, you swine! And stick your hands up!"

I obeyed. "Put the bike down." So they won't think of—— My heart beat wildly, but I already had my nerves under control. They felt my breeches, especially the wide material round the knees.

"Empty your pockets!"

I did so. Not a soul in the street—— If they should . . . ? And if they ask me where I lived? What was I doing in this district? My brain worked feverishly. I was allowed to replace the bunch of keys, the comb, and the two handkerchiefs. What could I have hidden? I was only wearing breeches and tennis shirt! "Best to act as if scared; they will then be impressed by their own importance," was my anxious thought. They had forgotten the punch on the jaw in the meanwhile. But the revolvers were still there—they were standing in a semicircle round me. Did they think I'd escape? Nonsense. The one in front, on the left, seemed to be in command. Aha, a star on the collar of his uniform—a Group leader!

He thrust the handle of his revolver at my shoulder-blade.

"Where have you been?"

". . . I was with friends . . . a birthday . . ." I stammered.

He looked at me threateningly for a second. The others? Were they expecting an order?

"Go on, then!" shouted the Group leader. "Now you know! When an S.A. man calls you, you must stop immediately. Do you understand?"

"Yes," I said anxiously.

The Group leader looked at the others and grinned. " He's dying of fright," said that glance. The others all grinned as well.

Let them grin, for all I care. I kept silent.

" Go on ! Quick ! " he shouted at me again.

I pushed the bicycle a few paces further, and then mounted. Mustn't ride off too hastily. Remain calm. They were sure to be looking after me—the material in the tyres.

· · · · · · ·

Rothacker had called for me. We want to go to the Unemployment Exchange together to collect his dole. It would be quite safe if I came along, he said; the Exchange was as crowded as ever, and the officials at the desks had their hands too full to take any notice of individuals. He has often told us in the last few weeks how the unemployed were not so frightened of the Nazi terror as at first, and that they have started, although very carefully, to criticise Hitler's dictatorship. We had reported this in our illegal paper.

As we pass the Power Works, Rothacker nudges me. In the narrow alley that runs between the Power Works and hut settlements, and along which Franz had fled, stands a lamp-post with " Zauritzweg " written on the street sign. The new name hasn't been there long. It occurred to the Nazi bosses rather late in the day that the comradeship which they have talked so much about between Maikowski and the policeman Zauritz who fell on the " victory night " should be given an outward symbol. So they have put up a bronze plate for Zauritz as well under the tablet erected in Maikowski's memory. It was inaugurated by a parade of the Thirty-threes and a division of police.

We turn down the Berlinerstrasse. Rothacker looks round.

" Why, that's . . ."

Of course it's Ede ! He has already seen us and comes towards us.

" 'Day, you blighters," he says, and shakes hands. What a handshake !

"All dressed up before dinner?"

Ede is wearing a blue suit and a light felt hat. A coloured tie hangs down over the checked shirt. He is wearing his glass eye.

"You sees everything, you does," he grins.

His one eye winks at me.

"Got anything special on—a 'job' for us?" asks Rothacker.

Ede bends his head sideways and looks at him slyly.

"No, not ter-day. I'm goin' to the little 'un. She's got 'er day orf ter-day...."

"So that's it," I answer. I have to laugh. He had once told me about the girl. She has a job as a cook. The "sandwich machine," as he had christened her.

"Gotter 'ave a bit o' fun now and again too," nods Ede. He wipes his glass eye with his handkerchief.

"It 'urts like blazes—but I daren't come along wivout it," he explains. And then, "Cheerio, boys. Mustn't keep the girl waiting!"

We continue on our way. Past the Charlottenburg town hall. Two huge swastika flags hang limply from the tiny windows in the turret. On the left, a black-white-red flag. People are going up and down the wide stone steps. The street pavements are crowded with the busy everyday life. No one looks up at the flags. We are the only ones who always blaze with rage at the sight. Do the others just accept things as they are? Has it already become part of their lives, something that seems unchangeable?

In front of us, small groups of unemployed are standing in the hot sunshine in the Wilhelmplatz, close behind the town hall. They can be recognised at a glance by their worn clothes, their downtrodden shoes. The sight brings back pleasant memories. Our groups used to stand here, about this time, and start a discussion with the others.

The Exchange is in the next street. Hundreds of unemployed move about the square. No one dared to stand round here for the first few months after Hitler's Government started. They would have aroused too much suspicion. We stop at one of the groups. I can see clearly that quite a number of men were taking part in the talk. Now they are standing with their hands in their pockets, listening to a slim black-haired chap. He goes on talking, the others backing him up in the deception.

" . . . and when I pulled out the line "—he measured a distance on his left arm with his right hand—" a pike as long as this, gospel truth." The others laugh loudly. It sounds too forced to me. None of the men seem to take any notice of us, but they are weighing us up all the same.

" Wanting to do a bit of eavesdropping " is what their glances are saying.

We leave them.

" They've got over their first fright, haven't they ? " says Rothacker.

In the short street that leads to the Exchange stalls and barrows are lined up one behind the other. The owners call out their goods to the queue of unemployed. Thick crowds stand round a few stalls. " New Inventions for Everyday Use " are being demonstrated. Trade is only carried on with small coins here; it has to be adapted to the purchasing-power of the buyers. Five razor blades for ten pfennigs, " best veal sausages " for the same price. " New patent " tie-pins for fifteen pfennigs. A few fruit-barrows stand in between, and even a stall that proudly bears the placard, " Shoe Repairs while You Wait." The artificial rubber soles cost one mark. They can be stuck on at once if desired. " There's still a lot of idiots knocking about," remarks Rothacker, pointing to a fortune-teller standing under a tent roof. A closely packed mass surrounds him, mostly women. His turban consists of a coloured cloth tied round his head, and he wears a gown pasted over with bright silver paper stars. Long yellow rings dangle from his ears. He keeps on pulling at a chain that makes the tiny figure of a man in a glass bowl bob up and down.

> *The little man from Amsterdam,*
> *Wise and clever, tells all he can.*

"Look into the future—only ten pfennigs," is written on a large board. A box of horoscopes stands near it.

The fortune-tellers spring out of the ground like mushrooms. They are especially thick in Kurfürstendamm, the fashionable district. They call themselves "Scientists of the Future" there, and their fees are correspondingly high. Dozens of astrologers' papers are published in the new Third Reich. Hanussen has started a new school of thought.

The Unemployment Exchange is housed in a closed-down factory. We cross the first cobbled courtyard. A bright light flashes in the ground-floor rooms on the right, an experimental laboratory for steam-driven apparatus. Long rows of people near that. The hopeless look of those who have been out of work for years has not been printed on their faces yet. Their clothes are still in quite a good condition. This is the section for those who have only been workless for a short time. They will land at the Relief Centre in a few weeks. Rothacker has to go across to the second yard, to the section for unskilled workers. He has had himself entered on the register here in order to save himself the long journey to the offices for skilled workers. A weather-beaten wooden shed stands opposite the paying-out room: the central kitchen for those receiving charity from the Relief Centre. "The spoon dole," as the unemployed call it. A swastika flag hangs above the door. S.A. uniforms are to be seen behind the glass pane. The place will be crowded out by the unemployed in less than an hour. The Relief Centre distributes food cards which entitle the holders to a bowl of food for a few coppers. Quite a number of shamefaced lower-middle class are among them; they carry their food home in double-handled pans. In former times the unemployed often used to make a protest by carrying their bowls of food to the aldermen in the town hall. The food is usually a dark brown liquid with a few bits of potatoes and other vegetables floating on the surface. It is entirely free from meat, and half cooked. The protest marches to the town hall have stopped, but the bad food has remained.

"If yer takes that standing, yer only a connectin' tube," Ede had once commented.

The signing-on office is full of people. It is a dirty grey room. Proverbs are printed on the walls in large lettering: "Honesty is the best policy," and, "A rolling stone gathers no moss."

Long rows of low benches stand in the middle of the room. They are all packed. The men sit and argue in groups. Others snap worn cards down on the seats. The several hundred voices fill the room with a dull buzzing sound. The air is thick with smoke and smells of tobacco and sweat. Officials sit behind a wooden barrier in front. One is wearing S.A. uniform. They cry out names at intervals. Long rows of men are queued up on both sides, waiting for their cards to be stamped. Rothacker joins them.

"I'll wait at the side here."

"All right." He nods.

The place looks like a queer gathering of conspirators. The low benches on which the men are almost crouching. The clouds of smoke, the whispered conversations which fill the air with a monotonous hum. Here and there a few have decent clothes, but those of the majority shine with age and are covered with patches. Young faces, old faces, unshaven, all wearing the same haunting expression. I recognise a few comrades. One of them smiles across to me. He still wears our blue Defence Organisation cap. There is a darker blue mark in the middle of the peak, where the blue cloth has not been faded. The anti-Fascist badge had been pinned there. A few put their heads together; their expressions and gestures tell me what they are talking about. Politics. Do the S.A. bosses allow this gathering together? Do their spies report the conversations? But the others are sure to camouflage their subjects. A board is hung above one of the desks. Chalked in large letters:

LAND WORKERS WANTED

No one goes up to that desk.

A hand on my shoulder. I jerk round.

"You here, Jan!"

"And you, Kurt?"

Kurt shakes hands, draws me to a bench. Three men are already sitting there. They stop talking. One fills his pipe self-consciously. He looks at Kurt questioningly.

"Carry on talking," says Kurt. "This chap's all right."

The three stick their heads together again.

"How's 'business,' Jan? We don't hear anything at all about you these days."

"What can you expect? Good to-day, bad to-morrow. I'm not the boss; don't know everything."

Kurt pushes his cap back. He laughs sympathetically. What fine teeth he has. He looks as brown and healthy as ever.

"Yes, that's right," he says.

Kurt is a young comrade from Strubbel's hut settlement. We had often pasted up posters and painted on the walls in the old days. But it's a long time since I last saw him. Our contact with the settlement is now the cripple, the one I visited together with Strubbel. Kurt won't know anything about that, though. It's the rule now. We only meet in twos and threes in our street to arrange things, and to print our material. The other comrades in the groups of five then get the finished results.

"Have you heard anything about Strubbel?" asks Kurt.

"No. Nothing."

"But I have."

"Have you?"

"He's in Königswusterhausen. He's built himself a mud cottage. He's just hanging on—but he's got no 'bugs' after him any more."

"Have you seen him?"

"Yes. I rode out on my bike." Kurt laughs dryly. "They've given him 'bread and wages'! Helping on the land. Forced work. But he's got to do it. And the wages! Thirteen marks a week, with a wife and child. He got almost the same amount on the dole here."

He moves closer.

"They hunt about to find them work, I can tell you. They drain village ponds and carry off the mud. Pave the roads with stones from the field!" He bangs his knee. "And that's supposed to help the farmers. You should just hear *them* cursing; they're just mad about it, I can tell you! Because they have to pay the whole cost of it all. The ducks swim about in the ponds even if there's mud on the bottom, and the roads were good enough for the farmers before," he adds dryly.

"But we don't understand that. That's Arbeitsbeschaffung!"[57] I answer ironically.

Hope he knows more details; we can use them in our paper. Kurt's neighbour must have heard the last few words. He turns his head. He has fiery red hair and his face is covered with freckles.

"Did they send 'im out from 'ere?"

"He moved out himself. Had to. Didn't feel ' well ' here," answers Kurt.

Redhair points to the board in front. "Workers wanted on the land," he says. "Sounds very good, don't it? They've sent thousands out. They stops yer rotten bit of dole if yer won't go. The blarsted swindle! An' one of these fine days yer finds yerself struck orf Berlin's register; yer ain't a Berliner no more!"

"What? Skilled workers as well?"

"O' course. It don't take long ter become a farm labourer that way. Yer've done what they expects of yer, and then yer gets forbidden ter move back ter Berlin."

Kurt gestures oratorically. "Throw the newly emigrated eastern Jews out of the towns! That's what they used to say. Now they chuck the born Berliners out! And what happens to the families?"

I glance round carefully. The other two are talking a bit too loud. It's not worth the risk if—— But no one's taking any notice of us.

"What do they care about that—families?" answers Redhair. "I knows of some families where they've all bin taken from one another. They've stuck the kids in 'omes, the women on the land. Most of 'em takes their families with 'em at the first go off. And then the Nazis feel sure they've got rid of 'em fer good."

"Skilled workers," says Kurt thoughtfully. "But that's mad—to send the specialists of a highly industrialised country——"

"It's all mad," interrupts Redhair. He turns right round to us. "My lad's in Arbeitsdienst.[58] Came 'ome on 'oliday a few days ago. They 'as ter cultivate wild land. 'E ses it's all sand and stones. What's goin' ter grow there, I asks yer?"

He pokes his head forward as if waiting for an answer.

"They loads the sand an' stuff onter lorries with spades. 'Ills, mind yer. 'Ole 'ills and mountains. Where the spade won't go in they uses an excavating machine. But that don't throw the muck straight inter the lorries—oh, no; that'd finish the job too soon. The chaps then 'as ter lift the 'ill on to their spades inter the lorries."

He taps Kurt on his chest with his finger.

"They drags these jobs out as long as they can. They dunno 'ow ter find the chaps work. They don't cost anything. They lives on soup that's only stinkin' water. And sleeps in wooden sheds. It's the bloody same everywhere, wherever yer looks. So long as the figures of the unemployed look all right."

"You sometimes get a chance of seeing how they really look," says Kurt.

"What 'ave yer got on yer chest now?" grins Redhair.

I look round for Rothacker. He does not seem to have finished yet. I have been keeping the line in view all the time.

"Listen, Jan."

"Carry on. I'm listening."

"Our neighbour had a cousin visiting him from East Prussia two days ago. He's a mechanic. Wants to find a job here. Has always wanted to work in Berlin, and see the sights, he said. His relations were fairly staggered by his optimism. 'But, Paul, don't you know how many unemployed there are in Berlin already?' He didn't understand at first. Then he fetched a local paper from East Prussia out of his pocket. Started reading: 'The metal industry in Berlin is now employing full one hundred per cent of all the metal workers in Berlin, within a few months of Adolf Hitler's prosperity Government taking over power. Skilled workers for the metal industry are now being drawn from other parts. . . .' "

Redhair thumps his knees, laughs uproariously.

But it's getting too noisy now. Where's Rothacker?

" I've got to go, Kurt ! "

" Cheerio. Keep your pecker up, Jan."

" I'll see to it ! "

Rothacker is now quite near the pigeon-hole. There are only three men in front of him. I stand by the side.

" Are you a Jew ? " the S.A. man at the pigeon-hole asks a pale lad wearing a peaked cap whose papers he is just finishing off.

" Why ? Do I look like one ? " the latter asks dryly.

The S.A. man thrusts his face nearer the pigeon-hole.

" I asked you if you are a Jew," he roars. He waves the boy's insurance card about in the air. " It's to do with land work. Jews aren't sent out."

" Oh, that's why—— Well, no. Pity I ain't, though," the boy answers.

" You'd better be careful what you say," says the S.A. man angrily. " Room 2, on the first floor, to the transport offices. Your card stays here ! "

The youngster leaves, mumbling something that I can't catch. I was watching the men in the queue during these exchanges. They nudged each other and whispered remarks. A few sitting on the forms had stood up, their attention drawn by the raised voices. Their faces quite clearly show their sympathy for the boy. The S.A. man could not have failed to notice that ! Rothacker nodded smilingly at me as if to say:

" You're surprised, aren't you ? "

His card is stamped immediately after that.

"That was a mouthful. Fancy them not arresting him," I whisper.

"They'd have to arrest dozens a day if they started on that track," answers Rothacker.

We walk slowly to the exit. I tell him about the talk with Kurt. Rothacker listens carefully.

"He's O.K.," he says when I finish. "But he knows nothing about our new contact with the hut settlement."

"That's what I thought. I acted accordingly."

Rothacker suddenly grabs my arm as we walk down the stone steps outside.

"Jan, there's something wrong!" he pants.

He lets go of my arm and takes great leaps down the stairs. What's up? What's up? Danger. It seems to strike me like a sudden blow. Then I see Rothacker running across the yard to a woman who is pushing her way to the entrance among the crowds coming and going. She keeps on turning her head as if looking for someone. She's seen Rothacker now; runs up to him, takes hold of both his hands. I can see her excitedly telling him something. Rothacker draws her aside.

Stay here. If something's wrong—we are both—but where have I seen the woman before? That round face, the dark hair? I think hard, but I can't place the woman. She must have come straight from her job; she's still wearing her blue apron. She's talking away. Rothacker stands quite still in front of her, his mouth half open. Whatever is it? It must be something to do with him. I look round carefully. No one is watching them. The unemployed are still coming and going in streams. I wait and wait.

The woman goes at last. Rothacker looks round and then comes towards me. Something terrible must have happened. His face is deathly pale; the eyes behind the glasses are staring and yet seem somehow dimmed. He takes hold of my arm in silence, draws me out into the street. His lips move. I want to ask him what's wrong, but the words won't come. I have a choking feeling in my throat. At last Rothacker starts talking, brokenly, and almost inaudibly.

"Our neighbour—Else sent her—to catch me here——"

A pause. I press his arm.

"S.A. at our place—they went away for a short while—Else was able to tell the neighbour. She wanted to go to the police with the child—two S.A. men caught her in the doorway—they're sitting in the flat—waiting."

Rothacker is silent and stares straight ahead. S.A. ! S.A. at Rothacker's ! Why just at his place ? I pull him away from the noise round the stalls into a side-street. He lets himself be led like a child; doesn't seem to notice it.

"Else asked for the police warrant. They only laughed at her. S.A. on their own. Thirty-threes ! Not even special constables ! " He looks at me. " Can you understand—without any reason we know of——? "

"Must be another case of an informer," I say chokingly.

Rothacker nods silently. An informer ! I can't get rid of the thought. The chap who delivered the newspapers—whom no one knows—arrested two weeks ago—and now Rothacker ! I think of each individual comrade. Who could—— But it's no use now; got to attend to Rothacker first.

"Of course you can't go home, Erich. Ride out to Franz's new district. You can stay at the place he's arranged for in cases like this. At Lamprecht's."

Rothacker does not answer for a long time.

Then he says : " It's not as easy for me as for Franz. What's going to happen to Else and the child ? And the flat ? The Relief Centre won't pay up any more ! "

"Erich, you know we'll look after them. We can't say now what'll happen later. The first thing is, you've got to go away at once ! "

Rothacker jerks his head round, looks me straight in the eyes.

"And if they arrest Else ? Because they can't find me ? "

I put my arm on his shoulder.

"I don't believe that, Erich."

He is silent for a while. We turn a corner. The street is empty here.

"Only S.A.—no police warrant!" says Rothacker. "I *must* find out whether the police know about it; everything depends on that!"

"But you can't . . ."

"Why not? I'm going to our police station. My place is 'clean'; there can't be any special reason—— What can happen to me, in any case?"

I try to put the idea out of his mind. But Rothacker is obstinate.

"Well, all right then. I'll see you to the corner. I'll wait for you there."

Rothacker has gone into the police station over the way. I walk slowly up and down. The police! They've become quite harmless enemies compared to the S.A. I know of cases where comrades who were being searched for by the S.A. gave themselves up to the police at the last moment. The Polizeischutzhaft at least often saves them from being "shot while escaping."

At the police station Rothacker asked to see the superintendent. The official on duty looked at him enquiringly.

"In what connection?" he asked.

"I was at the war, and I want to ask for a special favour that I can only tell the superintendent."

The official reflected for a while. "Just a moment, please," he said.

He returned a few seconds later, leaving the door of the next room ajar.

"This way!"

The superintendent was a man with grey hair. He was sitting in front of a writing-desk over which hung a photograph of Hitler. That made Rothacker feel a little less sure of himself.

The superintendent wearily indicated the chair near the writing-desk.

"Sit down, please"; and then: "What can I do for you?"

Rothacker gave his name and address and then told him about the affair. He watched the other man's face all the while. It remained expressionless. The man listened without saying a word, his hand playing with a paper-knife. Rothacker mentioned his war activities again, described his wounds, winding up with, " I can't understand it at all. Wanted to make enquiries whether you've got anything against me here, and, if so, what ? "

The police official looked at him. He had clear eyes under white bushy eyebrows.

" You haven't been home yet ? " he asked.

" No. I heard about it on the way."

" Shouldn't have said that," thought Rothacker, as soon as the words were spoken. " But how could I have heard of it otherwise ? " The question had been put very skilfully. The superintendent stood up, paced up and down the room, then stopped in front of Rothacker.

" We have nothing against you here, Herr Rothacker," he said.

And then, after a short pause:

" We can't alter anything ! "

He started walking up and down the room again, came back to Rothacker, and said in low tones, so that it should not be heard outside:

" I repeat—I can't give you any advice, Herr Rothacker."

" He's one of the old type," was Rothacker's contented thought. He knew that the police were powerless against the S.A. But he was now absolutely certain that the police had no part in the affair, which meant that they knew nothing about his illegal work. He thanked the officer politely. The latter even accompanied him to the door. . . .

When Rothacker told me what had happened, I argued again with him that there was now only one thing for him to do—to go to Lamprecht's. He agreed at last. I could see that the thought of what would happen to his wife and child was his main anxiety. I promised to do everything I could.

. . . .

The situation remained the same. True, the S.A. went away from Rothacker's place, but they returned every other day, and we ascertained that the flat was under continual observation. We fetched the easily movable things out with the neighbours' help. At an appointed moment Else and her child also disappeared. The rest of the things in the flat were confiscated by the landlord to pay the rent.

A previously arranged letter arrived a few days later from a village on the Silesian frontier. A relative described this year's good harvest. She wrote that the others were all well and happy, and then told us at the end of the letter about the death of the old village shepherd. We were sure to remember him well; he was now happy in the Lord's presence.

Rothacker had emigrated with his family.

. . . .

With the district sub-committee's consent we have suspended all newspaper and pamphlet propaganda. (It was only through their central organisation that we were able to send Rothacker and his family away so soon.) The comrades of the committee, and Franz too, are convinced that our recent losses were not due to chance. We are sure now that we were right in suspecting a traitor when our paper distributor was arrested. How else could the S.A. have come to Rothacker, a member of the group committee? Moreover, two other comrades have been arrested since Rothacker's disappearance. Sympathisers, who were only subscribers to our paper. And nothing was found on them.

I have gone into the matter very thoroughly with Schwiebus and Teichert. While talking it over, we decided that two of the comrades did not seem genuine enough in the light of recent events. We have dropped them, for the time being, without their knowledge, and we shall keep them under careful observation. We then went to all the reliable comrades and told them to keep to verbal propaganda in the meanwhile. We arranged new meeting-places for them, and also for the district committee, and we even went to the extent of giving these jobs to other comrades. We have warned them all not to make any notes. Telephone numbers, dates, and hours of the meeting spots, must be learnt by heart. At the most, small pieces of tissue paper that can be quickly swallowed may be used. We have suggested sufficient topics for discussions to the comrades. The rise of prices is still continuing. Dissatisfaction is spreading far up into the middle classes. There are now many thousands of grumblers who used to vote for Hitler. Those who still have their jobs lose a quarter of their wages through the exorbitant deductions and the continual " voluntary " levies. That makes things even dearer. But the unmarried are even more outspoken. Their deductions are increased by the taxes on bachelors. Two remarks that I heard recently while shopping are typical of the new situation. A well-dressed woman, wearing a Nazi badge, asked for a pound of dripping.

" Dripping " ? repeated the assistant, who seemed to know her, obviously astonished.

" Of course. Who can afford butter nowadays ? " answered the woman.

" But you've got a very nice new flat."

" Yes, that's true," said the woman, and broke off the conversation. She must have realised that she had already said too much.

And the other case. A middle-aged man complained to the fruiterer that he had to pay nine marks a month bachelor's tax alone.

" The only thing to do is to get married," answered the woman.

" That'd be a fine idea ! " exclaimed the man. " Don't you know that the monthly wages for a married couple and a child have been fixed at a hundred and twenty marks a month ? And if the wife has a job as well, and their joint earnings come to more than that, it's considered double earnings."

" You're right," answered the fruiterer; " *they* wouldn't marry on that either."

I was astonished. The business people have always been the most difficult to pump. They quite rightly feared they would lose their living.

Before Hitler came to power the Nazi papers used to call these same deductions " nigger taxes."

Yes, the comrades have plenty to talk over. The Maikowski trial is drawing near. They held an examination in our street recently. The police closed off a wide circle, so that we were unable to recognise the accused comrades. What will happen to them ? And what will happen to Richard Hüttig—our Buildings Defence Group leader ? And yet something has happened that makes public interest forget the coming Maikowski trial; that stirs every comrade to the very depths. The trial over the burning of the Reichstag has begun ! At first we had only heard Dimitroff's name, nothing more. Yet this name has suddenly become an inspiration, the symbol for an idea. Dimitroff's bold and daring words have re-echoed right through Germany—through the whole world. We know this from the foreign newspapers, from foreign wireless reports. Every word gives us new courage. His sentences are passed from mouth to mouth; are carried along the streets, into the houses; are re-echoed from the tiniest worker's flat. Not only that: something unbelievable has happened. Public opinion, crushed in a thousand ways, has suddenly returned, in a night. I see for the first time people talking politics in the trams, in the squares, in the shops, everywhere.

" What did Dimitroff say to-day ? " This question is heard everywhere. The papers with the latest trial report are almost snatched from the seller's hands. We anti-Fascists know that a Communist who has been kept in chains for months is now before the highest court of the Third Reich. A Communist who learnt the foreign language, even the laws of this foreign country, with superhuman effort, in order to fight the " evidence " and the accusations of the " packed " court, with clear-cut arguments. But not only this. Dimitroff switches over to the offensive. He cross-examines, and forces the hearing of witnesses who tear the masks from the faces of the Nazi fire-raisers.

What a revolutionary ! He fills the many thousands of German workers with renewed strength, brings back their faith in the power of their class. Hilde tells us that Dimitroff's words don't fail to impress the toughest Nazis. She is certain, after having overheard a few talks between her brother and his S.A. pals, that many of them are beginning to have their doubts over the real causes of the Reichstag fire. She says that these S.A. men, who are the bitterest enemies of his political views, express their unconcealed sympathy for him. They admire his courage. " We've none like that—could do with a few of his kind," is the way they refer to him. We hear the gramophone record of the trial reproduced on the wireless regularly now. The commentator tries to spoil the effect of Dimitroff's already cut-up sentences with mean and spiteful remarks every time. But he can't wipe out the impression of those few broken sentences! He achieves exactly the opposite effect, with his sneering and mockery. We know every time what Dimitroff must have said in coherent sentences. To-day, the majority of the German people recognises who are the real incendiaries. The Nazi Ministers and the leaders stand in the dock. They realise that very well, and are now trying to hide what can yet be hidden. The papers have not dared to print any more extracts from the speeches for some days. They contain only a general report of the proceedings. On the wireless, the gramophone records of the trial have become very rare.

In fact, there have not been any at all for the last two days. What a lot can sometimes be done by one individual!

· · · · · · · ·

It is Sunday morning, and glorious weather. I am standing with my bicycle at a street corner in one of Berlin's suburbs. There is only enough food for one day in my small haversack. But this cycling tour into the country is not a pleasure-trip. I am waiting for Bruno, the one-time boxer with the flattened nose. I have to think of that morning in the dance-hall, when Franz and I, as " assistant mechanics " to Rudi and Bruno, printed our newspaper. Franz has told me that the red-haired Rudi with the freckled face, and Bruno, are inseparable friends and the boldest comrades in the district, apart from being work-mates. They are well suited, too. Rudi's detailed judgment of every situation is the complement of Bruno's " Berlin tongue " and habit of rushing at things.

We had arranged this ride when I discussed the new situation with Franz at the beginning of the week. The comrades have come into contact with those who have remained in an S.A.J.[59] group there.

One of these young comrades works in a Charlottenburg factory. To-day's outing is only to give us the opportunity of getting to know them for a start. Bruno and Rudi have talked to two of these comrades so far. They are willing to work with us, and they were the ones to suggest the picnic, but they added we shouldn't rush the other comrades at the first go off; they still have the wind up badly. Rudi's job took him elsewhere, Franz did not want to meet the S.A.J. comrades for the first time for tactical reasons, so they asked me to come along. Franz thought that I would be able to get things working with the youngsters better, as I had been a leader of a youth group in the past.

" Mornin', Karl."

I jerk round. Bruno has arrived. He has ridden along without a sound, and now rests one leg on the pavement; the other is still on the pedal. Karl—it still seems strange to me, but they only know me by this name. He has a lovely bicycle, a light racer. The enamel and the bars gleam in the sunlight.

" I thought you'd be coming that way ! "

I nod in the direction from which I had expected him. Bruno shakes hands vigorously.

" In the ordinary way—but to-day "—he grins slyly—" I 'ad ter fetch the fireworks fust."

" You've really got it with you ? "

" Course I 'ave, when I sez so." He taps the leather case strapped behind the saddle. " It's well packed up, too."

We ride off. So he's got the " fireworks " with him—the small closely printed book—the illegal *Brown Book* of the Reichstag fire and the Hitler terror. We have heard about it for some time. The president of the court had continually attacked the " notorious " *Brown Book* during the Reichstag trial. Our controlled Press has raged for weeks about the " filthy lying publications " of the emigrants.

We are as happy as school-kids each time. We are used to reading between the lines. What a blow the book must be to Hitler's dictatorship ! Comrades have learnt more details about it from Moscow, on the wireless, and heard how successful the book has been with its indisputable facts. I heard about the book and the counter-trial in London from comrades in the neighbouring district. It was a splendid encouragement for us. We feel that we are not fighting a lone battle. The comrades abroad are mobilising world opinion on our side ! During the first few months, some of our members called the emigrated comrades " lazy cowards." But they have given up this wrong view of things since they heard of the success of their work against Hitler Germany. I saw the book at Franz's place for the first time. Everything runs so smoothly in that district ! They even get the illustrated workers' paper regularly from Prague. And they've got eager subscribers for it too. Franz is delighted when he sees my eyes open wide with astonishment. If we could only fetch similar stuff to our street ! But it's impossible—now.

My feet work the pedals mechanically. I look at Bruno. He nods, smiles. We are cycling rather fast. Still suburban streets. So he has fetched it along after all ! I was opposed to the idea at Franz's place. What do the papers write ? Fifteen years' penal servitude if found in *possession* of a copy. And for *spreading* the information ? Taking it with us to the S.A.J. comrades ? Read it out to them ? I disagreed with Franz. Bruno and Rudi have known them for years, Franz explained. They are all absolutely reliable. It will be a new experience for them. They will be all the more ready to work with us when they see what we are doing, and what material we've got. Well, we'll see if it is so to-day. Franz was always the one to accept responsibility, and if he sees it like that it's sure to be all right.

We turn left. A main road. Bruno now cycles on in front,

leading the way. He rides well. I keep on having to glance at the leather satchel at the back of his bike. Fifteen years. How old am I now? Absurd! Bruno looks at his wristwatch. He turns his head a trifle, his feet still pedalling away.

"We're just in time—got to meet 'em punctually," he calls out. The trees on the roadside fly past. The leaves are beginning to change colour. Autumn. The sun is still hot— or is it the speed? I am sweating. A lorry comes towards us. S.A.! The brown uniforms are closely packed in the open truck. There's one of them sitting on the roof of the driver's box holding a fluttering swastika flag with both hands. We raise our arms in salute! On and on. Left, and right, wide stretches of agricultural land. Now and again a plantation of young trees comes right up to the high road. I read the figures on the milestones.

A goodish way yet. A church tower appears. We come to the village soon after that. Bruno jumps off his bike.

"Behind the church, on the left, one of 'em was to wait." He wipes his forehead and his short black hair with the back of his hand.

"Only one?"

"Yes, 'e'll take us to the others. They're sittin' near the lake."

We push our bikes slowly along the road. An old peasant sits in the sun in front of his cottage door and puffs at his pipe. Near the inn on the left stand a few S.A. uniforms. Well-built lads. "The Communists want to confiscate your land, the last goat in the stable is to be divided—divided, divided!"

Franz told me how the comrades have once more started working at the landworkers in the north. It'll be a difficult job. How our comrades must have suffered in the villages, in the little provincial towns. They were well known to everyone!

A wooden sign on a brightly coloured post: "Adolf Hitler Square."

The square is a broad patch of grass with a dirty-looking

pond in the centre, where ducks are swimming about. The wooden fence, with swastikas set in all the way along, is probably supposed to make it imposing. A thin, weakly-looking tree grows in the middle of the fence. A sign announces: " Hitler Pond."

But there's the village church.

" There 'e is," says Bruno, as we come round the church.

A young lad sits on a white painted stone by the edge of the road. He jumps up and comes towards us. He is wearing short knickers and a blue open-necked shirt. An old army pack hangs over his left shoulder. A fresh open face, long brown hair. He can't be more than twenty. The hiker type. Like Heinz Preuss. They all look alike. Where's Heinz now—in a concentration camp?

" Ahoi," says the youngster, and shakes hands.

" Ahoi," grins Bruno back at him.

(Ahoi: **A**dolf **H**itler with**O**ut **I**nterest.)

" Did yer 'ave long ter wait, Alfred ? "

" Only just arrived."

" Is it far to the others ? "

" Ten minutes."

We soon turn right off the main road through a path between the trees. Along the banks of the lake. Tents are standing there, and boats near the banks. Most likely a camping-ground for rowers.

" A bit further. We're on our own," says Alfred.

" I 'opes so," replies Bruno.

Alfred turns his head in surprise.

" Have you brought it along ? "

" Sure thing."

" That's great," says Alfred, delighted. " But you've gotter talk carefully; the others are all under Herbert's influence."

" We'll see ter that," remarks Bruno. He jerks his head towards me. " Karl's from Charlottenburg. You works in a Charlottenburg shop, don't yer, Alfred ? "

" Yes."

" The two of yer must 'ave a talk afterwards."

"O.K."

So this is the Alfred with whom Franz suggested we could work. Seems a decent sort. There should be another one here who is willing to work with us. " The others are all under Herbert's influence." That will be the leader of the group.

We push our bikes across a clearing. A tent has been put up close to the reeds. They are lying near it, on a narrow strip of grass at the edge of the bank, browning themselves in the hot sun. Two, three—six men and two girls. We lean our bikes against a tree. The comrades offer their hands, mentioning their first names only. We do the same. Young, fresh faces. The girls look their part of belonging to a youth movement, in their short dresses. One of them has thick plaits of fair hair.

" Yer've picked out a nice spot," praises Bruno.

He is still as affected by the strangeness as I am and wants to keep the friendly conversation going.

" We always do," remarks Alfred.

So that's Herbert. He half whispered his name. He is tall and scraggy. Wears spectacles on his pale face. Seems to be the oldest. His dark hair is carefully parted in the centre. He is wearing a plus-four suit, the others shorts.

I sit down. Bruno whispers something to Herbert, then comes towards me and claps me on the shoulder.

" Fetch our things; can't leave 'em over there."

We walk back to the edge of the wood.

" We'll stick our things a bit on one side. If anything goes wrong, the others don't 'ave to be caught as well."

" Did you tell Herbert about the book? "

" Yes. An' Alfred prepared 'im fer the shock too. That 'Erbert'll never get excited over anything. The others were quite surprised, but not 'im. ' We'll read it afterwards,' was all 'e said."

Funny, I had the same feeling about Herbert as soon as I saw him. He'll be a hard nut to crack.

We put the bikes and the cases down on the left of the bank, hidden in the reeds.

"The one wiv' the rope is the other chap who's ready ter work wiv us—Alfred's friend," whispers Bruno.

I look towards the lake where a small thick-set lad is skipping, his feet barely touching the sand, his hair flying in the wind.

We rejoin the others. Bruno tells them that it has taken us less than an hour and a half to cycle out. It is the first time he has been here. Do they know anything about the place, what feeling among the country people is like? I ask a few questions too. We both try to start a conversation. Without success. The comrades reply to the questions, but I have the feeling that none of them is sufficiently interested. We are still strangers.

There is a big gulf between us. They have been on the other side of the lake, but have never stayed with the peasants, one of them answers. Bruno's racer was fine; he was saving up for a bike, another remarked. Then silence falls again. Herbert is lying on his back and looking up at the sky. He has not said a word so far. Alfred's suggestion that we play football is greeted with enthusiasm. The division into two teams is accompanied by cries and noise. But Herbert explains that he wants to continue sun-bathing. I help Alfred to tie a string between two trees.

"You've got to work up contacts with them first; they are only used to one another," he whispers.

"We could meet somewhere and talk things over. Where do you work?" I grasp the opportunity of saying.

He mentions a large metal factory. Ties the knot tightly, and remains silent. Is he already regretting having agreed to our suggestion on the way here? Then he says slowly:

"I mustn't lose my job. My mother is old and my father's dead." And then, "I've got to be very careful at the factory—want you to know that from the start."

I put my hand on his shoulder.

"We know that, Alfred. If you'll only tell us what they think of things in the factory, it'll mean a lot to us. But we can talk about that another time. Are you free on Tuesday after work?"

"Tuesday?—Yes, that'll do me."

He mentions the train and station by which he goes home in the evenings. I am to wait at the corner, near the baker's. We play for a long time. It is almost midday and the sun is very hot. With a noise we rush into the water. We form a chain and pass the girls along for a dip. They shriek with laughter.

"Don't drop me, Karl!" "Lift me up, Karl!" The cries and the expressions on their faces all go to show that we now belong to their group; we are their friends. Herbert gives us the cold shoulder again. He stands on the bank and stares across at us. He still has the same earnest expression on his face. Bruno stands near me. He laughs. His nose broadens; the water runs down from his hair.

"We'll start off afterwards," he whispers.

I nod.

We all get our food ready. The two girls make coffee on two spirit stoves. I watch them. I was at the Havel last Sunday with Käthe. We had separated at the station in the evening. Can one have a girl these days? I can't go to her place; she can't come to mine.

"Let's mix it all up; there's more ter choose from, and it tastes better too," says Bruno.

We had always eaten collectively in our youth groups. Bruno isn't used to anything else. I can see by the pleased way they agree that they all accept his suggestion as new proof of our comradeship. We all munch away, our mouths full. I wink at Bruno. He nods his head the slightest trifle.

"We've gotter meet more often, pals," he says. "Not only while 'iking; in town too. We younger folk 'ave gotter stick together; we'll be needed one o' these fine days!"

"Yes, he's right."

"That'd be fine."

"The walks in the open aren't enough," puts in Alfred; "we've got to arrange proper talks, get hold of something worth while to read. . . ."

I watch the faces closely. They all seem agreed. But Herbert? He does not say a word; his face seems veiled, all except for the eyes behind his spectacles, which survey the group as if trying to judge the effect of Bruno's words.

" I could get 'old o' summat ' worth while ' ter read," says Bruno. " It'd be best if we arranged something to-day. We might be able to meet one of your lot. If we can't, I could . . ."

" I'm against that ! " interrupts Herbert. He puts his cup down. They all look at him. " We would be dragged into your activities of propaganda and agitation. That's all your suggestion means ! "

" What d'yer mean, ' dragged ' ? " asks Bruno quietly. " That might happen in time, but it all depends on you; we would o' course be mighty pleased if you'd join in the work."

" We want to maintain our Socialist groups, and not run into idiotic dangers like you do ! " answers Herbert.

I see two of the lads nodding agreement. If we don't succeed now in convincing them, we'll never win them over.

" I don't think we oughter talk about you and us like that, comrades. The Nazis every day prove by their terror that they look on us as *one* enemy. We've gotter come together. Us younger ones specially. Remember Karl Liebknecht, 'oo called up the youth to oppose the war. And I can tell yer this much: we think over every step afore we decides on anything. We none of us exposes a comrade to unnecessary risks."

Pause.

As no one says anything, I start again.

" Do you really think that Fascism will collapse of its own accord ? Do you only want to come together to prove that you still have the same opinions ? The working-class youth always stood in the front ranks, comrades. It's got to be the same to-day. We've got to fight together ! "

Silence again. The quiet makes me think of the possible dangers. I look round. Not a soul to be seen far and wide. The lake is calm and smooth. The sun's rays flicker on the surface of the water. Herbert breaks the silence.

"Sure you've always 'fought.' But against our leaders, always."

I look at his mouth pressed together. Why don't the others say anything? Do they all share Herbert's opinion?

"Comrade 'Erbert, that sort o' talk won't get us anywhere," says Bruno pleadingly. "We've got enough ter talk about what's been going on for the years before 'Itler. And 'ow your leaders voted for Adolf in 'is first Reichstag. 'Ow they called the workers out fer 'is May Day celebrations. But we don't wanter talk about all that, I tells yer. That belongs ter the past; we wants ter arrange for the future now."

Silence again.

"That's my opinion too," says Alfred. He turns his head questioningly towards the others. "What do you others think?"

He has found his tongue at last.

"You're right." Willi supports him. "It's thanks to Herbert that the group has kept together—but that's no longer enough."

"Me too," announces one of the comrades sitting near him.

"And me."

The girl with the long plaits!

"I'll arrange everything with 'Erbert and Alfred," says Bruno quickly. "They'll let you know what we've decided." He looks at Herbert. "But let's start reading now. It's getting late."

He did that well. He was right to respect Herbert as the group leader. I notice Herbert pulling himself together.

"Lounge about as you are doing now; we've got to appear perfectly harmless. The comrades have brought very important documents with them—the *Brown Book*," he says.

The comrade near me jerks up from the blanket. The girl on the other side opens her mouth in astonishment. Their eyes gleam; they nudge each other.

"The original *Brown Book*?"

"The one that . . . ?"

"Shut up! You know what that can mean to us!" says Herbert roughly.

He is quite right. He has a lot of good points.

They are all quiet now. All eyes follow Bruno, who goes across to our things. All heads are turned when he comes back. They all want to see the small book.

"Someone's got to stand watch by the footpath at the back; we've got to guard ourselves against being surprised," I say.

No one wants to go. They are all too eager to listen to Bruno reading. I stand up.

"Let's take it in turns. You can start when you see me sit down up there."

The lake lies below me, a broad glistening expanse. There is no wind. The grass is pleasantly cool here in the shade. They really only look like week-enders down there. Bruno is lying on his stomach, his elbows planted firmly on the ground, his head resting on his hands. I strain myself to listen. Nothing can be heard up here; he must be reading very softly. How pleased they were! Franz was right; we will be able to encourage them to join us in our work. Who's that calling? I can't see anyone. It comes from the tents in the front. Dance-music floats up. They've even got portable gramophones. . . . The third watch has gone up to the path. Bruno is reading softly. The faces of the young comrades are very serious. They don't look at each other. A few lie stretched out with their eyes closed. A large stone suddenly splashes down into the reeds in front of us. Bruno breaks off. My head jerks round. The young comrade comes leaping down from the slope.

What is it? Danger? And he's running? That only makes us seem all the more suspicious.

"Sit down! Sit down!" orders Herbert. He has remained calm. The book has disappeared into Bruno's sports jacket. The comrade has reached us now.

"At the back there . . . two S.A. men . . ." he pants.

We sit paralysed for a few seconds. Bruno is the first one to pull himself together.

"Herbert! Start playing with the ball. But keep calm, all of yer! We're going to our things."

Herbert nods.

We wait and wait. Bruno has turned his bike upside down, fusses about with the wheels. The others are standing in a circle over there and throwing the ball to each other.

"Can't you catch? Quicker—quicker!" That is Herbert's voice. He has himself well under control. If the S.A. come to us, how will the youngsters react? They're too young. Have never been in such a tight corner before. We should not have—— What had I read: "Well-known Communist camping-ground raided." It'll make the police more suspicious of the hikers—the *Brown Book*—fifteen years' penal servitude.

"This chain is blasted sandy!"

Bruno! How calmly he says that! Does he notice that I— is he trying to bring me back to my normal senses with that simple remark? I am terribly ashamed. There they are! Two police and two S.A. men. So it's a raid! They come slowly down the slope and then go towards the group. One of the S.A. men stops near the tent and looks into it. I look at Bruno. He is turning the pedals mechanically with his right hand and looking across at the others. His lips are one thin line. The blood throbs in my head. We can hear every word.

"Who does this tent belong to?" asks one of the police.

We can only see his broad back and the short thick-set neck under the green helmet.

"It's mine," answers Herbert.

"Have you got a tent licence?"

"Yes. Just a second."

He runs to the tent, crawls inside. The boys and girls stand motionless round the four uniforms, their arms hanging limply at their sides. One of them has the ball pressed against his chest. They ought to go on with their game! Carry on! I can see one of the S.A. men casting searching glances all around, then nudging the policeman and whispering something. The latter turns his head quickly, looks towards us. If they come to us—but they are not searching the others. There's Herbert back again, hands the policeman his licence.

"Haven't you read the rules? Don't you know that the tents may only be pitched on the sites reserved for the purpose?" says the man sharply.

"I thought all this was public woodland," answers Herbert.

"What do you mean, public woodland? Pack up at once!"

"All right."

The policeman hands the licence back and turns round to us.

"Do you belong to this group?" he calls across.

Bruno straightens—but Herbert is before him.

"Yes, we're all together."

He means well—doesn't want to leave us in the lurch. But he should not have done it all the same.

Bruno's mouth remains half open. My hands tremble. I must do something. The back wheel of the bike is still revolving. I stop it.

"Now you know! If I find your tent on the wrong ground again I'll have to summons you!"

The words seem to come to me from a long way off, and then:

"Heil Hitler!"

"Heil Hitler!"

My right arm jerks up in the air, as if someone has pulled it with a string.

The four uniforms disappear behind the trees. I feel terribly hot; my mouth is dry. Bruno gives me a long look. He takes a deep breath. We wait a bit and then go across to the others. The two girls stand close together, as if supporting each other. The boy is still holding the ball pressed against his chest. It's Alfred. He is very pale. Not a word is said. Bruno offers Herbert his hand.

"Thanks, Herbert. But it was the wrong thing to do all the same. We should have been strangers."

Herbert doesn't answer. But his eyes brighten behind the spectacles, a gleam of pleasure flickers over his face.

The tough-looking Bruno with his roughened face, his broken nose, and Herbert, thin and pale, a proper bookworm.

"We're buzzing off now," says Bruno. "We'll see each other this week all right. I knows where ter get hold of yer now."

"Yes," is all that Herbert says.

We shake hands all round.

Push the bicycles slowly along the wood path. Bruno stops behind the camping-pitch in front of us.

"Let's sep'rate, Karl. It'll be best," he says. "Yer knows the way now, don't yer?"

"Yes."

I shake hands firmly.

"Remember me to Franz and Rudi."

"Sure thing."

I stand and watch him until he disappears among the trees.

. . . .

We have kept the two whom we suspect of betraying us under observation for weeks. One of them, Robert, is a young locksmith. He joined the Party from the youth organisation a short while before the Fascists came to power. He always begged to be included in dangerous work. We have put that down to his youthful spirits. But when our newspaper distributor and the five subscribers who had not yet received their copies were arrested, and for the first time we suspected treachery, we were struck by Robert's curious behaviour. Although we had warned all the comrades to be especially careful now, he was still as daring as ever. One night he cycled past a wide trench in the street where workmen had been working and threw a packet of pamphlets in as quick as lightning. But Robert's eagerness for illegal work makes us suspicious since the S.A.s unsuccessful attempt to catch Rothacker. And then the people he mixes with. He talks a lot with a number of S.A. men. Our comrades confirm that he still keeps it up. It's true we have always known about these contacts. Robert used to report all these talks, and sometimes was able to provide us with important inside information on what the S.A. were thinking. He knows a lot of them. From his apprenticeship days, and from the continuation school. They even know that he was once a Communist. But the old friendships weather that, and, besides, Robert told them that the political events have proved to him how false and useless his work for the Commune was. That sounded very plausible to them, Robert told us. Hadn't the *Führer* declared that he was prepared to offer a conciliatory hand to every misled Volksgenosse, they said? It had only been idealism that had attracted him to Communism, and useful Volksgenossen could develop from chaps like him.

But we now view Robert's S.A. talks in another light. It's true that we have nothing definite against him, but we have dropped him all the same. I have met Robert a couple of times in the last two weeks. I can't, I just can't get rid of the feeling that we are misjudging him. He does not know anything definite about my work; only that I am a reliable comrade, or was. For I told him on the first of these occasions that I am not interested in these things any more, and I have had enough of politics. (His first words were, Why didn't he get his paper any more, and when were we going to use him for another " job " ?)

I regret the years I have lost, I told him. I should have used the trouble and efforts for my own personal gain; would be in a better position to-day if I had. And, in any case, it was absolutely useless and crazy to attempt to oppose the present firmly entrenched regime. Robert showed a worried face, grabbed hold of me by the shoulder in the open street, and shook me. Did I realise what I was saying? he demanded angrily. I had to pull myself together to remain unmoved. I knew quite well, but the facts which were already history had disproved all our abstract theories. Robert looked very upset, and he kept on attempting to persuade me. But I stuck fast to my opinions. Every word went through me like a knife, but I forced myself to remain uninterested. There was too much at stake.

And then I met Robert again yesterday. And again I felt we had made a mistake. Robert's young face has become lined and haggard in the last two weeks. " What the devil is wrong with you, with the other comrades ? " he asked. He couldn't understand it at all. The other comrades talked just the same rubbish as I did, didn't want to work any more. He grabbed my arm, and looked so despairingly at me while saying this, that I became thoroughly puzzled. " Is it a remarkably clever attempt at spying ? " ran my troubled thoughts. But he couldn't act like that. I have developed an extraordinary sensitiveness for judging people during the last few months of illegal work. It has never let me down. The man is genuine.

But I overcame my feelings and kept up my attitude. " That is all over and done with," I explained again. Robert swallowed hard a few times. I had been one of the best comrades; it was enough to make the best of them despair, he said in a dull voice. Then he started off again excitedly. I had been in the workers' movement for twelve years; I couldn't have suddenly lost my senses. I left him quickly after that. It sounds absurd, but Robert behaved so excitedly in the street that it might have become dangerous for me. For me, who am acting the part of indifference to him ! I came very near to telling him everything yesterday. But then it occurred to me that a traitor would behave in exactly the same way as Robert did. Besides, it would be breaking all our disciplinary rules. I mustn't give way to my feelings. The thought steadied me.

Three days later.

The comrades are still watching Robert. He goes to and from his job alone. He seldom leaves his house in the evenings. The affair has got to be cleared up one way or another.

The other comrade whom we suspect is Kranz. He is a bricklayer; has been out of work for a very long time, and has a family. He would be better able to judge which comrades are now occupied by important work, as he has been in the Party for years. Since we have been forced to work illegally he has only been given papers to distribute, but we have stopped even that during the last two months. Kranz has become absolutely unreliable. Often he did not come to fetch the papers, and when he did he was always late, so that it became too risky for the other comrades who were in contact with him. These comrades were relieved of *all* work from the moment our suspicions were aroused. Until to-day nothing has happened. But we know that that does not signify anything. For, if Kranz is really a spy, the Gestapo won't arrest the men who connect him with us. That would only expose Kranz to us. Arrested comrades nearly always stick to their guns at the Gestapo " trials," so that they are not interested in arresting individual comrades straight away. They have made it a habit to watch the suspects for weeks, in some cases for months. In this way they hope to get behind the individual links in order to rope in the whole organisation at one go. That is why we confine ourselves to methods by which even the best comrade only gets to know those with whom he has to work. He must not know anything else. I continually have to prevent myself getting to know things which are not absolutely essential. We know that not everyone is able to withstand the physical torture. So we prevent the individual from being able to make complete statements. Kranz can only draw conclusions about us from our activities in the legal days.

He is out of work. But his bald head with the ears curled up like dead leaves (they were frost-bitten one cold winter) can be seen every hour of the day and night in the beer-house. It is a riddle. Where does he get the money from to pay for the many beers and spirits and games of cards? It's true his wife never saw much of the few coppers he got from the relief. In order to get any household money at all, she used to go with him to the Relief Centre with her children, carrying the youngest on her arm.

Our comrades are keeping Kranz well under observation: at the beer-house which he frequents, at the Unemployment

Exchange, everywhere. And this is not an easy job. If our own suspicions are correct, we can't afford to put him on the alert.

Kranz carries on with his drinking. He never tries to get into touch with us again. It really seems that he is nothing more than a weakling going to the dogs, that he has become completely indifferent to everything else.

. . . .

I met Alfred, the S.A.J. comrade I had spoken to on Sunday, yesterday evening. I was not sure whether he would keep the appointment. He might have consented in order to get rid of me. He had already said that he was afraid of losing his job. (But I could understand that.) And then he came after all, kept his word. He's quite serious about working with us. We walked the streets for ages. I arranged a new meeting with him, but with a longer interval; hinted that we were experiencing "stormy weather" at the moment. He told me that I could meet him here every evening at the same time, on the way from the station, apart from our arrangement.

He also told me important details about the production and feeling among the workers in his factory. I shall pass this on to our district committee, and shall ask them whether we have any other comrades in this particular factory whom Alfred could join. I would very much have liked to use his report for our street paper, but we are unable to print one in our street, nor can we distribute any other material.

. . . .

Something awful happened to-day. Robert's mother went about crying, telling everyone that her son had been arrested, and was at the Alexanderplatz police station. He had gone to his work yesterday morning as usual and had not returned. She had run to the factory late in the evening, worried to death. The night porter could not remember having seen Robert leave the factory. The police supplied her with the facts. Robert was arrested yesterday evening. Caught painting Communist slogans on the walls.

We are all deeply moved. We had wrongly suspected a loyal worker. Robert had been unable to stand the inactivity any longer. He had gone off by himself, without taking anyone to keep a look-out. How he must have suffered the last few weeks, to have made such a decision! He must have known how small his chances were of not getting caught when on his own.

I keep on reproaching myself. I should have told Robert the truth that time when instinct warned me that he was genuine. It's true the decision to drop him was not mine alone. We are only human, can all make mistakes. These confused times are the cause; we are hunted from pillar to post; we do not know whether we shall still be safe the next moment. I keep on repeating all this to myself. But my conscience will not let me rest. Robert has been arrested—that is a fact that cannot be altered. Not now.

But, come what may, we are fighting for a Socialist Germany. The Brown Shirts have proclaimed that love for Germany belongs to them alone. They say they are fighting for the German people—and they destroy the finest Germans!

How could we help loving Germany—we workers of Germany?

It is *we* who built her railways and her towns, who cultivated her fields, and who remained poor, who have no share in her beauty. Robert. He must be doubly hit by his arrest.

You are sitting in your dark cell and thinking that we have all become cowards. That there is no one left to take your place. That your sacrifice has been in vain.

I shall always see your haggard, desperate face in front of me. Shall always hear your words ringing in my ears. " Do you realise what you are saying, Jan ? Why, you were one of our best comrades, Jan. It's enough to make anyone despair. . . ."

No. We do not despair; not even now, Robert.

·   ·   ·   ·   ·   ·

Alex says good-bye and leaves us.

Alex is the comrade who used to direct one of our dramatic groups. The district sub-committee sent him to me some weeks ago. He had been able to get in touch with some old members of the former Social-Democrat branch in our district. He wanted to bring our two groups together. I have met Alex regularly since then, but there has always been some hitch. He has told me each time how suspicious the Social-Democrat comrades are of meeting strangers. It was difficult to persuade them to establish contact with our groups. I must be patient and wait a bit longer.

And now Alex sent me a message two days ago to say that he had brought things so far, and naming a meeting-place.

The Social-Democrat comrade is walking along beside me. We saunter towards the Tiergarten. The tall trees fringing the bridle-path have already shed their foliage. The dried leaves crackle beneath our feet. I must start talking. I know that his shyness is acting as a barrier between us.

" We must first decide where we got to know each other."

" Eh ! Why ? "

" In case anything goes wrong. That's usually their first question. Both our answers have got to be the same."

The comrade looks at me.

" I didn't know that," he says quietly.

We consider a few possibilities, only to reject them. Our first meeting must sound plausible. Then I make a suggestion that we both find suitable.

I tell him my name is Karl. (It's enough if our own people know me as Jan.) He is called Ewald. We then agree that we shall only address each other with the polite form *Sie* if we are ever arrested. The familiar *Du* immediately makes the Nazis think of the " Reds," I tell him.

Was it too much, all this talk of probable dangers right from the start ? But he has remained quite calm, so that I don't think anything more about it. These precautionary measures are essential.

I keep glancing sideways at Ewald while we are talking.

Don't I know him from the old days? That red face, the bags under his eyes, the scar on his left cheek. But the grey hair at the temples? Ewald walks on beside me in silence. I am still trying to think where I have seen him before. And then I remember.

" Didn't you use to come to our meetings, Ewald? In the Türkischen Zelt.[60] Don't you live—— ?"

" In Rosinenstrasse, in the People's House," he interrupts. " I've been wondering all the time where we'd met before, too. Of course, that's where it was. We often had long discussions, Karl."

Ewald smiles, and I feel pleased about it as well. I notice that he has got rid of his feeling of shyness, of distrust. He looks at me in a friendlier way. In the People's House—now the Maikowski Barracks!

" But you've changed a lot—there's a different look——"

Ewald takes his hat off and passes his hand over his hair.

" I've gone grey," he says. He stares thoughtfully in front of him.

" In the Rosinenstrasse——"

Silence.

Then Ewald continues in grim tones:

" Our windows look on to the courtyard. They keep a close watch on the windows, but we can see down into the S.A. cells through the curtains. Comrades scream nearly every night. My wife can only sleep with cotton wool in her ears."

We turn down a footpath. Motor-car horns can be heard faintly from the Charlottenburg Chaussée. A few ducks swim about lazily in the pond on the left.

" Things have got much worse since the S.A. special constables have been disbanded. When the car comes along, they have to drag the comrades out."

Ewald thrusts his face very close to mine. He presses his fingers into the flesh of my arm so that each separate finger can be felt. His voice is hoarse with suppressed anger.

" But the faces of these S.A. men are printed on my memory. When the time comes . . ."

Every one of our comrades has taken special note of one or another of the brutes, but Ewald . . . ?

He goes on.

" We wanted to gain power by peaceful methods; they've knocked *those* illusions out all right."

(I had had a long discussion with him in December 1932. He had been for evolutionary democracy then.)

" I spent all my time brooding over things at first," he tells me. " And it was about the same with the other comrades. We felt desperate, and gradually we became completely indifferent to everything. Only seven comrades remained loyal in our branch. We never received any help from the central Party office. The whole organisation broke down, fell to bits. Only the seven of us kept together. Then one of the others fetched Alex along. He told us about you. Said that we ought to get into touch with your groups. We hesitated for a long time."

" I know, he told me."

" Yes, Karl. We kept on asking ourselves whether it was worth risking our lives for such a rotten lot. All that crowd that ran around our meetings, always talking, doing nothing but talk. They hang out swastika flags now and run after the Nazi demonstrations. That was enough to make us lose our faith in humanity. They voted for Hitler in spite of our warning. ' Let 'em stew in their own juice,' is what we thought."

Ewald breathes heavily. I keep silent. He looks at me.

" A good many of your lot have deserted to the S.A. as well. I know one of 'em quite well. When I see his bald head going into the Maikowski Barracks . . ."

Bald head? Bald head? Can it be . . . ? I grab Ewald's arm.

" You said bald head. What does he look like ? "

" Why ? What about him ? "

" What's he like ? Describe him in detail; tell me what he looks like ! "

" He walks bent. Has a bald pointed head, and funny-looking curled-up ears."

There's no doubt about it—that's Kranz! I feel very excited.

" And what about him? "

" I've seen him cross the yard a lot of times with the S.A. men," answers Ewald. " Didn't you know that? "

" No. He's a traitor—has given away our comrades."

The words echo in my ears. That's where he gets the money for his drinking from.

Kranz! The dirty swine!

This revelation has an unsettling effect on both of us. Makes us both silent.

" We shall have to warn all the comrades," I say at last. " You see how important it was for us that we met to-day, Ewald? "

" Yes," is all he says.

Is Ewald worried by doubts now? Because we are being spied upon? I know how the Social-Democrat comrades always think that some of our people are unreliable.

Ewald is the one to break the silence.

" And what about our group? "

So he's not backing out. I'm glad. He said that as if it's a matter of course.

" We'll fetch you papers to start off with."

Pause.

" And later on one of you can take part in our committee meetings. You'd be the best one for that, Ewald."

" All right. I'll let the others know."

We arrange our next meeting. It's to be in another district. I tell Ewald to be there at the same time, and on the same day, each week, if I am prevented from coming the first time. He shakes hands firmly. We walk off in opposite directions.

· · · · · · ·

October 17th, 1933.

The Maikowski trial began to-day. Ernst Schwiebus showed me Goebbels's *Angriff* yesterday evening without a word. He had marked a few lines in the article on the trial. They run as follows:

"When this trial is over, the scales will be balanced again. Bloodshed can only be avenged by bloodshed."

We walked up and down the streets for half an hour. But we didn't mention the trial. We only arranged to issue a circular about Kranz. A heavy weight seems to hang over us all. What is going to happen to the accused comrades? " Bloodshed can only be avenged by bloodshed." They are all innocent of Maikowski's death. I know that I was there in the street that night!

. . . .

October 22nd, 1933.

A member of our group wanted to be at the court. But only a limited number of the public is admitted, and their names and addresses are taken, which means that none of our comrades can attend the trial. A few witnesses who gave evidence in favour of the prisoners were arrested in court. " Suspected of being accomplices." The accused are guarded by S.A. in court. An S.A. man sits next to each one. The papers print the Public Prosecutor's declaration: " I will on no account permit the register of the examining magistrate and the detectives to be presented as freaks of the imagination by these young hooligans. The men standing in the dock are disguised Bolshevists. But the strong arm of the Third Reich threatens them. The days are past when it was possible openly to adhere to Bolshevism. I shall not permit of any protests on the part of the defence to this charge!"

Again a terrible threat. It is clear that the comrades are retracting the statements wrung from them during the months of torture at the " preliminary examinations." How they must be standing up to the judges! How boldly they must be speaking!

. . . .

We have produced a circular. In this the workers are informed of Kranz's spying and treachery. An exact description of him is included. We have given this leaflet to reliable workers at the Unemployment Exchange, for them to pass it on. It has reached the homes in our street. Where this seemed dangerous we stuck it in the letter-boxes. The Berlin central committee has incorporated the text in its list of spies and informers. In this all the working-class districts are warned against Kranz.

Pamphlet and newspaper propaganda is still held up in our street. We have given all the comrades strict orders to keep themselves and their flats " clean." We are expecting the showing up of Kranz to be followed by sudden house raids, perhaps arrests as well.

I met Ewald as arranged and explained our present difficulties to him, with full details. I hesitated at first, because I did not want him to get anxious. But this did not seem to disturb him either. The last year has hardened us all. I had misjudged him.

At our request the neighbouring district has taken over the delivery of papers and material to the S.P.D. comrades for the time being.

. . . .

So far the exposure of Kranz has not led to action by the S.A. in our street. This is either a tactical calm intended to lull our vigilance, or else the S.A. have their hands full with their Party's latest moves. A new wave of propaganda is flooding Germany.

PLEBISCITE ON NOVEMBER 12TH

Germany has left the League of Nations. A " plebiscite " is to approve this step and give Hitler a free hand in his home and foreign policies. I am strolling through the streets. Huge flags hang across the road. They have erected tall wooden masts in the squares. The banners stretched between these poles blow out in the wind.

Wir wollen kein Volk minderen Rechtes sein !
Für Ehre und Freiheit ! Am 12 November stimmt Ja !
Die Kriegsopfer stimmen mit Ja ![61]

Six-feet posters are stuck on the walls of the houses, on the advertisement boards.

LLOYD GEORGE ON GERMANY!

This is followed by a list of quotations from the British statesman's speeches in which he describes the position of Germany "robbed of honour and arms." At the end, in terrific letters:

JEDER DEUTSCHE EIN LUMP, DER NICHT FORDERT, WAS EIN ENGLÄNDER IHM ZUBILLIGT! ALLE STIMMEN JA![62]

I have to read a paragraph more than once. It describes the vital part. Less than twenty years have elapsed: the crash of aeroplane bombs, the booming of artillery, can return in a night.

There, another banner:

MIT HITLER FÜR DEN FRIEDEN DER WELT![63]

Cannon, aeroplanes, tanks—for peace! I can hear them talking again as they did then: "We don't want it. This war has been forced on us. We are only defending the Fatherland."

That banner again:

THE WOUNDED EX-SERVICEMEN....

The war-wounded are expected to demand new instruments of destruction! Cripples still limp along in the streets, begging, if they are not to starve on their miserable pensions, *dem Dank des Vaterlandes*.[64] I once saw photographs from a military Home for Incurables. Half the face torn away, armless and legless, living stumps. They are still lying in their closed institutions, waiting for death to release them. They have been buried alive. The men and women of to-day would have plenty to think about if they saw them.

I glance instinctively at the people hurrying past.

Indifference, the daily struggle for existence—that is all that their faces hold. And those two? He whispers something; she smiles archly up at him. He may be buried somewhere in a couple of years' time, and she will be opening an official letter: " Auf dem Felde der Ehre. . . ." [65]

I walk back aimlessly, as if my legs were functioning automatically. Will it always only be a few thousand who realise what is happening? I can see the long rows of demonstrators in front of me quite clearly, as if it had only been a few months ago and not the first few years after the war.

" *Nie, nie woll'n wir Waffen tragen,*
 Sollen die Herren sich alleine schlagen," [66]

they had sung then.

Songs, only songs. They had not wanted to realise that they must first get rid of the " Herren "—the people who cause war. Instead, they looked on while those who wanted to transform the semi-revolution into a proper one were murdered.

Karl Liebknecht [67]—Rosa Luxemburg. [67]

Thousands of them!

Spartacus!

Epp, the whole Fascist gang that flourished then, they are the rulers of Brown Germany to-day. *They* always knew what they wanted!

Two days before the plebiscite. The papers write that Hitler is going to speak to " his " workers to-day. At the Siemens-Schuckert Works. They are the largest industrial works in Berlin. Hitler knows now where the real weight lies. I remember what Franz said the first morning after the nomination of the Reichs Chancellor: " A Party leader should have spoken here, to-day, at Siemens'."

I go to Siemensstadt towards midday. Three-quarters of an hour's walk from our street. I pass Jungfernheide station. We met here that morning after the nomination. Tried to start a discussion in the trains; distributed pamphlets. It was here that Rothacker was almost arrested. Rothacker. We have heard from him twice. He is in Prague with his family. Getting on fairly well. They are supported by emigrants' committees. His wife sells newspapers in the streets. She is able to sell a lot because she is such a pretty blonde.

So a comrade who had seen them told us. They had not got on well together towards the last. The continual money worries—and then she wanted to get some pleasure out of life. And, in addition, Rothacker is almost twice her age. Émigré life will be more difficult for the woman. And then there's the child, the four-year-old Inge. . . .

A long wide road, the Nonnendamm. Banners are stretched across the street here, too. Hut settlements on both sides. Swastika flags flying from a few. They've got to be hung out for the parade to-day. This or that one is, maybe, genuine. There is Strubbel's colony. We used to call it " Little Moscow." We went to the cripple at dusk that time. The typewriter, the cyclostyle—hidden in the seed-box. Strubbel has left; the cripple has taken his place, still works for us.

It was here that the S.A. had lost control of themselves. They gave chase to Herbert Ziemeck on their motor-bikes in broad daylight. Dragged him to the Maikowski den—dead. Twenty-one years old.

" A cottage for each warrior from the Front," Hindenburg had once said. A number of " returned warriors " live here, in their little cottages. They had to build them themselves. With boards and roofing-felt. Nearly all are out of work, like Strubbel was. He lived in his hut in winter as well. Had no rent to pay. The same with nearly all the others.

One of the Siemens electrical railway bridges spans the road here. The Siemens Works start on the other side, on the left. The new office building is thirteen storeys high. A huge box-like erection of glass and concrete. Five minutes further on, on the other side, stand the old offices. This is another giant building. The yard-long hands of the clock on the big square chimney point to twenty minutes to twelve. The *Führer* will be coming along soon. Adolf is to begin his speech at twelve. The new offices have only been built during the last few years. An investment for the company's surplus capital. I glance up at the long row of windows. Teichert says many of the yards are empty now, as a result of " the national economic reconstruction." He works here. Will he and his mates be listening to Hitler's speech? Long rows of white houses begin on the right side of the street. All newly built, up to date and practical. The old Siemensstadt residential quarter was composed of clerks and undermanagers. The works knew what they were doing when they settled their employees here. The shadow of the factory looms large over their free time, never lets them lead a private life. Everyone knows everyone else. These new buildings have nearly all been put up by Siemens and have doubled the number of inhabitants. It was inevitable that this lower-middle-class suburb became a Nazi stronghold.

The hut settlements of the unemployed extend right up to the white houses. How they have always hated each other! The political and economic extremes of a town are seldom so close to one another. Tall wooden poles have been driven into the ground on both sides of the street where the first houses appear. They are plastered with green garlands, and have a huge banner stretched in between them:

SIEMENSSTADT GREETS THE FÜHRER!

People are standing on the pavements. Two, three, and more rows deep. Yet, I had expected more at this spot. Long files of S.A. close the street. They have unfastened their belts, which they are using as links between them. A crowd stands outside a wireless shop. I join them. An outsize loudspeaker has been fitted above the door. Eighty per cent women, and the rest mainly schoolchildren accompanied by their teachers. They've probably got a school holiday for the occasion. The women are all, without exception, well dressed. Somehow the salaries are made to last the month. Margarine is eaten the last few days. Any sacrifice in order to be able to present a " decent " appearance.

" He'll drive past, quite near us, right by us," says a

plump, fair-haired woman in tones of gleeful anticipation to her neighbour.

The latter smiles excitedly. They are behaving as if this were the greatest moment in their lives.

The proprietor of a butcher's shop comes out with his shop-girls. They are wearing white overalls, and caps with the shop monogram. The butcher is very stout.

" We'll keep closed as long as it lasts. This doesn't happen every day," he says loudly to one of the girls, gesticulating with his sausage-like fingers.

Let 'em all hear that; that's what you want, old man, isn't it? The quarter of an hour's patriotism, with no additions to the till, will pay sufficient dividend later on, won't it?

Sudden movement in front.

" They're coming . . . they're coming ! " is passed from mouth to mouth. The S.A. grasp their leather belts more firmly, push the crowd back. Cries of " Heil." It's only a single car. Goebbels. He raises his arm indolently—gone. A few minutes later his voice comes from the loudspeaker. Introductory talk explaining the deep meaning of to-day's " *Führer* speech " in the home district of " his German workers." While he is still speaking, the crowd pushed forward to the edge of the pavement. Wild " Heil " cries fill the air; the arms jerk up; mine, too. Hitler. He stands up in the car and returns the greeting. There is only three yards between us. Hitler's face is flushed from the wind. Fat and spongy. He looks a damned sight more " energetic " on the " *Führer* pictures." Two other cars follow close behind him. S.S. men stand on the running-board, ready to jump down at the crowd, their free hands in their revolver pockets. Gone ! The cries swell out along the street in wave after wave of frenzied sound. Three yards away ! That's why some people talk of an assassination. Madness ! Hitler's death would not alter anything. Goering, Goebbels, or someone else would just carry on in his stead. And on that very same night thousands would be put to death in the concentration camps. . . .

The shrill, enraptured voice of the woman near me interrupts my thoughts. She claps her hands in delight.

"Doesn't the *Führer* look lovely? Oh, doesn't he look splendid? How can anyone help being fond of him?"

The crowd pushes to the loudspeaker again. More people have come along, press forward to listen. An S.A. man stands next to me. He has the chin-straps of his short helmet buttoned under his chin. It looks more impressive that way. He thinks himself very important. The cries of "Heil" still come from the loudspeaker. Then silence, and at last Hitler's voice.

"Fourteen years of struggle . . .

"Marxist trade chaos . . ."

Always the same! And now:

"I am speaking on purpose to all the German workers who are gathered round their loudspeakers in all the factories at this momentous hour. We want to offer the hand of friendship to every opponent who is prepared to stand up for Germany's honour. . . ." The voice becomes shrill, is almost at breaking-point. " I know you only receive low wages—I know that!"

The next few sentences reach my ears without my understanding them. "Every opponent." He can say that to "his" workers! "I know that——" That won't help to fill the pay envelopes—but he realises that it is high time to play the "Socialist" card again. To show how he sympathises with the "little man's troubles." I give a start. The voice in the loudspeaker dies away. There is only a crackling and buzzing to be heard. Finished already? But why are the others running about so excitedly, waving their arms?

"Jamming... sabotage... it's a plot——" a few are calling out. Two S.A. men run to the shop door. The proprietor appears in the doorway. Raises his arms and lets them drop helplessly, shrugs his shoulders in despair. "It's the same everywhere—it's not my set," he defends himself.

The break has lasted a few minutes already. The S.A. man near me plucks nervously at his chin-straps. His face is distorted.

" Sabotage again—the blasted Reds ! "

I turn a disbelieving face towards him.

" But it's not possible—not nowadays ? The amplifiers are sure to be guarded ! "

" What else can it be ? " he says angrily. " But they'll get caught, they'll get caught sure enough ! "

The excitement grows. And then the *Führer's* voice suddenly bursts out again:

". . . long enough without honour and respect . . ."

I walk home slowly. The S.A. man's first thought was the " Reds." Everywhere, all the time, they are harassed by the feeling that there is an unseen enemy round them, waiting to jump at their throats.

I had a talk with Teichert in the evening. Told him about my *Führer* tour.

" Did you see Adolf too, you Siemens turner ? Didn't he shake hands symbolically with one of the workers ? "

" An' I don' fink," answers Teichert. " Just listen to uncle telling you all about it." He laughs contemptuously. The black stumps in his mouth show themselves.

" None of our gang was there. They chose carefully selected delegates from all the works. All foremen, and reliable Nazis as well. The workers from our yard were there, of course, but they 'ad to stand at the back. And the loudspeakers ! They were safely fitted up on one of the high dynamo sheds, you can bet ! They'd built a special ladder round it. S.S. men guarded the steps ! And now you know how the *Führer* talks to ' his ' workers, don't you ? "

. . . .

Election Sunday.

Groups of Hitlerjugend and the S.A. marched round the courtyards early in the morning blowing fanfares on their trumpets and then crying out election slogans in a chorus. The broadcasting stations interrupted their programmes every half an hour, repeating the same questions each time: " German men and women ! Have you done your duty ? Have you given your vote for Adolf Hitler's Government ?

If not, do so at once!" That's been going on for weeks. Wireless, newspapers, cinemas. Goebbels pours out his election propaganda a million times all over the Reich. They brought slips of paper to every home this morning: "This house is under block warden Meyer's supervision, House No. 38. Vote 'Yes.' Then give up this slip at the election box. You will save yourself the bother of being questioned by us later in the day."

Teichert's polling station is the same as mine. We have arranged to go there together; want to see what things are like. At first we thought of meeting in another district. Teichert said it was not advisable to let ourselves be seen together here, since the affair with Kranz. But our places are " clean "; we should be daring; that is the best cover, I argued. It would be sure to excite suspicion if we suddenly became " strangers," after having lived in the same street for so long. The unmasking of Kranz has had no further effects. We learn that he does not sit around the pubs so much now. Hasn't got the money. We are still on the alert, but we know that exposed informers lose their value for the Nazis. They despise them inwardly as much as they are impressed by the courage of our comrades. Hilde had reported such talks between her brother and his fellow S.A.s. Those who are cowards themselves, and most of them are (they never come down on us alone), always find the bravery of the others twice as strong as it is. So I insisted on Teichert fetching me.

And now we are carelessly sauntering down our street.

The flags have increased in number. They hang from the attic windows of the century-old houses, under the low moss-covered roofs.

We come to the bend in the road. Sunday quiet reigns in our street. This makes the drone from the machines in the Power Works seem louder, clearer. A swastika flag hangs from one of the big fluted windows of the tall red-brick building. The wooden fence of the rubbish-dump is stuck over with the Lloyd George poster.

" Every German a rotter who does not demand what . . ."

"We'll have quite a number of 'rotters.' You can be sure of that."

Teichert smiles. The black teeth stumps show beneath his upper lip. He nods his head slightly in the direction of two windows.

"Volksgenossen—special edition," he says mockingly.

I glance up at the two flags he is referring to. Two comrades live there. We have advised them to hang them out. We must prevent the slightest possibility of suspicion being drawn to any of our comrades in the present situation.

"It's got its advantages, Paul, our rooms looking out on the back."

"I should say so. We none of us want to be in the limelight."

We have reached the stage where every window facing the street is under S.A. control. Especially in our street. This morning the S.A. came to the houses that were sparsely flagged and asked if the front tenants who had no flags were Jews. It's a good thing Ede doesn't live in a front room. He had kicked up enough fuss as it was.

"Good tactics? What d'yer mean, tactics? Our comrades advertising the Nazis now!" had been his indignant reply, when we told him of the two comrades who were to hang out flags.

We turn down the Berlinerstrasse. Hilde lives over there. Must ring her up at her office some day soon. She sees Franz more often than I do. The flags hang closer to one another here. Only the lower middle class live here.

Clerks, lower-grade civil servants, small tradesmen. It is curious how our workers' quarters are so shut in. Only a few streets.

Charlottenburg is a civil servants' district. The representatives of the working class on the municipal council, even the workers' organisations themselves, have always had to fight against the middle-class majority. In the years before the war too. That's why the Charlottenburg workers are so revolutionary, always on the attack. I look at Teichert. The pale skin drawn over his prominent cheek-bones, his thick hair growing square at the temples. A worker's face. Nothing specially arresting about it; like all our faces. They all come from the same moulding-pan.

"And how's your wife, Paul?"

"What do you want to know about her? She doesn't know much about us. The same as in the old days."

He says that as if he has accustomed himself to the inevitable. His wife is a small, energetic woman. No longer young. She has never been interested in politics. Her home is her world. She would most certainly have implored him 'not to risk bringing such misery' on her if she had known of his illegal work. How can they live like that, side by side, yet not together? My idea of a comrade's marriage is different. Teichert draws a slip from his pocket.

It is the block warden's controlling slip.

"They get the results they want with this. Take it from me." He strikes the palm of his one hand with his fist. "They want to find out those on the voting-lists who haven't voted. And nearly everybody believes they find out *how* they've voted at the same time!"

I only nod. What must things be like in the country, where everyone knows everybody else? Even here in the town our propaganda is of necessity restricted by the powerful means at the disposal of the Nazis.

We have scattered tiny leaflets in our district with only a hammer and sickle and the word "No" printed on it. The same has been done in all the Berlin districts. Ede had the most difficult parts to do, as usual. Without his glass eye, the blind man's ribbon round his arm, and with his stick tapping in front of him. But we have not scattered any in our street, and have only discussed the plebiscite with a few of the tenants. We don't want the S.A. coming down on us so soon after the Kranz affair. Despite the terror, these slips will not only be a call to vote "No": they will have a moral effect on every Hitler opponent. Will show him that we can't be suppressed.

Teichert nudges me. He wants to tell me something, but can't do so as two S.A. men stand in front of us.

"Heil Hitler!"

"Heil Hitler!"

"Have you got your voting badge?"

"Voting badge? No," replies Teichert.

"So you haven't voted yet?"

"No."

"You'd better go at once. Otherwise you'll be stopped all over the place!"

"You can get the voting badges over there," explains the other S.A. man. He fidgets with his glasses. "Pin them on! It proves that you've voted."

They raise their arms, continue on their way.

"Come along, Jan," says Teichert angrily, when we are a bit further on. "They can have our answer at once!"

We pass a tram stop. The S.A. men are questioning the people waiting here. A fat woman talks excitedly.

"But I've got to go to Spandau—to my relations!"

"Go to your polling station first. You'll be questioned in Spandau as well, and then it'll be too late!" we hear one of the S.A. men saying.

"But they're expecting me to dinner . . ." The woman starts off again.

"Are you deaf or what? You can't go anywhere without the badge to-day!" the S.A. man shouts at her.

The woman angrily picks up one case and goes off. And now we see that a small man is with her. He carries the other case. We walk behind them.

"I told you so. Didn't I want to go by train?" the woman scolds the little man.

"Of course! By train! Yer don't seem to 'ave 'eard what Fritz there said. They don't let anyone past the barrier that 'asn't got 'is badge!" the little man defends himself; "they watches 'em even closer there!" The polling station is a pub. The people stand outside in a long queue, which continues through the bar to the next room. We are able to look into this room when we come to the doorway. The officials sit behind the table at the other end. They are all wearing National-Socialist badges. Immediately on the left, behind the open folding doors, stand three boxes, each on a separate table. Green curtains partially divide them. Two S.A. men stand on both sides of the door; one has a collecting-box in his hand, the other a cardboard tray with the voting badges. A man turns the pages of a long list at one of the tables. He repeats the names loudly, sometimes asking the date of birth to make sure. A Nazi official in uniform sits near him and ticks the names off each time on a list of his own.

They have a copy of the district voting list. *That's* how they can check those who don't vote. And then they fetch them.

" This house under the control of block warden Meyer——"

The voters go up to the boxes behind the door with the envelopes containing the voting slips. They mark in their crosses behind the curtain. Some of them are so agitated that they leave the curtain half open. A couple of yards behind them stand the two S.A. men. They keep their eyes glued to the boxes as if to prevent them being stolen ! The rules are followed. The S.A. are not in the voting room—only on the threshold.

Teichert winks at me. He shares my thoughts. It must have an intimidating effect on the hesitating " No " votes. I glance round involuntarily at the others behind us. Working men and women. Their clothes, their rough hands, show that. Their faces are serious, set.

The S.A. man with the cardboard box offers us the badges as we leave the room. The other one pokes the collecting-box forward.

" We're out of work," answers Teichert.

They give us the badges for nothing. They are made of tin. A " Yes " is punched across them.

Outside, Teichert turns to me.

" Their blasted cheek makes me sick ! We've got to pay them for the badges they check us with ! What next ? I'm not going to wear their bloody medal."

· · · · · · ·

Two days later.

Hilde tells us that her brother and his S.A. friends have been having furious arguments. They were shocked to find practically five million " No " voters almost a year after taking over power.

" Under the circumstances, and according to their figures," says Teichert.

" No one can test them, though."

" The Charlottenburg result is one of the best," I tell them. " We've got thirty-eight thousand ' No ' voters. Why, even the much larger workers' districts, like Friedrichshain and Wedding, have only forty thousand."

" In spite of the Thirty-threes. Perhaps it's because in Charlottenburg the workers are having the hardest time from the Third Reich."

. . . .

I have been unable to carry on working at this book for some time. It was impossible for me to write in my own room any more. My neighbour—her room is only divided from mine by a thin wall—had remarked to the landlady that she heard a typewriter in the house. The old woman passed on the harmless explanation that *I* had given *her*. Of course, she didn't have the slightest idea what it was that I was always typing. As far as she is concerned, I am a tenant who pays his rent punctually, and a " nice person " into the bargain.

There had been similar occurrences some days previously. Officials had called at our flat a few times while I was writing. I was able to hide the written pages quickly, but they saw the typewriter. We know that the Nazis give the officials whose duties take them to private homes strict orders to take careful note of the tenants' gossip—in fact, of everything that they see and hear. A typewriter in the possession of an " ordinary " private person—and one who lives in a workers' district at that—is sure to invite attention.

That's why I have been looking for another room to work in. A sympathiser of our movement who lives in another part of the town has now offered me the use of a room. I hinted that I am writing something " forbidden." I had to do this in order to be fair to him.

I now go there for a few hours at a time. Have devised a mechanism by which I can make the manuscript and my notes disappear at once in case of need.

. . . .

Franz had to change his quarters two days ago. The blow fell on the Lamprechts. The family where I had taken Käthe that time. Franz told me about it.

He was standing in Lamprecht's kitchen yesterday, shaving. Lamprecht's wife wanted to go with him to one of their secret cyclostyling places, to collect the papers. Rudi, the fitter with the fiery hair and the freckled face, printed the papers there together with another comrade. (We had printed our paper that time in the night-club with Rudi and his friend " Boxer Bruno.")

Franz, who had just started soaping his face, told her to wait until he had " scraped off " his beard.

" I'd rather go on first," Erna Lamprecht answered. " The baby's asleep, and Kurt will be home from the coaling yard in less than an hour. Otherwise his supper won't be done in time. I'll take his papers to the distribution centre. That'll save Kurt the journey. He's so dead tired in the evenings."

I know this printing place well. Had often gone there with Franz. It is only a small shop. Electric fittings hang in the window, with gas and water taps, and electric bulbs. Above them in the shop window hangs a Hitler portrait wreathed in green stuff.

GAS AND ELECTRIC INSTALLATION

is written on the window-pane, and underneath in larger letters:

GERMAN SHOP!

The proprietor, Comrade Schwante, is an old man. He always wears a faded blue mechanics suit, and a pair of thin, old-fashioned nickel glasses. He is very short-sighted, and has a brown face, deeply wrinkled, like old leather. He goes fishing in the country every Saturday. That is the old bachelor's one passion. Long shelves, holding copper wire, pincers of all sizes and shapes, and pieces of lead piping and other similar articles piled up in confusion, are fitted round the walls of his shop. Old Schwante never tidies up. Probably because he's got no time to do it; he only just manages to earn a bare living with the small repairs as it is. " Old Schwante provides the comrades of the district with food and keep in his own way," Franz had once said jokingly to me, referring to the cyclostyle.

It stands on a long table in the back workroom. A large modern machine. It automatically inserts the unused sheets and piles the printed ones behind the rubber roller, and even has a device on which the number of sheets that have gone through the machine can be read off. Works quickly too. Of course it makes enough noise for three other machines, but that does not matter there. The shop is a place where you would expect noisy repair work to be going on. Franz went to Schwante's shop ten minutes after Erna. What he saw a short way before he got to the shop made him jump. A crowd had collected on the other side of the pavement. Had something happened at Schwante's? Franz was horrified. He stepped up behind the people. He was not known in this district! And then he saw it. Drawn up on the pavement outside Schwante's shop was a black Maria!

He trembled; his knees threatened to give way.

They had been caught. They're in for it. Mustn't let anyone notice anything; it won't help things if you are caught. Is Erna already in there? What now? ran his thoughts.

Franz told me afterwards that his head seemed to be spinning round. Then the door over the way was jerked open. Men wearing pale-green uniforms with bright nickel badges on their chest came out. Goering's Feldpolizei! They were surrounding the three civilians, pushing them into the car. Erna Lamprecht—old Schwante—and a tall, haggard comrade. Franz only knew him by sight; he had once met him with Rudi. But where was Rudi? His red head was not among the others. Yet he was to have helped them with the printing. Had he left earlier? The other one there—the fourth civilian—wasn't that—of course it was—Seifahrt! And he's talking to the Feldpolizei—they don't push *him* into the car! Franz felt paralysed. The car on the other side drove off. The crowd dispersed, talking in low tones. Franz pulled himself together; he must walk on. He forced himself to walk calmly—until the next corner. And then he started running. He suddenly knew what he had to do! He ran for more than a quarter of an hour, with straining lungs. To the coaling yard! To warn Erna's husband!

Too late. He heard, twenty minutes later, that Kurt had run direct into the Feldpolizei's arms. They were waiting for him in his flat when he came home. Lamprecht's neighbours wanted to take charge of the little girl. The Feldpolizei did not allow it. The only result was that their own place was immediately searched.

Franz went to see Bruno the same evening. To Bruno, Rudi's best friend. As soon as he opened the door, he saw by Bruno's gloomy face that he knew everything. But he had no idea that he himself did not know everything. Bruno led him silently to his room, and then fell into a chair, hiding his face in his hands. Franz saw Bruno's shoulders heaving with tearless crying. Bruno, the Fichte boxer! The strong man, whose sense of humour never failed him, even in the most difficult situations. He had remained so calm and collected when the S.A. arrived on the scene while we had been reading the *Brown Book*. That we are at all able to link up with the S.A.J. comrades is due entirely to him. The silence in the room had a nerve-racking effect on Franz.

He had to break it at last.

"Seifahrt—the rotter—the traitor!"

Bruno shook his head up at that, glared at Franz with wild eyes. His face became distorted.

"What's the matter with him—doesn't he know that yet?" was Franz's thought.

"He went along with the Feldpolizei—was talking to them. But where is Rudi?" he asked. "He wasn't with the others?"

Bruno jumped up suddenly, turned the chair over with a crash.

He shrieked, shrieked at the top of his voice—as if every wall didn't have ears these days!

" Seifahrt? Seifahrt? So Seifahrt is his murderer!"— and fell back on to a chair.

After a while he said quietly.

" Rudi—Rudi—he was with the others—shot by——"

Franz lives with Bruno now. He says that the latter has changed completely. He has become terribly thin. At mealtimes, when the others are talking excitedly, he just sits there without saying a word. He eats listlessly. Worst of all, he can't be trusted with disciplined jobs any more. Like a tireless animal, the one thought revolves in his brain at every hour of the day and night: Rudi's death must be avenged! He is always out; comes home late at night. The district published a circular a few days after the incident. Bruno kept at the others until he was given the whole pile. The other comrades told Franz that wherever Seifahrt goes, the circulars appear with him. Bruno follows him like a shadow. Seifahrt changed his flat. He only goes out accompanied by S.A. now. But he was found on his doorstep badly knocked about one evening, in spite of all these precautions. Bruno came home with a scratched face that night.

He did not even leave Seifahrt in peace in the hospital. Stickbills describing his treachery appeared on the walls. In the very ward where Seifahrt lay. He moved to another street after he was discharged from the hospital. The S.A. organised a regular supervision service in the meanwhile. They surprised the people entering his house, searched their pockets. But Bruno was not to be shaken off. A few days later the following words were deeply scratched on the wall of Seifahrt's hall:

ACHTUNG! DER ARBEITERMÖRDER SEIFAHRT WOHNT JETZT HIER![68]

That's how Bruno, the ever-present accuser, chases his victim through the town. That's how he makes every further spying activity on Seifahrt's part impossible. Seifahrt is like a hunted wild animal which never knows where the enemy may be lying in wait for him.

He does not know Bruno.

Bruno's campaign of vengeance gives the comrades new faith in the strength of their class.

He shows them that in spite of the terror of the S.A., of the police, they are *not* powerless against traitors.

Seifahrt gave the game up at last. He disappeared quietly from the district one day. Even Bruno was unable to trace him.

" But we'll find him one day—and then no one will be able to save him," he told Franz.

. . . .

I am waiting near the Wittenbergplatz Underground station. For Käthe ! I rang her up at her office. How long is it since I last saw her ? Our private lives are submerged nowadays. Not only ours; that of all the comrades. Do the others feel the same as I do ? The longing to see Käthe comes more frequently these days. To know that there is someone who understands things, with whom one can talk about everything—absolutely everything. True, it means a lot to have the comrades. People who have still kept a clear head in this country where everyone and everything seems to have become changed into brown robots. The frenzied whirl of events, the uncertainty of the next day, have greatly strengthened our personal friendships. Yes. We realise to-day better than ever what a lot we would lose if we had to stand alone.

The illuminated advertisements of the store across the way glitter dazzlingly. The whole Tauentzienstrasse is lit up with red and blue lights. The memorial church looms up at the end of the street, large and clumsy. The pedestrians move slowly along the pavements, past the windows, in crowds. Quite near me two Schupos brandish their arms covered in the white cuffs about in the air, directing the long rows of cars round the square.

A crowd of people come out from the station. Käthe ! Her brown eyes sparkle.

I take her hand. She tucks her arm firmly in mine. We walk slowly through the throng. We have been looking forward to seeing each other again for weeks, have so much to tell each other. And now we don't say a word. Just look in each other's eyes, squeeze each other's hands. No, not now—afterwards. We want to sit down somewhere. Käthe takes short steps; I shorten my own to match. The warmth of her hand—it seems to me as if we were quite alone here in the street. She is pale and looks worn out. Her face has got thinner. Or does her very fair hair give that impression, or is it the bright light here?

I wonder what I can tell her. Something pleasant. But all I can think of is:

"That ought to open the eyes of small shopkeepers. First they boycott the Jews—' Down with the big multiple shop!' And now, 'All Nazis are forbidden to disturb business in the large stores.'"

"I keep wondering about it myself. Do people really forget things so quickly, or do they just close their eyes to things?" Käthe replies.

A Salvation Army group is standing at the corner, singing. A woman holds out a collecting-box. Her fat red face under the large bonnet smiles unctuously.

"Do you remember the old woman who does the ironing at our corner? They even stuck a boycott poster on her place."

I nod.

"The assistants were standing outside a large shoe shop not long ago. I asked one of them what it was all about. They wanted to enforce the dismissal of a Jewish apprentice. The Nazis in the place force them to protest, she told me. And none of them could afford to lose her job."

"It's the same everywhere," remarks Käthe. "There's one of our employees in the office whom I used to have long talks with now and again. I know he used to vote for the Left Parties. He's been steering clear of me for some time now; greets me with a loud 'Heil Hitler.'"

In a café, we choose a table near the window. Behind the

window, the stream of passers-by flows along without stopping. The noise of the traffic comes to our ears like a continuous dull buzzing in the background. Käthe moves quite close to me. I am conscious of her warmth. She stirs her cup in silence, gives me smiling glances.

I light a cigarette and inhale deeply. Fine. Käthe gives me another of her glances.

" Mother is ill. She's been in bed for some days now."

" Ill ? I hope it's nothing serious ? "

" No. The old trouble. But she keeps on asking for Franz. I haven't told him she's ill. He'd only worry."

" When did you see him last ? "

" Yesterday. Hilde was there as well."

" I saw him last week. Is everything all right at their place ? "

" Yes. He looks quite well."

I breathe more freely. So he did not tell her about Rudi. He didn't want to upset her either.

We sit there for a long time without a word. Then I tell Käthe that we shall be able to go away for Christmas after all. Somewhere in the country. Her face flushes with joy. She puts her arm on mine. Her eyes brighten. We make plans for the journey with all the excited feelings of looking forward to the future. Käthe says she'd prefer to go to Mecklenburg. There are thick woods there and many lakes. We calculate the probable cost. Our " holiday savings " will be just enough, we discover with satisfaction.

I see her along two streets, and then we separate.

I return to our street with very slow steps. It might snow by Christmas-time. We'll chase each other through lonely woods. Romp about. Throw snowballs at each other. What fun to throw stones on the frozen lakes. We might take our skates along too. And then we'll spend the evenings in some village. It will be like discovering a new country when we walk through the quiet village street after dusk. Friendly lights will be burning behind the low windows. We'll suddenly be longing for the warm parlour of the country inn. Käthe !

We shall be together at last.
For days and days.

. . . .

The Maikowski trial has lasted for weeks. The Press previously wrote that the Public Prosecutor's summing up was to be expected by the beginning of January. It will soon be a year since the night when the Chancellor was appointed, when the Thirty-threes marched through our street. The verdict is at all events to be pronounced before the anniversary of that night. It is to be a " symbolic vengeance." The newspaper reports show us quite clearly that the prosecutors have not yet succeeded in convicting the accused comrades of murdering the Stormleader Maikowski and the policeman Zauritz, despite the fact that the whole machinery of the State has been set in motion, that the events of the night in question have been dissected into their minutest details. But all that the controlled Press can write about is the *Mordüberfall der Kommune*.[69] The idea of *kommunistischer Mörder*[70] is thereby to be impressed on the public's mind. Not one single line in any of the papers mentions that the S.A. marched through the Wallstrasse, although their way back to their Storm quarters from the torchlight procession lay through streets in the opposite direction. By marching up our street the S.A. were responsible in the first place for creating the opportunity for a conflict. We know quite well that they wanted to " take our street by storm " in the first flush of victory. And the accused comrades must have referred to this during the trial; for the Press hints at denials and counter-arguments on the part of the accused, which " are, of course, deliberate lies and distortions." The trial must be a terrible mental torture for the comrades, in addition to what they must have suffered during the months of cross-examination. In the trial reports that appear in the papers, this sentence is often printed with cruel lack of emphasis: " The proceedings had to be adjourned because one of the accused again had an attack of screaming . . . because one of the accused, as has so often happened during the trial, fell down in an epileptic fit. . . ."

The National-Socialist papers have, in fact, made a "national hero" of Maikowski. They always describe the S.A. Storm 33 as the *Ehrensturm Deutschlands, den Sturm der alten Kämpfer*.[71] Goebbels recently "consecrated" a new Party flag in the Tempelhofer Field *Durch berühren mit der Blutfahne Maikowski*.[72] The pictures in the papers show Storm 33 as the guard of honour lined up in front of the speaker's platform. Up till now there had been only the *Blutfahne vom 9. November 1923*[73]—the flag they had carried during the *Putsch* in Munich. And there had only been one "national hero"—Horst Wessel. Their second "martyr" is now Maikowski, shot by his own S.A. men! All this has intensified our anxiety for the accused comrades. The more so because the Nazi publications shout for the heads of the accused. Yet, in spite of all this, the Maikowski trial is by no means the centre of the public's interest. The Reichstag trial puts it more and more in the shade. After Goebbels and Goering gave evidence the strain of waiting for the result of the trial almost reached breaking-point in all classes of the population. Didn't Goering angrily answer the cleverly worded questions Dimitroff put to him with: "You are in my opinion a scoundrel; the gallows is the only place for you"? And on another occasion he shouted at him in obvious fury: "Get out, you rogue!"

The German Press had to pass over Goering's threats with what has now become easily understandable silence. But I can vouch for the fact that these threats are not only discussed by us, but in much wider circles as well. People get hold of the reports in the foreign papers. There has never been such a demand for them as now. Everywhere, in the trains, the cafés, the parks, people sit and read foreign papers. They pass from hand to hand in the cafés; everyone waits impatiently until the others have read them. For we haven't all got the money to buy foreign papers.

But even the German Press has had to give dictator Goering a telling off. When Goering spoke about the criminal Communist philosophy, and when Dimitroff boldly asked him whether he was aware that this criminal philosophy was at the moment ruling a sixth part of the earth, namely the Soviet Union, Goering jumped up again. He said he was quite aware that the Russians paid with credit bills, but he was not aware that these were afterwards cashed. An official denial appeared in the German Press the next day which had to admit " that the Soviet Government has up to the present day punctually paid all its debts in Germany." The announcement was published in all the papers in very small print, and in an inconspicuous part of the paper at that. But our comrades passed it on with grins and smiles from one to the other. And we weren't the only ones who appreciated it. I heard the people talking about it in the grocer's, hinting at the Nazi methods of buying goods without paying for them.

Public attention is focused on Dimitroff. There would be found to be hundreds of Dimitroffs in all parts of Germany, if the records of their trials were ever published.

All the official denials and concealment of news cannot prevent the truth about the real incendiaries reaching ever wider circles. Where the illegal pamphlets and papers do not penetrate, the Moscow station brings the news on the radio. Listening-in evenings have been organised everywhere. In our street as well now. We hear the report of the trial every evening. The comrades then pass it on verbally. Hilde told us that even the S.A. who visit her brother talk about the news from the Moscow station: some because they are furious, others in order to be able to report " something new." Goering is well aware what dimensions this listening-in has taken. He issued a decree to the effect that " The wireless reception of foreign wireless stations with the intent to listen-in will be considered as hostile to the State, and punished accordingly." The decree will remain printer's ink at least as far as we are concerned. Goering's " partner " Goebbels is most helpful to us here. At his orders the German wireless industry has undertaken the production of so-called *Volksempfängern*[74] at a comparatively cheap price. It is possible to obtain these small sets for a few marks down and the balance payable in small monthly instalments. But only

German stations can be heard, and that is what was intended. However, our wireless amateurs soon discovered that the range of these sets can be greatly increased by fitting a small additional component costing not more than a couple of marks. Many comrades who were unable to raise the money for an expensive set can now listen in to Moscow.

. . . .

It's Christmas Eve. I have an appointment with Ede. Ede wants to go to the " Winterhilfswerk "[75] distribution. To the National-Socialist People's Welfare Centre.

" Yer can come along all right. They all lines up down the street. An' when it's my turn, yer just stays where you are. Nobody'll notice anyfing," Ede said, brushing my doubts away. " Then yer'll 'ave a fine chance of 'earing what the others ses about things."

This was my only reason for considering going with him at all. But we are only going to meet near the offices. They are less than ten minutes from our street.

Winterhilfswerk. Teichert told me that every worker at his factory had to " sacrifice " fifty pfennigs each week. One of the many " voluntary " deductions. The Nazi officials pass the list of names round on pay-day, with the amount to be filled in at the side, so that no one dares to give less than his predecessor. Voluntary contributors receive a Winterhilfs emblem. The round paper rosettes covered with pictures and the inscription " We Help " are stuck on the doors in all the houses. On mine as well. They have a different colour every month. There is quite an exhibition on some doors. They are the signs, for the swarms of collectors who run in and out of all the houses rattling their boxes, that this tenant has already " sacrificed." Teichert says that the workers do not get the paper rosettes for the fifty pfennigs for which they sign the list. These are, in a certain sense, *Pflicht Groschen*.[76] They have to give another fifty pfennigs for the badges. In his opinion the majority do that so as to have peace and quiet in their homes.

Hitler opened the Winterhilfswerk with great pomp in the

Kroll Theatre. He addressed Krupp, Siemens, Thyssen, other high financiers, and the Party bosses in their gorgeous uniforms, on the subject of this " practical Socialism." He toasted Goebbels as the organiser of " the greatest deed in history." Our unemployed comrades told me what they get from the N.S.V. A few stones of potatoes, a hundredweight of coal, and a pound of margarine—to last them a month ! And the margarine is not even free. Sold at a " reduced price." A certain amount has to be paid for the potatoes and coal, too. " I uster get that from the Social Welfare in the old days, and the dole they gave was bigger, anyway," Ede added.

The farmers have to " contribute " the potatoes, the coal merchants the coal, the small tradesmen the groceries. They call that *Pfundspenden*.[77] No business man dare risk refusing. They give to the poor what they can extract from the small tradesmen and call it " Socialism." And what happens to the cash collected ? It must amount to millions each month !

Goebbels seems to realise that ordinary collecting-boxes have lost their effect. Loudspeaker vans now patrol the streets. Canvassing columns march in procession through the town, with camels, monkeys, and other strange animals. In Tauentzienstrasse, the busiest street in Berlin, the S.A. collectors are on horseback. They hang the collecting-boxes round the horses' necks and stand on the pavements barring passage. We have also collected in our street, twice. A couple of twenty-mark notes was the result. We sent them to Karl Kurgel's and Heinz Preuss's mothers, for Christmas parcels to be sent to them both. Preuss is in the Brandenburg Concentration Camp, Kurgel in the Oranienburg. They stuck Kurgel in the camp without any cause at all. The Thirty-threes only arrested him because they wanted to know from him where Franz was. X of the S.A. Reserves told me about it. All that we have been able to find out during the many months is where they are. Nothing else. I stop. Ede—where's Ede ? But this is the wrong corner; we'd arranged the next one !

Eintopf[78] Sunday. In no household is the midday meal to

cost more than fifty pfennigs. The collectors come into the homes and examine the saucepans.

" The *Führer* eats a one-course dinner as well, and passes the rest of the money on to the Winterhilfswerk," they declare.

But they served themselves a bad turn everywhere with their pot-peeping. I have never seen old Frau Zieschke, who lives in our house, so upset as she was on this particular Sunday. She brought me into her kitchen, pulled the lid off her saucepan, and started a regular scolding.

" I gave that collector what for, I did. I draw a small pension, I told him. ' My dinner's not to cost more than fifty pfennigs,' I told him. ' Is that it? The *Führer* eats the same? Well, I'm glad if I can afford a meal at Christmastime that costs fifty pfennigs,' I told him."

Frau Zieschke railed and grumbled, while I was asking myself what had made her fetch me in; she doesn't know anything about me. Then she asked me quite suddenly whether I knew the *Eintopf* song.

" No."

She started singing in her thin old voice.

Wenn am Sonntag Morgen der Reichskanzler spricht:
Eintopfgericht, Eintopfgericht, Grünkohl,
Und der dicke Göring macht ein langes Gesicht,
Eintopfgericht, Eintopfgericht, Grünkohl![79]

The old woman sang that to the tune of the German folk song, " Wenn am Sonntag Abend die Dorfmusik spielt," in her piping old voice. She still held the saucepan-lid in her left hand. It looked so grotesque that I couldn't do anything else but laugh. Of course I knew the song; we have all known it for some time.

But where in heaven's name did Frau Zieschke hear it?

There's Ede! He shakes hands in that energetic way of his.

" 'Ello, Jan. An' now let's be orf. Let's see what I can skin from 'em."

He clears his throat and spits.

" I've got the doings wiv' me too. And if them nobs don't 'and out enough I'll give 'em summat for all their trumpet-blowing ! "

" Now, just listen; we two don't know each other. And do be careful with what you say. *We've* got to be extra careful ! "

" Sure thing. Don't I know that ! "

The Groceries Distribution Centre of the Winterhilfswerk is housed in an empty shop. A long queue four deep stand in front of it. We take our place at the end: are part of a long row a few minutes later. New arrivals keep on coming along. I take a look at the others. They are mostly working women and unemployed men. I can see by the clothes of a few that they have seen better times. I would take that little man with the bowler hat and dark coat for someone with a safe income if I met him elsewhere. The coat has a good velvet collar, and seems quite new. And the elderly woman on the left wearing the fur jacket ? What a proud face she has. It's labelled middle class even here. It's sure to be " painful and lowering " for her to stand here. Absolute need must have driven her to this. We stamp our feet. It is cold and windy.

It's the same as during the war years. I queued up then for a few grammes of margarine, for the turnip marmalade. Father was at the front, mother in the munitions factory. She came home dead tired and hungry in the evenings. Her face was always yellow. From the sulphur.

An S.A. man opens the shop door and lets a swarm of people in. We all push forward.

" Get on a bit, you in there ! "

" 'Ow long 'ave we gotter stand aht 'ere in the cold ? "

The shop door has already been closed. Ede winks at me. He is now standing on my left, at the extreme end of the rank. He was right. I can stand here quite safely. No one will notice if I go in or not. In any case, they all push forward when they get the chance. I took a good look at the two men who just shouted out. One of them wears an Arbeitsfront[80] badge ! Those in front must have been standing here for an hour at least. There are about sixty of them ahead of us.

The S.A. man didn't let more than a dozen in. The boots stamp away on the pavement. It starts snowing. A fine drizzle, half snow, half rain. What next! How many are there behind us? I count the rows. Seven, eight . . . more than thirty. How long till their turn? We've been here twenty minutes already! That first batch only brought us two steps forwards.

A young man walks past the rows. All that I can see is his head and the soft felt hat he is wearing.

"Hallo, Erich," he calls out.

The little man with the bowler hat two rows in front of me jerks his head.

"Yes, here!"

"Come out for a second!"

The little man pushes his way through the throng. I can't see the two, but can hear what they are saying. The others in the queue also turn their heads towards the two.

"Have they finished with you?"

"Yes."

"Well, what do we get!"

"You can carry it in one hand. A pound of onions, half a pound of box cheese, and a grocery voucher for one mark."

A smacking sound. The young man must have slapped the parcel.

"What am I going to do with onions, I ask you?"

They continue their talk, but I cannot hear the rest.

In front of me, to the left, a tall, haggard woman starts grumbling. She places her arms on her hips.

"A pound of onions—half a pound of cheese! And that's what we've been standing here for hours for?"

She starts waving her arms about. The others step back involuntarily.

"What do they do with it all? . . . what do they do with it all? . . .They fetched a whole lot of fat from my butcher, and sausages, this size!"

She bends her left arm to demonstrate the size, holds it up for the others to see. She looks at everyone in turn, as if demanding an answer.

" They wants to celebrate Christmas, too," says one old man with a white beard bitingly.

" It was just the bloody same in the war. Nothing to eat in the bleeding trenches—but the 'eadquarters 'ad their swell food ! "

Ede ! Can't he hold his tongue ? And, anyway, he shouldn't make such a strong remark. I frown at him. He grins, shakes his head lightly. He even fancies that his remarks were especially clever tactics.

" It's the same old shop. Only a new firm's taken it over ! " says a voice behind me.

The little man wearing the bowler hat pushes his way back to his place. Isn't he wearing a Party badge on his coat ? He must have heard the last remark, for he pushes his hat on to the back of his head and says excitedly:

" I shall report the matter, you can take it from me ! A report on the distribution centre Lützow here ! . . . To the director of the Berlin Winterhilfswerk . . . to Spiewok personally ! "

" There's honour . . ." the man with the white beard leaves the sentence unfinished. " Among thieves " he wanted to say. But he has seen the Party badge. I notice that broken sentence has a warning effect on the others. They first looked at the old man in astonishment, but they are now weighing up the little man. I look at Ede and then at the little man. Stand on my toes so that he can see me. I draw a small circle with my forefinger on my coat lapel. Ede gives me a long look. At last ! He nods. He's understood me at last. He'll hold his tongue now at least. Maybe the little man has been sent here to eavesdrop. What's he saying now ?

" It's a disgrace, the way they share out things here ! I shall send in a complaint ! I shall demand redress ! "

He is really annoyed at the thought of the meagre " share " he will receive ! But there is also pride in his voice ! He fancies himself as a " semi-official " person compared to us. My opinion may be wrong. The faces of the others bear relieved expressions again. In front the shop door is opened.

The jostling starts again. An S.A. man stands in the doorway and glances searchingly down the rows.

" Don't let any more come along at the back ! " he calls out. " We're closing in an hour ! "

His words release a tumult of cries and expostulations.

" Do you think we're standing here for fun ? . . . We won't all get in in an hour. . . . Let other people do the job, if you can't do it properly ! "

The four-abreast queue suddenly becomes disarranged, turns leftwards. The people move towards the door in a block. Arms holding unemployment cards gesticulate.

" If you're not quiet at once, we'll close now ! " shouts the S.A. man.

" Oho . . . that'd jest do us ! . . . But yer can't do that wiv' us—not wiv' us, yer can't ! "

The doors of the shop bang to. The key screeches in the lock. I have been pressed against the shop windows. A large poster has been stuck on from the inside.

BECOME PRACTICAL SOCIALISTS ! JOIN THE N.S.V.

And a smaller notice underneath :

WANTED
A cylindrical iron heating-stove.
A child's pram in good condition.

The S.A. man must have used the back door. He comes round to the street, stands in front of the excited mass and starts pushing the people back. They all struggle back to their old places to the accompaniment of bickering and insults. The tall, haggard woman now stands next to me, the little man with the Party badge in front of her. Ede is further forward. He has gained two rows.

" That's all they can give when they've got so much money." The tall woman starts off again. " My brother's working; they knock off the Winterhilfe subscriptions before he gets his wages ! "

"That's so," nods a young woman near her. "When all the deductions are taken off, a quarter of the pay's gone!"

She pulls her shawl closer. She has thrown it over her head to keep out the wet.

A few days ago Teichert told me a rhyme that is making the rounds of his factory. It is a parody of the usual grace before meals.

> *Komm Herr Hitler sei unser Gast,*
> *Und erfülle die Hälfte von dem*
> *Was Du uns versprochen hast.*[81]

"Yes, and then there's the indirect money!" says the tall woman again.

"Indirect! What do you mean?" asks the younger woman.

The other takes a deep breath, looks round to make sure the others are listening.

"In the grocer's a few days ago. A woman asked for a small box of cheese—the kind wrapped in tinfoil "—everyone is paying close attention, even the little man—" and then she noticed the price, and started complaining because it was dearer again. Prices were being raised all the time, and it wasn't fair. The assistant said it wasn't dearer. Of course it was, insisted the woman, getting angry; she wasn't going to be swindled like that! Twelve pfennigs, and it used to cost ten!"

The tall woman looks triumphantly at the interested glances of the rest of us.

" 'Buy one,' said the assistant, ' and then I'll explain it all.' And what do you think the reason was? The two pfennigs rise had to be passed on to the Winterhilfe!"

Heads nod meaningly all around. The old man with the white beard laughs dryly. The little man fidgets with his bowler. He certainly seems embarrassed. To think they should dare talk like this—with the little man wearing the Party badge listening without interrupting! In the shops, in the weekly markets, I have often heard the women grumbling about the rise in prices—but here, right outside the Nazi offices!

" You get a chance of seeing how things work sometimes," says the young woman with the shawl. " We applied for a marriage loan. They talk such a lot about it. They had us medically examined to see if we'd be likely to have healthy children "—she shrugs her shoulders—" and then, to satisfy their ideas about race, my husband had to get certificates of our family tree from our home towns. It took months, and the cost nearly ruined us."

" Yes, and what happened? " the older woman interrupts. The younger one looks back at her. She has a thin, pointed face, like a child's. And dark brown eyes.

" And then they said, ' Ah, you are unemployed? Then you don't get a thousand marks, only five hundred. But you've got to bring somebody along first who'll guarantee you'll pay it back.' "

She laughs mockingly.

" Of course, it fell through. If we had anyone in the family like that we wouldn't have needed *them*."

The queue laughs. I can sense the feeling which they all put into that laugh.

" And now unemployed even *with* somebody to guarantee them don't get their loans any more!" said the young woman with emphasis. " Quite a lot only dared to marry because of that—it was the same with us." All heads jerk round towards the front. The S.A. man is looking through the window. I nod to Ede. He smiles, nods back. He has pushed himself forward quite nicely, is sure to get in with the next batch. And then it'll be time.

The S.A. man in the shop turns the key, opens the door. A general rush forward. I slip unnoticed out of the row. Ede has got in all right.

I pace slowly up and down past the street corner. It's cold. Another five minutes, and if Ede doesn't come then— but people are coming out of the side-entrance. Ede isn't among them. Yes, there he is, the last one. He looks round for me, then walks slowly down the street. I let him go on a bit in front Catch up to him a few seconds later, grab hold of his arm. He jumps round, startled, and then surprised. I thought you was gone a long time ago, Jan."

" Was just thinking about it. It's damned cold. But where is your ' share ' ? "

Ede is not carrying anything. He laughs, claps me on the shoulders.

" They give me my share on paper. Look 'ere ! "

He pulls a few slips from his pocket. I read.

" Voucher for one pound of sugar, one pound of rice, half a pound of cocoa." And a grocery voucher value one mark as a finishing-touch.

" How did you . . . ? "

" That was a gyme ! " laughs Ede. " I 'eard the bosses doing the sharing out telling the people there was only the one-mark vouchers left; them groceries 'ad all bin shared out. The folks grumbled a lot, but they were glad enough to git the vouchers. Well, I pulls me doings out, I does. And when 'e starts telling me the same tale, I just lays that there Fust Class Iron Cross, that there gold medal for wounded, and that there certif'cate of blindness down on the table in front of 'im. ' Just take a li'l look at that stuff,' I sez ter 'im, I does. ' I was four years in the trenches, I was. I've been made a cripple for the Fatherland, I 'ave. An' now I ain't even goin' ter 'ave summat decent ter cel'brate Christmas wiv'. Oh, no, that don't go down, that don't. Just you tell that ter the marines, but not ter me,' I sez. ' They collects the Winterhilfe subs from my two uncles, they does, and from my sister too. They sez ter me yesterday they was goin' to give me them deductions themselves, so as I'd 'ave summat ! ' I tell yer, Jan, I never said all that quietly, too, I didn't. 'Fore I could say Jack Robinson all the others 'ad come crowding round."

We turn a corner.

" Not so loud, Ede . . ."

But Ede is in full swing.

" What's the trouble ? I can tell yer that, can't I ? Well, that there nob got excited all right, I can tell yer. ' Yer can't let 'em give you that money without our permission,' 'e says ! ' If yer does that you'll be 'ad up fer sabotaging the Winterhilfe !' An' then 'e thinks things over a bit, and sez I can 'ave a Christmas-tree. ' What d'yer want me to do wiv' a tree ? I can't stick that in a saucepan,' I up and tells him. Then 'e stands up and opens the door in the counter, an' tells me ter come in wiv' 'im ter the next room. An' then 'e fills in the vouchers for me there. But I wasn't ter tell the others anyfink, 'e warns me. . . ." Ede laughs loudly. " An' I didn't tell 'em anyfink eiver. But when I comes out I 'olds them papers out in my 'ands. The others in the shop comes running up ter me. ' Did yer get something ? ' they all asks. I never told 'em anyfink; all I did was to wave them papers about in their faces. Most of 'em ran after me, they did, and the shop was full up too. I sez to 'em at the street corner, ' 'Course I got summat. All yer've gotter do is ter kick up a bloody row like I did.' I sees 'em from the door a'terwards, the 'ole blasted lot rushing at them there nobs ! ' "

I return to our street alone, making a detour first. In front of me, at the street corner, stands a newspaper kiosk. The man is just hanging the *B.Z. am Mittag* out. Thick headlines.

TORGLER AND THE BULGARIANS ACQUITTED !

LUBBE SENTENCED TO DEATH !

It seems to go right through me. Must keep calm.

" In an atmosphere of tense excitement the President of the Senate, Judge Bünger, this morning pronounced the above verdict on the Reichstag trial. It is in accordance with that generally expected because . . ." The rest of the text is hidden by the folds of the paper. Shall I buy one ? Afterwards, when I have calmed down a bit.

Käthe ! We are going away to-night.

Dimitroff acquitted !

What a wonderful Christmas! Nothing else could have made us so happy.

. . . .

We are at Teichert's.

He told Ernst Schwiebus to tell me to come. His wife knows us by sight, but she doesn't know anything about our illegal work. We sit at the round table under the gas-lamp. Frau Teichert greeted us very curtly. She sits by herself, knits with her back to the stove. Teichert rests his elbows on the table, supporting his head in his hands. The evening paper lies in front of him. Schwiebus fetched it along, showed it to me a few moments ago. No one speaks.

MORALLY GUILTY OF THE MURDER!
THE FINAL WORD ON THE MAIKOWSKI TRIAL!

In how many homes in our street, in how many streets in Charlottenburg, is that now being read? If only someone would say something! I look at Schwiebus. He is twisting the corner of the tablecloth. He won't look at me. We should not have come to Teichert. It all seems so strange to me here, such a lack of friendliness. I glance furtively at Teichert's wife. The knitting-needles click between her fingers. She is completely absorbed in her work. A small, round woman with fresh red cheeks. The dark plaits of hair that frame her face, the snow-white apron—the woman fits well into this room. It is so cheerless and clean. The grandfather clock with the shining brass pendulum, the small white lace antimacassars on the red plush of the sofa. Teichert suddenly pushes his chair back, stands up. He walks up and down. His wife stops knitting, looks up at him.

He sits down again after a while, reads the paper out to us.

" ' . . . Obsessed with the fanatical idea of keeping the Wallstrasse free of political opponents, a patrol and intelligence service had been organised, which announced the approach of the National-Socialists. As the singing S.A. were passing through the Wallstrasse, Stormleader Maikowski at their head, the attack started. . . .' "

There is quiet for a second. Frau Teichert still keeps her eyes on him.

"'... Why have the prisoners not been convicted of murdering Stormleader Maikowski and the policeman Zauritz? We must unfortunately give the answer, disappointing to many of our readers, that the results of the proceedings have not been able to prove that one of the accused fired the fatal shot. The penal code in existence at the time does not allow of the accused being sentenced to death. It would have been a different question if they had committed the deed half an hour later—that is to say, on January 31st. They would then, according to the " Schutz von Volk und Staat "[82] Laws, have incurred the death-sentence.'"

Even Frau Teichert is moved by the open brutality of the Public Prosecutor's speech.
" But, then . . ." she says.
Teichert interrupts her.
" He admits the fact himself that none of the accused fired the shot——"
" This Attorney-General Ranke expresses his regrets that he cannot sentence the innocent to death!" I interject.
" In the Third Reich," says Schwiebus gloomily, " human life is not worth that much "—snapping his fingers—" when workers are concerned!" Teichert scrapes his chair back, paces the room again. For a long time only the creaking of his shoes is heard.
Then Schwiebus starts talking. Without any connection to what we had been discussing.
" Hilde told me yesterday that there was a fight between the S.S. and S.A. At the S.A.'s New Year's Eve celebrations. In the Berlinerstrasse. In the Bamberger Hof beer-house. An S.A. man is dead. The S.A. haven't been able to stand the S.S. for a long time, eh?"
No one answers.
It's Schwiebus who breaks the silence again, mockingly.
" The *Angriff* published the obituary notice yesterday, eh? ' Our S.A. comrade, who died in the performance of his duty.'"

Teichert steps near his chair.

" Yes . . ." he drawls, his thoughts quite obviously otherwise occupied. And, after a pause, " The verdict will soon be given."

" In the Maikowski trial ? "

" Yes. They want to announce it before the anniversary of their march through our street."

. . . .

Heinz Preuss has been released from the concentration camp ! Heinz Preuss, the young comrade who was arrested in the spring while sticking up posters. Heinz Preuss, the hiker, who wore his hair long, right down to the back of his neck. He sent me a message through underground channels to say that he was back again, that he had been included in the Christmas amnesty, and that he wanted to see me. I then arranged a meeting-place and warned him to be particularly careful about the way he came.

I met him yesterday. At Franz's place. We were shocked when he arrived, but we did not let him notice anything. Franz gave me a long look, though. Heinz has become terribly thin. His cheeks are sunken, and deathly pale. He used to be so brown and healthy. When we used to tease him because of his long hair he always answered, " I'll tell my mother to cut it round the saucepan." His hair is now closely cropped. This makes him look worse.

He told us that the prisoners due to be released had to line up in the camp yard beforehand. The governor delivered a short address. Told them not to attribute the Government's leniency to weakness. They would wipe out anyone who was caught a second time working against the Government.

Despite this threat, and everything that he had had to put up with in the concentration camp, Heinz Preuss has remained unshaken. He wants to work with us again. We explained that this could only be in three months' time. For his and our safety. He understood that in the end, and agreed. He then told us that he had received a Christmas parcel from his mother, and was overjoyed when we told him that we had collected the money in our street. He had given the parcel to the other comrades. Had been released the day he received it. He then asked how all the other comrades were going on. Wanted to know exactly how things were, how we were continuing our work, etc. But we gave him only a rough outline of things. Not because we are mistrustful, but because we felt that he should not worry unnecessarily now. He ought to recuperate during the next few months; nothing else.

But it was impossible for him to be completely cut off from us now; he would not be able to stand it. We considered for some time whether we should agree to that. At last we arranged for him to meet one of us at longer intervals. Outside Berlin, and with the minimum amount of risk. For we know from other districts that the Gestapo keep a sharp watch on prisoners released from concentration camps.

He also told us that, except for a few, the comrades in the concentration camp had all remained firm.

" Do you know who was at Brandenburg with me? " he asked us suddenly. " *Erich Mühsam!* "

He had to tell us all about Erich Mühsam after that. His account stirred us deeply. I stayed with him until the early hours, long after the others had gone. I asked him to describe everything in detail. Even let him sketch the plan of the Brandenburg concentration camp building down to the most minute detail. The world *must* learn how Erich Mühsam was tortured. . . .

Yard 3 in the Brandenburg concentration camp. It had struck seven o'clock in the morning a few minutes ago. The forty men from Division 9 were lined up in two files, Heinz Preuss among them. An hour and a half had passed since they had been turned out, had cleaned their barrack-like cell, and had drunk the watery coffee. Yet they all stood there shivering as if they still felt the clammy straw sack that served them as their bed. All they had on was their thin shoddy clothing.

Heinz Preuss pulled his head deep down between his

shoulders. He always shivered at the back of his neck since his long hair had been cut off. They all had their heads cropped like convicts. The concentration camp had been housed in the old prison. It had long since been abandoned as a prison on account of its unhealthy condition. The lanky sergeant in his black S.S. uniform walked critically up and down the rows. He tried the effect of his command " Attention " on each one. Preuss looked past his face, across to the fifteen-foot-high red-brick wall. The sergeant took a few steps backwards, planted his hands on his hips.

" Form fours ! " The command was barked out.

The heads were turned sideways in short jerks. " If only the ' exercises ' won't be too bad to-day," was Preuss's anxious thought. " Erich Mühsam is sure not to be able to stand it; he looks as if he were going to collapse any minute now, as it is." He had caught a glimpse of him a second ago when they had had to turn their heads. Erich was the third man away from him on his right. He stood there, bent up, his chin almost on his chest. A new command.

" In groups, left wheel . . . quick march ! "

Erich Mühsam was at the head of their file. Heinz Preuss waited feverishly for the next command. " If only he won't start exercising at the double—with Mühsam ! And it's hardly possible to help him here. To have to stand by unable to help him ! "

The new formation had barely been completed when the next command cracked across the yard.

" To the church—at the double—march ! "

The whole length of the yard lay between. A hundred and fifty yards from the wall to the church. A hundred and fifty yards ! They were all weakened by the months of confinement, under-nourished as a result of the poor food. They trembled at the mere thought of exertion. Preuss glanced towards the right while running. Erich Mühsam ran with his head down, as if he were carrying a heavy sack on his shoulders. He was unable to keep in the straight lines of the row, lagged a short way behind the others. Were the others in front mad? Why don't they go slower ! This blasted fear of the warders. *He* wasn't running with them, *he'd* save himself that.

The wooden clogs clattered on the concrete! They were all panting. Preuss saw that Mühsam was dropping even more behind. Who the devil was running near him? Kanzow! Didn't he notice anything? Didn't he see what to do?

"Grab hold of him—grab hold of him," hissed Preuss. The two near him passed the word on. Kanzow faltered, hesitated. He was sure to be thinking: " Pull Mühsam along, take hold of him, when they are watching every move, if anyone helps another, the same . . ."

" Kanzow ! " called out Preuss sharply.

The former faltered again for a second, and then grabbed hold of Mühsam's arm. In this way they reached the church. But not quite ! A fresh command was rapped out when they were only a few yards away.

" In groups to the right . . . ! "

Back. Back again ! They were all thinking the same. With racing pulses, hammering hearts. But there was never much time left for thought. The sergeant had followed them to the centre of the yard.

" To the wall . . . at the double . . . quick march ! "

Always at the double, no rest. Pull and drag him along. Managed it ! Erich Mühsam reached the other side of the yard with the others. The sergeant must have thought that he had harassed them sufficiently, or perhaps he did not want to force things to breaking-point this time. In any case, this " physical training " passed off with endless slow step and group exercises after that.

It was the same every day. They all heard the next command before it was uttered.

" Left wheel ! Right wheel ! . . . Form fours ! . . . In groups ! . . ."

They were half an hour later than usual on their straw sacks this morning. Quiet ! Quiet until twelve o'clock ! The long morning hours that one could fill with personal affairs when not ordered off to work in the kitchen. To peel potatoes. There were eleven hundred and sixty men in the camp. Forty men had to peel ten hundredweights of potatoes. Twenty-eight pounds to each man!

Neither Heinz Preuss nor Erich Mühsam had to go to-day. They lay on their straw sacks, Mühsam's head resting on his stretched-out arms. Preuss saw how his back was shaking with the short, quick breathing.

" Can't I do anything for you? " he asked softly.

Mühsam turned his head, without raising it.

" No, that's all right . . . all I need is rest . . . rest. . . . I'm so worn out," he answered jerkily.

His cheeks were sunken, his face pale. The thin grey beard had been half torn off. He had closed his eyes, black rings round them. The bones of his head protruded at the temples, forming deep cavities. Heinz Preuss felt himself getting hot all over. Erich Mühsam. The old comrade. Now only a physical wreck kept together by his iron will. He beats all the younger ones at that. He has seen the inside of quite a number of concentration camps. Treated everywhere as the Jew, the hated " Jewish agitator journalist," who had to suffer daily the most hideous tortures. Preuss had known him for a number of years. He had attended a few meetings at which Mühsam, the anarchist, had attacked their political ideas. But that lay ages behind them. They had become loyal friends here. Comrades sharing the same afflictions, the same suffering.

But, despite everything, Mühsam's opposition had remained unflinching. He refused to hear of the word tactics, however little use could be made of it here as it was. Hardly a day had passed during the last few weeks when the will to express his opposition, the strong will of the dangerously ill man, did not achieve wonders.

" I have finished with life . . . I don't fear death. Only this slow wasting away. They want to drive me to commit suicide. But they will never, never succeed in that . . . ! "

Yesterday Mühsam had told him that. His glance had suddenly hardened.

" And I will not give way . . . I will not give way to them!"

"Things would not be so bad for him if this obstinacy did not stretch to the most unimportant orders," mused Preuss. So that insignificant things resulted in a whole train of punishments for him.

The stairs of the place were clean, the railings free of dust. "Dirty Jew. Mühsam, wipe the stairs! Dirty Jew. Mühsam dust the rails!" These were the continual tasks he had to do as punishments. That was why Preuss and the other comrades had voluntarily offered to do these jobs. That went all right for a couple of times. And then " S.A. Comrade " Rübach smelt a rat.

"What? You swine! Although you're Aryans, you help the Dirty Jew Mühsam!"

Blows and kicks emphasised the racial differences.

Heinz Preuss looked across the room. The narrow slanting windows above the thick beams of the roof. Division 9 was a bare room directly under the roof. Twenty yards long, eight yards wide. Straw sacks lined both sides. In the centre stood a row of long deal tables and benches, one behind the other. Two more rooms lay beneath the roof of the large red-brick house. They had only been " furnished " since the place had become a concentration camp. There were not enough of the cells with the long rows of barred windows.

"S.A. comrade" Rübach! There the fellow sat, swinging his legs indolently and on the look-out for what was happening in the room. He was sitting right near the doorway, which had a double door in a barred grating extending into the room. It looked like the cage of some wild beast of the jungle. Peepholes had been fitted into the wall on both sides of the door, so that everything could be watched from the corridor outside. " Comrade " Rübach was in charge of their room. An S.A. man arrested for theft, he felt himself to be a prisoner for an honourable offence compared to the others. The S.S. had had good reasons for making him the room senior. In reality, he was far from being the eldest in Division 9. What the S.S. wardens omitted as far as tyranny was concerned was made up for by Rübach. When anyone wanted to leave the room he had to apply to Rübach. And

stand to attention, hands on trouser seams, while doing so.
" Comrade Rübach, please may I be excused ? "
And the same procedure afterwards.
" Comrade Rübach, a man from Division 9, returning from being excused." They had to address the despicable oppressor with the title " Comrade " !

He was quite aware of his favoured position, and made the most of it. When the monthly food parcels arrived, then he purred like a cat, and sat next to the lucky one, begging for tit-bits. Most of them gave him a share. Fear was the only reason ! " He hates me like poison," thought Preuss. " He never gets anything from me. We know each other far too well." What a difference a proper senior would make to them all ! At the potato-peeling, fellow-prisoners from Division 6 had told Preuss that in their room a comrade, a one-time naval officer, was in charge. He had issued his instructions : " A respectful attitude towards all the warders and a brisk military way of speaking. That creates a good impression." Since then 6 was considered the model Division by the S.S. warders. Even their morning " physical training " was soon directed by the " officer " comrade. He directed them with " impersonal efficiency " !

They were rid of all oppression from then onwards. And his influence was soon felt in the sharing out of the food. " Model " Division 6 soon developed into a large commune. They shared the food parcels, swapped clothing. Not only that; they formed—small Marxist circles ! " Everything runs with impersonal efficiency," the comrade had laughed.

Preuss started up from his thoughts. In front, Rübach had jumped up and was standing to attention in front of the cage-like projection of the door. That was the signal for the rest. Bastwork and wooden things were flung aside. They all jumped up from their benches, from the straw sacks, and formed themselves in two long rows in front of their mattresses. It became quiet in the room. Someone tried to stifle a sneeze. From the passage came the tramp of heavy boots, then the rattle of keys. " It'll be the two new sergeants, the two-hourly reliefs," thought Preuss. He looked at Mühsam.

The latter stood there at ease, had even stretched out one leg. His whole bearing expressed lack of respect. The door flew open, the barred door of the grating the second after. It was only one S.S. sergeant. Ignoring Rübach, who clicked his heels together, he walked past him a few yards into the room. Then he looked down the rows searchingly. He held a pile of white paper in his left hand.

The post !

" Yes," he said, " hm . . . hm . . . yes ! "

He was behaving so strangely. As if he had something special in store. Had someone written too openly ? But the relations knew quite well that not a line was passed uncensored.

The men at the back did not notice his curious behaviour, but they were aware that he had come about the post. Their faces showed expectancy. The feet remained still but the bodies jerked impatiently. As if they all wanted to say, " Well, why don't you hand them out ? . . . Hand them out ! "

" Yes . . . hm . . ." repeated the S.S. man again, and turned the letters over. He then began to call out the names. The men in question stepped up singly. They received the letter standing at attention, moved a few steps aside and started reading. Their wives, their mothers, their children, had written.

Neither Preuss nor Erich Mühsam had post. Nevertheless, all those without post had to remain standing stiffly to attention until the sergeant left. He now had only one letter left in his hand. He unfolded it, and started reading. Then he glanced again along the row. " There's something wrong," was Preuss's thought. " But why doesn't he start shouting if some indiscreet words have been written ? " The sergeant still did not call the name out. The rank lined up opposite him showed their uneasiness. But those who had already received their letters did not trouble themselves with the mystery. Their thoughts were a long way away from here—a long, long way.

" Pascholke ! " the sergeant called out at last.

Pascholke stepped up, a man towards the end of the thirties. His broad, heavy shoulders seemed misplaced on his thin body. His face had a melancholy expression. Pascholke? Wasn't that the comrade who had applied for leave? But it had not been granted. His wife was ill in hospital.

"Here," said the sergeant, and held out the letter.

Pascholke took it, unfolded it . . . hid his face in his hands. The paper fluttered to the ground. Pascholke lay near it, sobbed and cried like a little child. All at once he started howling at the top of his voice, his back rocked to and fro, his head still resting on the large knotted hands.

The letter-readers all jumped round. The sergeant turned on his heels and left. Heinz Preuss lifted the letter up and read ". . . inform you that your wife has died."

They carried Pascholke to his straw sack. He was whimpering softly. Someone laid the letter on the table. It seemed as if waves of icy coldness were spreading out from the letter. Pascholke was still sobbing. A few of the men were sitting on their sacks holding their ears.

Another day. They had received their bread rations—a quarter loaf per man per day. They were supposed to make it last the day. They were all hungry after the food, tasting of soda and devoid of all fat. Preuss had been on kitchen duty to-day. A few potatoes would always find their way into his trouser pockets. They were being cooked now. In the washbasin on the only stove in the room. Two men stood on the alert keeping guard. The stove stood near the cage-like double door. This addition to the midday meal could not go on much longer. Fires were to be stopped in a few days' time. It would be all over then. There weren't enough potatoes for all as it was. A portion had always to be allotted to "Comrade" Rübach.

Potatoes as hush-money!

One of the two guards hissed softly and raised his arm warningly. Steps could be heard in the passage outside. They were all standing near their straw sacks the next instant. The bowl of potatoes simmered forsaken on the stove. It was to be hoped they would not notice anything. It was the two

Division sergeants—and the other two? They were new! Seemed as if the guards in the building were being changed.

The four S.S. men walked down the lane formed by the two rows of men. Rübach fawned behind them.

" Have you any Jews in this Division ? " Preuss heard one of the new sergeants asking.

" Jews ? I should say so ! "

Wasn't that the same S.S. man who had recently brought Pascholke his letter? It was ! The fatal word had been uttered. Jews ! The red peasant face twisted to an ugly grimace. He's going to show the new ones what a fine lad he is !

" Jews, step forward ! " he roared.

Four men moved forward, Erich Mühsam among them. The peasant spat on the floor, and then gave the nearest man a push.

" There, lick that up, you Jewish swine ! "

The two new sergeants' laugh pealed out in the room. The man shouted at, short and delicately built, showed a desperate face. His eyes looked from the floor to the S.S. man's face, and from there to the floor again. Preuss watched Mühsam out of the corner of his eye. His chest was moving agitatedly, his jaws working. His eyes behind the pince-nez were narrowed and blazing with hate. Whatever will happen when it is his turn . . . what ?

The rest were thinking the same. Their faces were very serious. " Well, what about it ? "

The sergeant raised his fist. His reputation was at stake before the two new reliefs. The short, delicate man was still hesitating, then knelt down in front of the worked-up sergeant and bent his face quite close to the floor. Preuss saw him wiping the spittle away with his sleeve. Peasant-face turned triumphantly to the two new S.S. men.

" There you are ! "

He turned back to the row of men, who were staring fixedly.

" There, you've had another chance of seeing what these Dirty Jews are like ! "

All four S.S. men laugh loudly.

"You stupid workers have to be shown your leaders in their true colours!"

The new S.S. men grinned.

"Or would you Aryans have done the same?"

Peasant-face glanced questioningly along the row. No one answered. The S.S. man grabbed the first man angrily by the arm.

"Would you, an Aryan, have done the same, I asked you?"

The man shook with fright.

"No," he whispered.

"There you are!" The S.S. sergeant laughed boomingly.

He then went across to two of the four men standing in front and pulled them to the group of uniforms. Erich Mühsam was still standing unmoved.

"Perhaps he'll be lucky to-day," was Preuss's relieved thought.

"Start massagin' yourselves a bit."

The two men looked at each other, troubled. Fear, nothing but fear, was to be read in their faces. Thirty pairs of eyes were fixed on the two. It seemed oppressively hot in the room.

"You've forgotten how the ear-boxing dance goes, have you?" Peasant-face screamed at them.

He pushed the smaller one aside, stood squarely in front of the other one.

"Just watch me. This is how it's done!"

He hit the man resoundingly on the face. He swayed, and fell, got slowly on to his feet again. Tears ran down from his eyes. Blood was dripping from his nose.

"How long have I got to talk to you? It'll be your turn too if you don't start," the sergeant bellowed at the little man.

The latter started hitting the other one. But he stood quite still. Until the sergeant gave him a blow from behind, then he started hitting too. The S.S. men laughed shrilly, and then one of them took hold of Peasant-face by the arm.

"Stop!"

The two men staggered back. They were both smeared with blood. Preuss's feet felt like lead. Human nerves couldn't stand that much longer. Week after week, always the same. He glanced at Erich Mühsam again. His head was hanging on his chest. He must have stopped looking for some time.

" By the way, what are your Jews' names ? " asked one of the new S.S. sergeants.

He asked that calmly and somewhat amused—as if nothing had happened !

" Hey, there, your names ! " Peasant-face pitched into the man standing in front.

Preuss did not hear the first three names. He waited, waited, feverish with fear. Now it was Mühsam's turn— Erich's turn—now ! And then he heard his voice. Ominously calm with rage.

" Erich Mühsam."

The new S.S. man who had wanted to know the names stepped forward in amazement. He jerked his head forward as far as his uniform collar would allow.

" That's Mühsam—the Jewish swine of a journalist ! Here, in this place, in Division 9 ! "

Preuss felt a lump in his throat. Now it would start off all over again from the beginning. It was the same every time the guards were changed. " That's Mühsam ? . . . Mühsam ! "

Erich stood there without changing his expression. He looked the S.S. man full in the face, with all the contempt and decision of a man whose only weapon was his strong will. His unconquerable determination not to weaken lay in that glance.

The other S.S. sergeant planted himself next to the first one.

" Yes, that's him ! " he said importantly, as if showing a rarity in his collection.

The new S.S. man recovered from his surprise. He rummaged in his pockets. Pulled a yellowed newspaper cutting out, and showed it to the others.

" That's what they gave me ! They told me to pay particular attention to the lad ! The revolutionary tribunal[83] in the days of the Münich Soviet ! "

He pointed with his finger to the newspaper cutting.

" There he is ! That's him ! "

He jerked round, waved the cutting in front of Mühsam's face.

" You're responsible for the twelve hostages [84] who were shot by your people then ! The twelve hostages ! "

His voice reached a high pitch, and then broke.

The other three uniforms stood close behind him. All four faces were blazing with fury. Cold shivers crept up Preuss's spine. " Done for, done for," was his only thought.

Erich Mühsam's words rapped out into the silence in the room. He stood with his head up.

" I had absolutely nothing to do with that. I had been arrested ages before that ! "

" We'll see about that downstairs, you Jewish swine ! " roared the new arrival.

He grabbed hold of Mühsam by the arm.

" Take him down ! Downstairs with him ! The other new guards have got to see this ! "

They dragged Erich Mühsam out with them. His head hung down; his shoes scraped the floor. The door in the grating clanged; the outer door slammed to. Silence. The others stood staring, listened with bent heads. Nothing more was to be heard.

The hours passed.

The evening soup was brought. Preuss could not touch his. They lay down to sleep.

The hours passed.

Preuss could not sleep. He could not get rid of his anxious thoughts. His head ached.

The hours passed.

Erich Mühsam did not return.

Heinz Preuss was awake for hours. Suddenly a ray of light came from the central passage outside. The door was pulled open. The uniforms, the shiny buckles of their shoulder-straps gleaming in the lamplight, were dragging something dark, something lifeless, along the floor. They threw it down on to the sack near Preuss. Preuss did not stir.

But as soon as the door had been closed he jumped up. The others had been woken. Soft whispering, the crackling of the straw, filled the darkness. Preuss bent over the stretched-out body.

" Erich ... Erich ..."

No answer. He felt about with his hands, shook him. Mühsam remained dumb. When he touched his head, his face, he felt something sticky on his hands. And then he broke down at last with the torture of the long, long hours, the horror of this moment. He leant his head against the still shoulder and wept.

No one could talk to Erich Mühsam from then on. They had bashed his ears to bits, so that the inner ears lay exposed as red shiny bladders.

During the following weeks Erich Mühsam and Heinz Preuss formed an even closer bond. Heinz Preuss always had pencil and paper on him. He replaced the missing sound words by written ones.

· · · · · · ·

The papers published the Maikowski trial verdict to-day. Fifty-three prisoners have been sentenced to thirty-nine years' penal servitude and ninety-five years' imprisonment.

The newspaper reports mention that none of the forty-seven witnesses for the defence was cross-examined on oath ! But none of the papers print a single word from the speeches of the official " counsel for the defendants " or from the final words of the accused comrades.

The *Völkischer Beobachter*[85] writes under the thick heading:

"NO DEATH SENTENCE FOR THE RED BANDITS !

" The verdict in the trial against the Communist murderers of Maikowski has been pronounced with a mildness which exceeds all expectations. This will be as incomprehensible as the verdict in the Reichstag fire trial. The embittered feeling that ' the pen can destroy what the sword has achieved ' must be prevented. We are convinced that influential quarters will still find the appropriate ways and means."

The *Angriff* prints the catch-line:

"MAXIMUM SENTENCE ONLY TEN YEARS' PENAL SERVITUDE!

" Even while the verdict was being announced shouts were heard from the public gallery, which increased to tumultuous scenes towards the end of the verdict, so that the president of the court had to adjourn the sitting.

" This verdict fulfils one condition: it is in accordance with the moderate letter of the law. However, the tremendous disappointment which it will evoke among the masses of the people, and especially among the Maikowski's faithful S.A. men and the noisy scenes in court which followed the announcement of the verdict, prove with all clearness and precision how essential is the establishment of a truly German Law, in accord with the natural feelings of the German people, in place of a cold and formal collection of paragraphs...."

The longest sentence—*only* ten years.

I recently had occasion to talk to the wife of a comrade sentenced to penal servitude some months ago. She is not allowed to send him any parcels. He is permitted to receive *one* censored letter from her every eight weeks. She, but only she, is allowed to see him every three months. For ten minutes and then under guard. In the few months her husband has become a mere skeleton as a result of the prison food. The monotonous imprisonment is undermining his nerves. There is no occupation for most of the prisoners, owing to lack of work. Every form of mental relaxation has been abolished as " too humane."

The " people " " protested " against the Maikowski verdict in the court. It had been Maikowski's bosom friends, the S.A. men from Storm 33. The president of the court had to adjourn the announcement of the verdict; the *Völkischer Beobachter* is convinced that influential quarters will still find the appropriate ways and means.

We were only able to understand the significance of this incident and this threat after X of the S.A. Reserves gave us his report the next day. The Thirty-threes present had sent delegates to protest to the Prussian Minister of Justice. The Secretary of State, Freisler, received them at once. He made a reassuring speech to the S.A. men. He said among other things, " We are building up a National-Socialist State, but our goal has not yet been reached, S.A. comrades. That is how we must consider the verdict that has been passed by the court of the National-Socialist State. What our opinion of this verdict is will be reported by those who are in the *Führer's* confidence. This case will be very carefully examined by his Ministers, and steps will be taken as a result of our decision."

.   .   .   .

New difficulties have arisen over my writings. The manuscript became so thick that it was not safe enough in my old hiding-place. I took it, therefore, to a political sympathiser. He returned it at the end of a fortnight. He did not feel safe any more, he explained. After that, I took it to another one who is to all appearances a " well-placed " person. But he has given it back to me now too. His porter gives him such queer glances, knows that he formerly used to read Left papers. It would therefore be better for us both if I took the packet back. I told them both that it dealt with an illegal subject. I had to do that. I had tied the parcel up carefully, though. But I am now convinced that they both opened it. They saw what it was about, realised what it could mean for them if the manuscript were by any chance found in their possession.

If this is the case, everyone who shares this knowledge can endanger me somehow at a later date. Perhaps they also thought that I was sure to bring the Gestapo down on them if I kept on taking them further completed pages from time to time.

In any case, I do not believe their arguments. They simply became frightened. So that I must now keep the manuscript at my place to-night. But I must, at all costs, get rid of it to-morrow. It can't be stored in my room in our dangerous district.

. . . .

The papers report.

"At a late hour in the evening of January 30th, the anniversary of the murder, a memorial service will take place in the Maikowskistrasse. The full West Standard of the S.A. and a division of the special police under Wecke will participate in the ceremony. Chief of Staff Leader Heines will greet Maikowski's parents. Then the major commanding the S.A., Röhm, will deliver a speech. Squadron Leader Prince August Wilhelm, Chief Commissioner of Police, Admiral a.D. Levetzow, Police Chief Beck, General Goering, Police General Daluege, the *Führer* of the N.S.K.K., Chief Squadron Leader Hühnlein, the Lord Mayor of Berlin, and Standard*führer* Dr. Lippert. The chief of the S.S., Himmler, will also be present."

Teichert stands up, takes his cap off the peg. His wife stands at the stove and stirs a saucepan. She turns round when we have reached the door.

"Be careful, Paul, please. They'll be coming along in thousands to-day."

Teichert goes back to her. He lays his arm round her shoulder.

"There's nothing to worry about. There'll be a lot taking a look at that hubbub to-day. Don't worry; go to bed afterwards."

The woman nods. She puts the wooden spoon down, sees us to the door. Looks after us as we go down the stairs. That I have called for him again to-day—does the woman suspect anything?

Three men are standing in front of the house door talking softly.

"You celebrating too?" one of them asks. He has his hands tucked in the deep pockets of his leather jacket.

The other two laugh mockingly. I pull at Teichert's sleeve. On no account stay here, get started in a discussion.

"Sure thing," answers Teichert.

"I seem to know the younger one," I say when we are a little way further on.

"Bernard Rutz," answers Teichert. "He's only been here for two days. He deserted from the Landhilfe.[86] He rode here from East Prussia on his bike—now, in winter!"

He looks at me.

"I only had a short talk with him. We'll let him give us a report; he's got something to tell!"

"Bernard Rutz? Wasn't he in the Youth Red Front?"

"Yes, of course. We must try to get the lad to become active again, too. But there's enough time for that. We'll give him a good look-over first."

It is long after lighting-up time. The street lamps are now dull yellow glares. Their rays fade away into the winter night. But through the tall rippled windows of the Power Works bright lights are burning, as usual. Our street is usually deserted when the weather is so cold and wet. But to-day plenty of people are walking up and down. We see a lot of faces we know. Greet the comrades dumbly with our eyes. Teichert nudges me suddenly. Ede is coming towards us. I see that he is wearing his glass eye, his blue suit. He's well rigged out as a "passer-by." He starts when he is quite close to us. He surely doesn't intend to "know" us! I look at him blankly, shake my head gently. He understands, passes on. A short way further on we see Ernst Schwiebus. He is with Emil Schmidt. They behave correctly; "don't know" us. It reminds me of Heinz Preuss. Emil Schmidt had been sticking bills up with him when he was arrested. He's been released from the concentration camp now—he won't be running around here to-day! It would be sheer carelessness if he were. But I soon reassure myself; we would have been certain to have seen him already; the street is not long. It seems as if all the comrades have come to a silent agreement. Their mere presence lends the street its old appearance for all of us. Of course, swastika flags are hanging close to one another from the windows. They are our covering. The S.A. put the finishing-touches to-day with their "well-known methods."

We cross the Krummestrasse, approach the memorial tablets. A dark mass of people stands in front of it. They extend right across the road. Rothacker. He had stood there with me six months ago, in the garage entrance, while the tablets were being inaugurated. How quickly the months have flown. We have not heard from him for some time. The last letter was from Jugoslavia. The Emigration Committee has sent the family there.

" Let's go across," says Teichert.

We join the crowd. No one takes any notice of us. The yellowish-red flickering lights are the flames from the zinc oil vessels. They are placed on both sides of the tablet. It stinks of burning oil. The fumes are overpowering. Two S.A. sentries stand motionless against the wall, wearing long brown winter coats, the straps of their flat helmets fastened under the chin. On the pavement, between the sentries, wreaths with coloured bows have been laid. The bronze tablets are decked with green garlanding, and right above them a swastika formed of fir-tree boughs. A laurel-tree has been placed to the right and left of the sentries.

Other civilians also come up like us without greeting. Others, again, for the most part in uniform, stop, click their heels together, and raise their arms in the Hitler salute before they come nearer. Spectators come and go. The street is slowly filled with lookers-on who want to watch the prospective march up.

I nudge Teichert. Two S.A. men are talking near us.

" . . . they're nearly all our enemies even now, although they hang out our flags."

" Everything should have been burnt down that night," returns the other one. " The worst thing possible is not to know whom you can trust ! "

The first S.A. man says something else, but we can't understand any more. The two walk off. We leave as well.

Maikowski has now become the " martyr." Yet he himself had been inconvenient for them at one time. Had refused to attend church with his troop.

"We must get back to the street. They'll soon close this part." Teichert interrupts my thoughts.

"Yes."

The activity has increased. Whole groups go in the direction of the bronze tablets, and come back from there. Mainly civilians. I see only a few solitary Hitlerjugend uniforms. The S.A. must be assembling somewhere else for the march up. They'll soon rope off the road; Teichert is right. What shall we do then? A solution suddenly occurs to me. "We could go to Mother Franke, Paul. She lives just by the tablets," I say softly.

Teichert looks at me.

"Mother Franke . . . ?" he asks questioningly.

"The old woman whose husband was a mail van driver. Zigalski still collects for the Rote Hilfe from her."

"You're right. That's a jolly good idea." Teichert is pleased.

We walk quicker. Behind the Krummestrasse, near the tablets, are more people. The door of Mother Franke's house is open. People, most likely other tenants, stand outside. I am back in a few minutes. Teichert has waited a little to the side.

"It's all right. She's still up; doesn't mind."

We go up singly. Mother Franke is pleased to see us.

"To think you've come to me for a change . . . to me . . ." she repeats the sentence a couple of times.

It must have surprised her. She is still shaking her old head in astonishment. Her eyes sparkle with joy. Her white hair is neatly combed. With a parting in the middle. Her face is covered with numerous small wrinkles. She looks very robust and alert, the old woman. Must be more than sixty.

Mother Franke trips on in front of us, beckons with her old worn hand. "Come along, come along, into the parlour . . . in front."

Mother Franke moves two chairs forward from the table, and then leaves us. I sit down. Opposite me, in a corner of the plush sofa, sits a large cat.

Teichert goes to the window.

"We've got a good view from here," he remarks, and comes back to the room. "But where's Mother Franke?"

I stand up.

Mother Franke is in the kitchen grinding coffee. The kettle is humming on the gas-stove.

"I hope that's not for us?"

Mother Franke laughs.

"Of course it's for you. Now go away, go on!"

I protest again, but she elbows me out of the kitchen.

We drink coffee. Mother Franke keeps on asking questions. She has not had a chance of talking to comrades for ages. Zigalski only comes for a few seconds. No, she would not have gone to bed yet, in any case. I am amazed to see how briskly the old woman talks, how well informed she is. She reads the papers regularly. "If you want to know what's going on these days you have to read between the lines!" She winks at us.

"Zigalski fetches other stuff along now and again." She smiles artfully. "If that weren't the case one wouldn't get to know anything."

We younger ones can take an example from the old woman. She does what she can. Pays her subscription, gives a mark more occasionally. Her husband had been in the Spartacus in the old days. She has remained loyal to us, perhaps because of his memory. He had driven a mail van. That's where he had caught pneumonia from which he had not recovered. That was many years ago. The Nazis would deprive the old woman of her pension if they got to know anything. A brave woman, Mother Franke.

Teichert has been standing near the window for some time.

"They're clearing the street now . . . they're clearing the street," he says suddenly.

We stand side by side. The ringing of bells comes to us across the silence. There—another one, only further off this time. We look at each other without speaking. That as well. It's all part of the show—the bells would not start ringing in the middle of the night otherwise.

From the right, from the bend in the street, where the Power Works stand, the dull beating of drums, the sound of confused singing, is to be heard. I bend forward out of the window. At the back they are just rounding the bend in the street. I can't distinguish people, can only see two rows of torches. As I bring my head back into the room I notice a dark group of people just under us, to the right. We had not heard them coming. Civilians? Or relatives? The song becomes clearer.

" *Die Strasse frei den braunen Batallonen*
Die Strasse frei dem Sturmabteilungsmann."

And then the head of the procession is below us. The song booms out in the narrow street. The solitary uniformed figure in front suddenly jerks his right arm at an angle in the air. They march away under us. Long, long rows of burning torches, raised arms, the uniformed backs and caps swinging up and down to the beat of the march.

" Clear the street ! " . . . But a year ago it was not yet cleared for you. You wanted to take it by storm then. You bring your songs, the sound of your nailed boots through the street. But you can't win it, not even now—after a year of the bloodiest terror ! You are still marching through *our* street, through enemy country. On the anniversary of your " revolution." On the anniversary of your " victory " !

There is a short gap behind the S.A. procession, and then —long rows of four-ranked grey Stahlhelm. White swastikas shine on the steel helmets, rifles slanting near them. Wecke's special police, Goering's picked troops. An officer rides a spirited horse in front of the police division. His steel helmet jerks up and down with the horse's prances. He holds a gleaming sword in his right hand. When level with the tablet wall he raises it in the air.

" Prrrrrre . . . sent . . . aaaarms ! "

A sudden jerk becomes perceptible in the Stahlhelm ranks. Hands simultaneously grasp the rifles. This is not a memorial service. It is intended as a new attempt at intimidating us. The force of the Fascist State.

" Division haaalt ! "
" Right turn ! "
The Stahlhelm are now facing the memorial wall. On its left wing. A single S.A. division comes from the right. Commands are again heard, shorter, clearer. The S.A. remain conspicuously on the right wing.
" The Thirty-threes," whispers Teichert.
The march past has not come to an end yet. Groups with flags come from right and left. Take up their position near the wall.
Complete silence falls. The officer's horse snorts, stamps its hoofs. The sound comes up to us quite clearly. Suddenly, from the right, hooters break the silence. New commands a few seconds later. " S.A., 'shun ! . . . Eeeeeyes right ! "
The police officer also issues his orders. The rifle butts scrape the asphalt. A small group of uniformed men—broad beams of light shine on to their uniform collars and capes—review the lines. A short fat man leads the way. He raises his right arm languidly. Röhm ![87] Close behind him the black uniform—Himmler.[88] The fat one with the swinging gait—Goering. To think he should let Röhm precede him !
Rattling of drums.
A voice starts to fill the silence.
The man waves his arms about. He greets the parents, the " guests of honour." It is Heines.
I close my eyes, lean my forehead against the cool pane.
And then another picture is there, clear and distinct. . . .
Men in faded field-grey uniforms, in blue sailor's uniforms, are coming along. Civilians in ragged, dirty clothes. Faces bleeding from wounds. Broken skulls; shot, stabbed bodies.
Spartacus fighters.
Workers from the Red Army on the Ruhr.[89]
Workers from the Hamburg barricades.[90]
German rebels.
Hundreds and thousands, tens of thousands of murdered fighters. A small group in their centre. A man and a tiny woman at their head. The man has closely cropped hair wears glasses. The woman has thick black hair.

Karl Liebknecht. Rosa Luxemburg.
Other well-known faces follow them. Leviné, Landauer, Sylt. And at the tail of this silent procession come the comrades from our street, from the last twelve months' struggle. Hans Klaffert, Otto Grüneberg, Paul Schulz, and many, many others. The procession stops now. The centre is directly beneath us. The man with the closely cropped hair and the glasses raises his arm.

" Is that what we died for ? "

" No ! " The cry comes from the thousands of voices.

The man turns round, points up to us.

" But you are still living ! " . . .

. . . .

The S.A. major-general is standing on the platform across the way, in front of the gleaming microphone. He rests his arms on his hips.

" Reich of Honour and Freedom . . . you two heroes now at rest up above are our champions and monitors. . . ."

I glance surreptitiously at Teichert. When the arms below are raised again, Teichert turns away, sickened. Takes a few steps into the room.

Silence.

When the first tones of the Horst Wessel song [91] float up from outside, Teichert turns to the window and closes it with a quick movement.

" They sing . . . and our . . . and our . . ." jerks out Mother Franke.

We sit in silence for a while. I glance down at the street from time to time.

At last ! They've gone !

Mother Franke gives us the house key.

" Wish you luck, boys. Keep at it," are her last words.

. . . .

February 1st, 1934.

The trial of Richard Hüttig and the comrades of his Buildings Defence Groups started to-day. As I mentioned in the earlier part of this book, they are accused of having shot the S.S. troop leader, von der Ahé, at a conflict with the S.A. and S.S. the 17th of February last year. The fight occurred during one of the many punitive expeditions the Nazis undertook in Charlottenburg. Our comrades attempted to defend themselves. They had no firearms; the S.A. had done the shooting. Ahé was mortally wounded. We know that twenty-four comrades have been arrested by Storm 33 and the police during the last months in connection with this incident. The Gestapo, together with the S.A. and S.S., suddenly closed our street and raided several houses as late as the beginning of September.

On that occasion alone, fifteen arrests were made. But the papers now write that there are only eighteen accused.

We have only one explanation for this. For, terrible as it sounds, the other six comrades must have been murdered; they would otherwise have most certainly been accused with the others.

I knew two of the missing comrades very well. Voss and Drescher are their names.

. . . .

I have decided never again to use my bike for the illegal work. On a previous occasion the S.A. shot after me while I was transporting illegal material hidden in the tyres.

The situation yesterday was a narrow shave.

I am riding to a neighbouring district—to the secret literature depôt to fetch pamphlets for our groups. We are kept well supplied with pamphlets these days. They are all cleverly disguised: sometimes as a railway travel advertisement, with the picture of a pretty woman on the cover, or in the form of " Rules for Protection against Aerial Attacks." Each one has a different cover, and the first and last pages are usually composed of genuine Nazi publications.

The literature depôt is situated in a lonely street. The thought occurs to me as I turn into the street that it is rather conspicuous riding a bike here. The houses are all modern detached buildings, mostly tenanted by civil servants who don't ride bicycles! And then I suddenly notice that another bicycle is already standing outside the house. Damn! Two bicycles! Someone else must have come to the comrade to fetch material. But if I ride up and down until the other one has gone it will look even more suspicious. I decide to go in after all and leave my bike beside the other one. A young woman opens to the pre-arranged signal—an unusual ring. I tell her the password and she invites me in. The comrade appears a second later. He knows me from the old days. I tell him immediately that I have come by bike, and ask if the other bike outside is by any chance . . . ? Yes, the other comrade is in the back room. That's unwise; he should have told me to come at a different time, I complain. It isn't his fault, the comrade tells me; the other man should have come the previous day. And, anyway, it's too late to do anything about it now. I urge him to hurry; it's best for me to leave as quickly as possible. He then fetches the leaflets and I hide them under my clothes. This takes only a few minutes.

While feeling in my pocket for the key to the safety-padlock on my bike I notice a small slip of paper stuck in my safety chain. I unlock slowly, unfold the note with my other hand, shielding the movement with my body.

" Two bikes!
Look out! Danger!

is written on the note. I crumple it together, pretend to be wiping my mouth—swallowed. Then I turn the bicycle round and stow the safety chain away with slow movements, while my brain works feverishly, my eyes searching the street.

The first two words are the same reproach that I myself made; the warning underneath? Does it really come from comrades—or is it a wild guess by some *agent provocateur*? In that case I should not have swallowed the note, should have let it drop. I wasn't upstairs more than a few minutes. . . .

Had those two been there before? The two men a good distance apart, who seem to be walking up and down the street at random. And there, on the right. Another two are standing on either side of the street at the corner. Trapped! The street is otherwise empty; not a soul to be seen. And I've got the pamphlets on me—damn—that's enough to earn a couple of years' hard labour! What now? Idiotic question! Ride off. You'll be arrested in any case. I push the bike slowly to the gutter, mount. One of the men on the other side stops, glances across at me. That heavy coat, the bowler hat, the tough-looking face—Gestapo! My feet push the pedals mechanically; my head hums like a swarm of bees. Five yards—eight yards—why don't they call out " Halt "? Why . . . ? I reach the corner, turn right slowly. The man there stands with his hands in his coat pockets; he has pushed his soft hat carelessly back from his forehead. We look into each other's eyes for long seconds. It's Harry! One of our party's committee in this district. Harry! Harry! Then the one on the other side must be a comrade as well. So *they* wrote the warning! But the two behind me are Gestapo detectives. I'm certain of that. One develops a sure feeling for that sort of thing these days—and, if not, then why the note?

I pedal and pedal; no one stops me. It takes me some time to realise that despite everything I have been in luck again. I feel as if I had been snatched from the gallows just in time.

I ride about for an hour, all over the town. Get off a number of times, look at the shop windows. I only return to our street when I am quite convinced that no one is following me, that I am really not being shadowed. But, however much I think the matter over, I can't piece the threads together.

But I soon got to know the facts. The comrades always " covered " the literature depôt with their sentries. The Gestapo had been there for the first time that day—but they did not make a raid then! They made up for this the next day—but when they arrived it was at a " clean," respectable flat. The place was turned inside out, but the search was in vain. The comrade was not even arrested. He was immediately " released " from our work, of course.

But I have ridden my bike for the last time while on illegal work. The Berlin Transport Co. can add me to its list of faithful passengers from now on. The fare money will just have to be raked up somewhere. Further, I shall only go about " respectably " dressed in the future. The Nazis are less suspicious of their Volksgenossen when they are well dressed.

It's surprising how quickly I have recovered my spirits.

Yet, is it really surprising? I notice the same with all the other comrades—and it's a good thing too! The illegal work places all of us in danger every day. But if your safety is continually threatened you lose your fear of danger to a certain extent. We realise that if we are caught in such situations we *must* force ourselves to keep calm. Most comrades succeed in doing this; they know that years of imprisonment, very often their very lives, are the penalty of failure.

. . . .

Ernst Schwiebus was here just now. He brought me two of to-day's papers. I have to write an article. For a circular on the Ahé trial, which is to be printed to-night.

For some months we have been anxious about Richard Hüttig and his Buildings Defence Group. Now our fear has become a certainty. They intend pronouncing death-sentences in the Ahé trial!

I pick out of a pile of old newspapers a few papers which I had marked and which contain reports on the trial. This was the only way of keeping them. Cuttings would have been too risky.

January 24th, 1934. Nachtausgabe.

" The aim of this trial is not only to expiate a great crime committed against the movement which has delivered Germany, but also completely to clear away once and for all the Bolshevist menace in Charlottenburg with all the might at the disposal of the law."

February 10th, 1934. Berliner Morgenpost.
" It must be left to the jury to decide whether the court will find that the fatal shot at the S.S. man, von der Ahé, was a badly aimed bullet fired by the witness, the S.A. man Amor. . . ."

February 10th, 1934 (the same day). Völkischer Beobachter.
" The firearms expert was unable to answer with certainty the question from what kind of weapon the bullet had been fired. The pistols shown him were very rusty and had no special peculiarities which could have helped him in forming an opinion."

I shall only add a few explanatory notes to these newspaper extracts in my article. For they prove quite clearly how the trial was run, and that it had one aim, and one aim only—that is, the death-sentence. I shall also mention that twenty-four comrades have been arrested in connection with the trial and that only eighteen have appeared in court. This means that six must already have been murdered, otherwise they would be standing in the dock.

. . . .

" . . . Hundreds dead ! Hundreds dead ! It'll be settled in the next few days. In the next few days, I tell you ! "

Teichert paces to and fro.

" ' Course it must ! An' it will too ! D'yer think it's the same wiv' 'em as wiv' us ? They've got machine guns ! They've got hand grenades ! "

Teichert stops in front of Ede near the table. Papers are strewn about on it. Thick headlines !

A FEW CENTRES OF THE REBELLION IN AUSTRIA SUPPRESSED ![92]
The Karl Marx Building Stormed By The Government Troops !
Heimwehr's Heavy Losses[93]

" Mussolini is concentrating troops on the frontier ! Hitler is most likely preparing for a march into Austria ! We are all hoping that the Austrian comrades will win, Ede. But it can also end the other way. It . . ."

" Don't care a bloody damn what them inkslingers write. The workers 'ave struck the first blow and we've gotter sit 'ere and can't do any bloody thing to 'elp 'em ! It's enough ter send us all dotty ! "

" Don't shout ! "

" Listen to me, will you ? Talk quieter, can't you ? You know what it can mean for us ! " " Ready-made " waves his arms in front of Ede's face.

Teichert starts pacing quickly up and down the room again. Ede rests his head in his hands. This has been going on all the evening; in fact, since the first reports on Austria arrived. Each one overwhelms the other with questions. Each one hopes. We argue for hours on end—shout at each other. The five of us have met to-day !

" The workers are fighting heroically "—Ernst Schwiebus starts the ball rolling again—" but is courage, machine guns, everything ? A general strike is essential—*everything* must be at a standstill. You've just read it; work is being continued in the factories ! "

Ede angrily sends the papers flying off the table.

" Jest read it ! Jest read it ! But they're bloody well defending 'emselves at least ! What the bloody 'ell did we do when Adolf came along ? Nuffing 'appened—nuffing. An' even if they don't win out, they've made a fight of it at least. They did 'ave a try ! "

Ede is right. It is better to suffer a military defeat than to let the Fascists grab hold of power without offering any resistance. *That* is always depressing; we've seen that ourselves.

" The Austrian comrades are trying out the strength of the workers. They'll learn from their mistakes; this will be useful in future fights. . . ."

" Future fights ? What d'yer mean, future fights ? They're still fighting ! "

" We know what you're feeling, Ede. But, knowing what we do, we've also got to talk about *that*, otherwise there's no sense in talking about things at all."

Ede hides his head in his hands again.

"The shops are open in some districts. The power stations are working again; the trains are running—the trains! Do you know what that means? That the Dollfuss Government can operate with its Fascist Heimwehr, with its army. The workers are confined in their bases. They are bombarding blocks of flats, the workers' homes, with heavy guns!"

Teichert stops short in his pacing up and down the room.

"You can't keep on telling the workers that the guns are to be kept for the last necessity—for when the Fascists start breaking up democracy. They've been steadily destroying it during the last few years! The workers have now started to use their guns without being told to. Because they realise that the crisis has been reached."

Ede jerks his head up.

"What did I say? 'Aven't I been saying that all along?"

"But Ernst has already said that. Only it's no good doing things by halves. It should have been planned *beforehand*!"

"Whichever way it ends, one thing remains, they are setting us all an example. We German workers can learn from them too. You're quite right there; we didn't bring things so far. But we didn't have the majority of the workers behind us. We have..."

"I'll tell yer what we 'ad! We kept on insultin' the Social-Democrats, that's what we did!"

"Of course we made mistakes, but we were quite sincere about wanting the United Front," Schwiebus interjects.

"We're learning from our mistakes too, Ede. But that doesn't alter things. We wanted to stop Hitler coming along! We couldn't do it on our own. We are only forming the United Front now. We've got the most difficult fights coming. We..."

"We'd better stop now. All you do is to keep on starting all over again!" the "Ready-made" interrupts. "It's gone eleven, anyway."

Our street is deserted. The machines in the Power Works are still humming.

. . . .

A Nazi at the barber's to-day:

"Civil war! Germans killing Germans! Adolf Hitler's Volksgemeinschaft[94] has kept us from all that. Dollfuss is responsible for the blood that has been shed. And all because he won't allow freedom of opinion!"

As if things are different with us! Blood, the thousands they have murdered, isn't that bloodshed? Isn't Richard Hüttig flesh and blood?

The Ahé trial—death-sentence demanded.

The Reichstag fire trial diverted attention from the Maikowski trial.

The Austrian rebellion is serving the same purpose for the Ahé trial.

. . . .

The evening paper lies on the table in front of me. I stare and stare at the page. I feel dizzy; the room seems to be revolving round me.

"VERDICT IN THE AHÉ TRIAL

RICHARD HÜTTIG SENTENCED TO DEATH

"Richard Hüttig sentenced to death and to lifelong deprivation of civic rights for breach of the peace and for attempted murder. Fourteen other prisoners sentenced to ninety-four years' penal servitude and eighteen years' imprisonment!

"... The special tribunal has had to deal with the same type of crime as the Maikowski trial. But, unlike the latter, it took only six days before passing sentences. It was able to examine one hundred witnesses during this time, as all superfluous matter was excluded from the hearing.

"The Public Prosecutor Dombrowski said, among other things, 'The prosecution has no hesitation, on the strength of similar trials and taking into account the fact that these and similar attacks continually show premeditated actions, in arriving at inevitable conclusions, *without* having to keep too precisely to the evidence submitted and to the results of the cross-examinations. The prosecution does *not* consider that it has been proved that von der Ahé was shot by Hüttig. After von der Ahé had been knocked down he got on to his feet again and received the fatal shot, in as yet unexplained manner, while standing. But the ringleader deserves the harshest punishment known to the law. The prosecution is convinced that those framing the laws would have intended the death-sentence for a deed like Hüttig's. If the other accused receive only sentences of one to fifteen years' penal servitude, it is because this special tribunal has decided to treat these prisoners with considerable leniency.' "

The president, Chief Justice of the Supreme Court of the Reich, made the following remarks:

" Conclusions arrived at by the prosecution were incomplete inasmuch as the prosecution was unable to bring forward incriminating evidence of the other accused against Hüttig. It has also to be taken into account that a year has passed since the deed was committed and that all the witnesses were in a state of intense excitement at the time. And, finally, the events of that night took place under bad lighting conditions. That is why the evidence of the witnesses was in many points at a considerable variance. The prosecution has, however, *not* arrived at the conclusion that Hüttig fired the fatal shot at Ahé. It has not been possible indisputably to prove who fired this shot. On the other hand, it has been proved that Hüttig was guilty of seriously disturbing the public peace, and had acted contrary to the Decree for Protection of the People and State, and was the ringleader in the latter offence. Moreover, he is guilty of attempted murder."

The Prosecutor merely remarked: " Ahé received the fatal shot in an as yet unexplained manner."

But at all costs one of the accused has to die: Richard Hüttig. He is no ordinary man in their eyes. He is the hated leader of the Charlottenburg Buildings Defence Groups. He is one of our finest and most valuable comrades—and they

know that. That is why they want to make an example of him. Richard Hüttig, our Richard, sentenced to death!
"The accused heard the verdict unmoved."
And now? We can't go out into the streets to shout to everyone that Richard is innocent, that a judicial murder by these Brown Shirts must be prevented. Are we really powerless? Is there no possible way of saving Richard?

. . . .

February 17th, 1934 (the next day).
Even the *Völkischer Beobachter* confirms in its report of the Ahé trial that Richard had not shot Ahé.

"It could not be indisputably proved that Hüttig, or whoever else had fired the shot. However, Hüttig had cast the bullet which put an end to Ahé's life, without taking into account from whose revolver it came!"

. . . .

"Ready-made," the comrade employed by Brennickmayer's, is already standing at the appointed corner.
"Alone?"
"I sent the other two in to Bunke's. It wouldn't have been safe for the three of us to have waited here."
We walk on slowly. There is a continuous flow of traffic, as usual. The cars drive past in long rows; the slowly moving crowds of pedestrians push their way along the pavements.
"Ready-made" looks like a young man from a betterclass family. The smoothly shaved cheeks, the dark hair glistening with brilliantine. He has turned the collar of his heavy winter coat up, but has no hat on. That's how the "better class" young people go about in this district.
"To Bunke's? It's an expensive place. And shall we be able to talk there?"
"Of course. They're always full, because of the music. I've still got enough on me to pay for our coffee."
"All right."

Whatever do Max and Erwin want from me? They are both "Ready-made's" colleagues. All that they had told him was that they wanted to speak to me. He was the best person to arrange that.

"Ready-made" has been supplying them with papers for some months now. They always ask for printed things. That's the best stuff for them to "trade with." They have organised readers' circles, each member paying a few coppers. And when the pamphlet has been read, they sell it. They sometimes get as much as two marks and more a copy. They settle with "Ready-made," who beams all over his face every time he brings me the money. We have given them theoretical books now and again, for their own use. Max is more advanced politically than Erwin. We have been to Max's place a couple of times. He has placed his furnished room at our disposal for discussions.

The café is packed. I lead the way between the tables in the large room. The people chatter loudly. At a few tables couples are sitting close together. The sound of crockery. Waitresses hurry from table to table. They are wearing tiny pink caps and fancy aprons to match. The band plays from a stage in front. But where are the other two? There, at the back, at the round marble table in the corner. They've picked a good table.

" 'Evening, Karl. Good seat, what?"

They are both pleased. They only know me as Karl.

"Sure thing. You're still as smart as ever."

"Ready-made" orders two cups of coffee. Who's at the next table? An elderly man. He is occupied with his stout partner. They are quite harmless. But over there—an S.A. Stormleader. He's also busy with his little painted lady—and, in any case, he won't be able to hear us in this din.

Max pushes a few coins across the table. Smiles proudly.

"Let's do this first. Six marks. For the last delivery."

"Received with thanks."

"When can we . . . ?" asks Erwin.

"Next week. As usual." I nod my head at "Ready-made."

"O.K."

Silence. Max takes a sip at his beer. Erwin plays with a pencil. They really must have something special up their sleeve. Need a pause to get going. Max told me recently that he was a Jew. The keenest *Rassenforscher*[95] would go wrong there. The straight reddish-gold hair. And he's tall and slim too. Has clever, regular features. Brave chap. If he's caught, he'd fare worse because of his race.

"Well, Karl, we want to discuss something with you," Max says at last.

"I'm listening. Get it off your chest."

Max is silent for a second.

"We want to join the family," he says quietly.

Erwin nods.

"Yes, that's what we wanted to talk to you about."

I let my coffee-spoon drop in surprise, stare at them both with eyes wide open. They want to join the Party? I was prepared for anything but that. I feel tremendously elated.

"Ready-made" is also surprised, glances from one to the other. I keep silent. They want to . . . Max perhaps; but Erwin? I take stock of Erwin as if I had never seen him before. The neat head, the slender hands. Why, he still has a boyish face; is under twenty. Erwin ought to be in the Youth Movement. But he lives in our district. The Youth Movement is weak there, is in the process of being built up. Max is older, cleverer.

But have they any idea what it means, to join the Party now? Needn't put them to work at once; they have proved their trustworthiness.

We have had losses—require new members.

They are still looking at me.

We are glad whenever new people come to us, especially these days. But that means more than just selling papers now and again; they have not had enough experience of the "work." They cannot be fully drawn into things at the start for this reason. That is in their own interests, and ours as well, I explain to them.

And do they realise how difficult it is for the "family" to

continue its work these days? I do not want to be pessimistic, but have they reflected how badly things might eventually go with them? Yes, they are quite aware of that, is Max's answer. They have thought it all over for some time. But the mere selling of "pictures" does not satisfy them any more, they cannot carry on with things as they are. It is to-day essential that everyone bring all their energies to the work.

I promise to arrange things for Erwin at once, because he lives in our district. He will receive a message through " Ready-made." Max's case will take longer. He lives in another district, so that I must first get into touch with the " colleagues " there. I arrange a meeting with Max when I can introduce him to the comrades in his district. They are both satisfied with the answer, shake hands silently.

We pay.

Max and Erwin leave first. The S.A. Stormleader is still sitting at the near-by table. He is stroking his lady's hand.

. . . .

I had difficulties in arranging Max's enrolment. The competent comrade in his district demanded that I bring three sponsors. He remained obdurate despite the fact that he knows me and that I explained that Max had been working with us for months. He insisted that this was doubly necessary since our work is illegal. I had to fulfil his conditions in the end.

Max and I met eight days later. He told me, his whole face beaming with joy, that he had already been drawn into the work. The district's paper was stored at his place after printing, and shared out from there. So the comrades trust him completely. I did not mention my doubts to Max. He would only have misunderstood them and would have thought that *I* mistrusted him. But I shall take the matter up with the comrade in question. He first demands three sponsors, and then stores our papers at Max's place a few days later. That is no way to work. Max is far too inexperienced in our illegal work. Yet he will now get to know quite a number of comrades. They are exposing themselves and their newspaper centre to risks. I know that Max is quite safe in his furnished room. He has a clean sheet with the Gestapo. I am fully aware how our work suffers through a lack of " clean " flats. This will have inclined the comrades to adopt the measure. But they dare not become careless just because of the scarcity of flats.

Our district committee has behaved similarly with two Social-Democrat comrades from Ewald's group. These comrades also wanted to undertake difficult jobs, and received them. I was glad to see what courage the Social-Democrat comrades displayed, but at the same time protested against this method of allotting work.

We are responsible for their safety, especially as we have had more experience of the illegal work than the two comrades in question. They must first be trained, and then gradually entrusted with internal work. But I feel confident despite these errors. We are beginning to feel that the Party is being built up again.

. . . .

I saw a new poster in our street to-day:

" GERMAN SCHOOLCHILDREN HUNT FOR DUMMY SHELLS !

" All German schoolchildren must play their part in Anti-Aircraft Defence. . . . Following duties . . . suppose an enemy attack took place from the air on Charlottenburg . . . enemy squadrons flew over the blocks of houses in the . . . streets, then turned their attention to the traffic in the streets . . . the target, the Charlottenburg Power Works, missed because covered in time by a smoke screen . . . a number of bombs dropped . . . blind shells lying about in the streets . . . these imaginary spots have been marked by the Luftschutzbund.[96] . . .

GERMAN SCHOOLCHILDREN, DO YOUR DUTY !

Dummy shell search. . . . Prizes offered for the best dummy shell finder . . . particulars from . . ."

Child soldiers! How often have I read in the papers, "They found a shell left over from the Great War... exploded... three were blown to pieces...."

The schoolchildren are entirely at the mercy of the Brown Shirt education. All the comrades have the same to tell of their children. The Fascist teachers nag them daily to join the Jungvolk, to join the Hitlerjugend. They are taught to treat "civilians" as belonging to an inferior grade. Continual "picnics" supplement the Nazi education. Here they learn to creep through barbed wire, to handle cases of munitions, and similar "exercises." Their clothes are always torn and dirty when they come home. These "lessons" are continued in their playground. Burning houses are extinguished with chemicals. Children who have been made leaders of groups are allowed to miss school whenever they have a long march on, so that they learn even less than the other children, yet they have to be passed in their exams because they are "officers."

The Nazis exploit the youngsters' romantic inclinations for their own use. The children's organisations are allowed to march through the streets at any hour they please shrieking out chauvinistic soldiers' songs. The Schupos even close all traffic for them. How important that must make them feel! What a lot the uniform, shoulder-straps, and trench-boots mean to a child. It gives them a chance of showing off in front of the other children, of playing "grown ups" out in the street.

Some of our comrades' children ask for uniform equipment for their birthdays as a result of this influence. While they are still very young their parents cannot talk to them about our way of thinking. They are afraid that they will talk to other people about it, and so their own children will expose them to danger. I know comrades who never carry illegal material on them because of their children. But they keep our Pioneer books [97] hidden away somewhere. They read from it to their older children in the evenings. "I must give my child *that* at least; he doesn't read anything else except the Nazi school rubbish," a comrade told me.

The Browns want to train a whole nation, from childhood to old age, for their war of conquest.

Teichert reports that the Siemens Works are working at top speed on war material. Some shops work three shifts. New metal experts have been engaged—toolmakers, turners, mechanics, etc. A number are sent on outside work. " Assembling jobs." New aerodromes ! They are all bound by oath—threatened with heavy punishments if they let anything be known. False prosperity in parts of the German industry—war materials. Germany, supplier of war materials to the Far East, we used to think. To-day the Third Reich is arming itself against the Soviet Union.

Many of our comrades have been able to get back to the factories because of this. Into the Fascist war factories ! We shall need them !

. . . .

We have again been struck a heavy blow.

Franz Zander, our Franz has been arrested. Yesterday evening in our street. Franz—in our street ! We know now how it happened. We made careful enquiries everywhere. We had to discover the details because we did not know whether the Thirty-threes came for him alone, or whether other comrades are soon to be arrested too. We know Franz was with comrades in the neighbouring district. In Moabit. He went to discuss a new method for printing papers, one which has been used for some time in his district. It is much cheaper and more copies can be printed. We know now that Franz came to our street for a few minutes to see his old mother. He learnt that she has been ill for months from Hilde. His sister Käthe had not mentioned a word about it to him. He was in the next district, less than half an hour away from our street. The temptation to visit his mother would come naturally. He must have struggled with himself for some time. It would be all right just for once; he wouldn't stay longer than a few minutes, and who would see him anyway, as it was already dark ? We can guess this now. But we still can't understand how Franz, who had trained us all to be so very cautious, could have come to our street. He knew that the S.A. had been looking for him here for a year.

. . . .

The loudspeaker was grinding martial music into the bar of the pub Africander, which is just opposite Franz's house. The fat landlady was sitting behind the bar knitting. Three men were playing cards at one of the round tables on her right. In the other corner, on her extreme left, sat a lonely customer. He was staring into his half-empty beer-glass. His bald head rested on his hands. The cauliflower ears protruded above his thumbs. It was Kranz, a regular customer. The landlady mentally reckoned up his bill. Three whiskies, four beers, two cigars.

Kranz stood up suddenly, took the cold cigar out of his mouth, and glanced round searchingly. The landlady threw her sock down on to the bar and went up to him. She struck a match.

" Here you are."

Kranz looked at her glassily. He took the match from her, turned the flame to the window, and puffed at his cigar. A second later he let the match fall. The cigar slithered down from the corner of his mouth. He stood there with his mouth wide open and stared across. The landlady looked at him in surprise. The other three were attracted by Kranz's curious behaviour. Then he pulled himself together and ran to the door.

" I'll pay afterwards . . . coming back later," he stuttered.

The landlady ran after him, wanting to protest, but Kranz was already outside; had not even stopped to close the door. Meanwhile one of the three men stood up. He saw Kranz running off in the direction of the Rosinenstrasse. As there was nothing unusual to be seen in our street they were unable to account for Kranz's peculiar behaviour. (Franz must have disappeared into his house a second ago. The customer who had gone to the door knew him. He told us that he had not seen him.)

"He gets crazier every day. Still, he'll pay his bill for sure," the landlady remarked to the others.

Soon afterwards S.A. men came running along our street. The mob of brown uniforms soon split up and formed a chain which stretched from the last two corner houses at the bend in the street right up to the narrow path between the Power Works and the Relief Barracks. A group of S.A. then entered Franz's house and occupied all the staircases and the doors on to the yard.

Nothing unusual had been noticed in Franz's house. But the quiet street was stirred up in the few minutes. The long rows of windows were packed with faces. Groups stood in the doorways and glanced across to the brown cordon with hate in their eyes. They were all standing a good way off, but it seemed that their silent protest had its effect on the Brownshirts. The S.A. men felt it quite obviously. They turned their heads nervously, looked along the rows of houses and windows. The business people peeped timidly through their shop windows, all except the fruiterer, who stood full square in his shop doorway. The same anxious thought was shared by all. Who is it for? . . . They've come so suddenly . . . who is in danger? Who? . . . Who?

. . . .

Franz rang at the door of his home. No one opened. Käthe was still at the office and his mother was in bed, unable to get up. The neighbour, Frau Schulze, heard him ringing. She was astonished when she saw Franz. Yes, she had a key to the flat; she looked after his mother during the day, she explained. She refused to go to the hospital and Käthe was away all day. Käthe ought to have told him that ages ago, Franz replied. He had only just heard it from his girl. At first she had only hinted at things, but he had kept at her until she told him everything. He wanted to see and speak to his mother for a couple of minutes; he would leave almost at once. He soon came out of the flat, but stopped to tell the neighbour that he had attempted to persuade his mother to go to the hospital. That was the best thing for her. She was even worse than he had imagined, was so terribly thin and weak. Then he took the stairs in flying leaps. A second later the neighbour heard a crash on the steps below.

A voice was shouting, hoarse with rage:
" We've caught you at last ! We've got you now, you b—— ! "

. . . .

When the Brown Shirts came out into the street, a sudden movement was noticeable among the people in the doorways; the heads at the windows jerked up with fear. A choking feeling came to their throats. It was Franz Zander—their Franz ! Everyone in the street knew him well.

The street remained silent. The men stood in front of the doors. But their pockets bulged with their clenched fists. All the windows were crowded out with spectators. Our street took leave of Franz in dead silence. It seemed that arms were outstretched from all sides, wanting to shake hands once more.

Franz must have felt that too. His face was calm. A smile even flickered on his lips. He nodded across the streets, up to the windows.

The S.A. pushed him along with quick steps. To the Maikowski Barracks, to the Rosinenstrasse. Children ran alongside the procession. That was the last time that Franz saw our street—that our street saw Franz.

. . . .

My first thought when I heard the news the same evening was that Teichert must be warned. Teichert, because he lives in the same house as Franz. And because we do not know which of us the Thirty-threes might still want to arrest.

The trams from Siemensstadt run along at short intervals. They are all packed. At this time of the day, knocking-off time at Siemens Works, many extra cars can hardly cope with the rush. I stand at the stop and cast flying glances at all the passengers getting off. Where is Teichert ? Perhaps he got out at an earlier stop to-day to buy something ?

Would it be better to wait for him at the top of our street? Too conspicuous. And if he comes from the other end he'll run unprepared into his flat.

Car after car comes along, stops, rolls off, empty.

Not there—and not in the next one. The minutes drag tormentingly.

I pace up and down—for hours, it seems to me.

Another tram rolls along. And in it, at last—Teichert!

He is surprised, fidgets with his dinner-basket.

" You here? " is all that he says.

It seems that the question " Why? " is about to follow. But he walks along at my side without saying another word. I feel very depressed. Steal a quick glance at him. There is a deep furrow between his eyebrows. He has become even paler the last few days, the cheek-bones more prominent. Seems to have aged years since Richard's verdict was pronounced. And now I must tell him this too.

" Why . . . ? It's sure not to be anything pleasant? " he says at last.

I don't look at him. Each step seems to hammer at my head.

" They've arrested Franz ! "

Teichert stops.

" Fraaanz? " He draws the word out, as if he had not heard the name properly. " Has his district been caught, or what—how . . .?

He grips my arm.

" In our street—an hour ago ! "

Teichert wipes his brow with his hand.

" In our . . . in our . . ." he says uncomprehendingly.

I drag him away. We daren't excite attention.

" The neighbour opened the flat for him—she said he wanted to see his mother."

Teichert does not answer; stares fixedly ahead.

" They surrounded the house quite suddenly—perhaps—"

I falter, but Teichert has already understood. He nods dejectedly.

" That's why I wanted to catch you."

We walk about. Teichert still remains silent. He presses his lips together, breathes heavily.

"We got someone to tell the neighbour to stop Käthe. It's too dangerous for one of us. Her mother mustn't get to know anything—not now. . . ."

"Jan," is all that Teichert says. He presses my hand. I avoid his glance. Käthe—she must get over it on her own. I dare not—not now——

"I'm going. Let's get it over. And if I'm—well, we'll see what happens."

He shakes hands again. I gaze after him, then walk round the block of houses in the opposite direction.

We'll arrive from different directions. But that won't save us either—if it's our turn now as well.

. . . .

Käthe had not been able to get much sleep while her mother had been ill. The old woman usually went off to sleep in the early hours of the morning. She had almost agreed to being taken to the hospital before Franz came. But since Franz had been to see her she keeps on refusing to leave the flat. With the obstinacy of the sick she repeated that she was waiting at home for his next visit. Käthe explained that Franz would be able to visit her just as often in the hospital. But no, she insisted on remaining at home. The days since then have been not only a physical strain for Käthe, but also days of mental torture. Her mother talks such a lot about Franz now. What he looked like, how he promised to come back again soon. Käthe dare not let her suspect, by the slightest signs of her real feelings, how things really stand with Franz.

Where is Franz now, and how is he being treated? Käthe has tried to make enquiries about him everywhere. At the local police station, which disclaimed all responsibility; at the Politische Polizei[98] in the Alexanderplatz Police Headquarters; at the Geheime Staatspolizei[99] (Gestapo), in the Prinz Albrechtstrasse, and in the Columbiahaus. They all dismissed her curtly. Franz Zander? The name was unknown there. No, they could not undertake enquiries; had enough to do as it was. We could not help Käthe either; it would only excite suspicion if we started making enquiries about him. We advised Käthe to tell Hilde that Franz had been arrested by the police and not by the S.A. For Hilde would only have blamed herself all the more because she had been the one to tell Franz about his mother. Hilde is quite desperate since Franz's arrest. She only talks about trying to do something for him. Käthe tells her every time that she does not know where he is. Hilde would only be dragged into the affair if she made enquiries about Franz. And if Hilde got to know that the Thirty-threes had arrested Franz she would have been sure to try to obtain information from her brother. We have to prevent her from betraying herself to her brother, the S.A. troop leader.

The Thirty-threes! Is Franz still in the Maikowski Barracks? The S.A. have not let Käthe enter the barracks. She could report to him after hours, the officer on duty had remarked mockingly. Where, where, is Franz? This "where" is Käthe's first thought when she wakes up in the mornings.

She rises early one morning. Dresses hastily and then fetches the basin and towel for her mother from the kitchen. On her way back across the hall her glance falls on the wire letter-box on the front door. Something white is lying there. A letter. At this time, so early in the morning? It must have come by the last post yesterday evening, and remained unnoticed in the dark. There is a printed stamp on the envelope. An official communication?—For Frau Elise Zander. Käthe does not know why, but the letter suddenly feels as heavy as lead in her hand. An official communication! She turns the letter undecidedly about in her hand, then tears the perforated edge.

"Died in hospital. . . . Death caused by a weak heart. . . . Will be released for burial on . . ."

Käthe reads the lines again and again. She whispers them softly to herself, without realising that she is doing so. Died

—but who? Died. . . . But the letter isn't for her at all. She turns it round mechanically. For Frau Elise Zander. . . . Elise Zander . . . Elise . . . for her mother. She stares fixedly at the sheet. . . . Died. . . . Above is written—a name; Franz Zander.

Franz—Franz.

" Kä . . . the, Kä . . . the ! "

Her mother is calling her in her weak, trembling voice. Käthe stands up. She stands there for a second with limp arms, still holding the crumpled letter in her hand. She raises her arm; it feels stiff and heavy, as if it did not belong to her. She looks at the letter again.

" Kä . . . the ! Kä . . . the ! Where . . . are you ? "

Käthe pulls herself together. Her mother ! She has not dared to let her mother know anything so far; this is an additional reason for keeping things from her. She hides the letter away in a drawer. Her mother is resting on her elbows. She must have vainly attempted to stand up. Her face is yellow, the cheek-bones protrude.

She looks at Käthe reproachfully.

" I keep on calling . . . and calling . . . and you don't come," she says.

She points to the wash-basin, the towel. Käthe brings her everything to the bed.

" Don't . . . you have . . . to go to . . . work soon ? " Frau Zander asks.

Yes, she has to go to the office. She won't go; she does not care about anything any more now.

" We've got—we've got a holiday to-day," she answers.

She is herself surprised to hear herself telling her mother that. The latter puts the flannel down, looks at her searchingly.

" Why are you talking like that ? . . . Don't you feel well ? " she asks. " You're so pale."

" There's nothing wrong with me—we've got a holiday to-day," Käthe repeats.

She must allay her mother's suspicions at all costs.

The news that Franz is dead spreads from house to house in our street like lightning during the morning. The street

is in mourning. No black is to be seen, but the death of our comrade is shown on everyone's face. His presence is felt in the talks, in the silent glances. Franz is taking leave of his street. He comes into the houses. He does not knock anywhere; no door opens, but he steps in everywhere.
An old woman is crying. He had often helped her, the young chap had. Carried things, fetched coal.
A comrade thinks.
"Do you still remember? . . . Neuköln—the meeting of the Reich . . . Friedrichshain, the free fight in the hall? Do you still remember? Good luck, Franz. You were one of the best. . . ."
They are taking leave of Franz everywhere, for ever.
Our street is long.
There are many houses.

. . . .

I walk slowly down the Berlinerstrasse. Hilde lives across the way. Mustn't forget to ask Teichert this evening whether he knows how she is. We must look after her more now that she has lost Franz. My glance falls on the electric clock in a watchmaker's shop. Plenty of time; I don't have to be there before twelve. I sit down on a near-by seat. The traffic goes past in never-ending streams. The sun is already quite warm. The trees! A few days ago yellow buds were still on the twigs. They have now unfolded to form tiny leaves. The change comes so quickly that one can almost watch it happening. How pleasant to lie in a green meadow—insects swarming. . . . Franz! He won't ever see all that again—won't ever come for a picnic with us again. It all suddenly comes back to me. I have seen Käthe only once since then, out in the Grünewald. She had gone to the Charlottenburg S.A. Standard doctor. He lives in the Kaiserdamm, in a luxurious flat. "The strongest man can die from heart failure," he had remarked ironically. She had received permission for herself alone to see Franz in the mortuary. They allowed her just to look through a window; the body lay some yards away, wrapped in white sheets. Only a small portion of the face was left uncovered, and that was thickly powdered. She had been unable to recognise him, had not known whether it was him at all. She told me all this between sobs. I could not utter a word; could only stroke her hair. I could not find anything to say which would help to console her. Franz won't ever return.

We shall not be able to meet at all after this; she is sure to be watched. It was difficult enough recently.

My thoughts go back again to the large Wald cemetery. The hundreds of workers who disorganised the traffic on their way, and then stood round the grave. Many had sacrificed their only coppers for the fare, for a few flowers. The faces filled with hate and sorrow appear before me again. The women weep; dead silence apart from that. A silence enforced by the threatening faces of the Gestapo guards. The young comrade from the Youth League rushes forward to the open grave, starts speaking. The arms of the Gestapo drag him away before he can say more than a few sentences. Yet hundreds of voices cry: " Revenge ! Red Front ! " . . .

I open my eyes. It is broad daylight.

You are no longer with us, Franz, my best friend and comrade. . . .

The Zoological Gardens are across the way. People are standing in front of the huge iron gate. They are all looking across at the elephants. Right in front, Jumbo, the oldest elephant, is receiving lumps of sugar with his trunk. Then he throws sand over his massive body, blows a jet of water into the air. The others near me are enjoying the scene. The grown-ups as well as the children. I pull my paper, the *Nachtausgabe*, from my pocket. Hold it in my right hand, keeping a good look-out. The hands of the station clock are exactly on twelve. The comrade will be arriving any minute now. He can't be here yet. No one else is holding a paper. I don't know the comrade, but he has been described in detail to me. He will also be holding a paper, and is to approach me with the passwords. I seem to be looking across to the elephants playing about like all the others here, but I am watching my surroundings all the time. A small pale man wearing gold-rimmed glasses soon comes along. He also joins the others at the cage. That's him! I have developed extreme sensitiveness to this kind of work. The description fits—he also has the *Berliner Börsen Zeitung* in his hand. I notice him stealing quick glances at the people round him. But it's better to wait a bit; it might still be a coincidence. I continue looking at the elephants, but turn the title-page of my paper more noticeably outward. A few minutes pass. Then the woman near me leaves. The little man takes her place soon afterwards.

Good guess; be careful.

" How old do you think the fellow'll be ? " the little man immediately asks in a thin falsetto voice.

The question seems to have been carelessly uttered. No one answers; they are all looking across.

" Difficult to say. Eighty, perhaps even a hundred years," I say calmly.

But even now! It might have been a random question. The answer—the answer now!

He laughs. A gold tooth gleams between his lips.

" If you wanted to make sure, you would have to keep a colossal animal like that as a pet. Like an Indian rajah, eh ? " he jokes.

The woman next to me laughs.

The answer was correct—especially " Indian rajah." So it's all right.

We meet a few seconds later a short way off. The little man gives me his paper.

" It's in there," he says curtly.

His voice is now deep. Quite a different person is walking at my side.

" Have you any news for us from your district ? "

" No. Our comrades are rather depressed after our last death. Things have got to get right again soon, though."

And, after a pause:

" He was one of our best."

The little man nods earnestly, shakes hands.

" Well, in a week, the same time," he says. " But we'll

meet somewhere else. I have been detailed for you now."
We then decide where to meet, and separate at once.

. . . .

I am at Teichert's place in the evening. He has let me know that his wife is visiting relations.

We read the Berlin district committee's Press Service, which I had received from the little man this morning. A detailed report of Dimitroff's, Popoff's, and Tanew's arrival and reception in Moscow. We are glad.

" And now it's Thälmann's turn ! He can only be saved in the same way as Dimitroff. Mass protests. Here, and abroad," Teichert says suddenly.

Thälmann. The last time we had seen him was at the Bülowplatz demonstration.

" The comrades gave a very good answer to the murder of John Scheer[100] and the three others. They stretched banners across two railway bridges during the night in Schöneberg. " REVENGE JOHN SCHEER ! " There's always a lot of traffic there. A couple of hundred workers saw the banners in the morning on their way to work. The fire brigade came along afterwards and took them down."

Silence.

It always seems so peculiar when Teichert talks like that, with such a home and such a wife.

He feels about in his vest pocket, fetches a small note out and hands it across to me.

It is a newspaper cutting.

EXECUTED !

is written in large letters above the column, and underneath in smaller letters.

Orders promptly executed.

I crumple the paper together, throw it down angrily.
" Newspapers in the Third Reich ! " says Teichert.
He stands up. Fetches the latest copy of our *Rote Fahne*.
I start.

"You've still got that . . . here at home?"

"Only got it back yesterday from Hilde," he reassures me. "I've got my reasons for showing it to you!"

I look at the paper. The text is crossed out on a few pages, underlined on others. "Rubbish" is written in large letters in the margin of an article on the building up of Socialism in the Soviet Union.

An article on maladministration under the Nazi bosses bears the remark, "Quite true. Just as bad as under the Marxist system!"

I look at Teichert enquiringly. He laughs. So that the two black teeth stumps in front again attract my attention.

"That is the criticism of the Nazi Party members!"

"Hilde gives . . . ?"

"Some of the papers she receives to the Nazis!"

He becomes serious.

"That has jolly good results, as you see. But the *way* she does that now!"

"How?"

"She has completely lost her head since Franz's death. Tries to forget things by throwing herself into the illegal work. She implores me each time to give her more papers, more jobs."

Teichert bends down to me.

"She used to give the Nazis papers before as well. But without letting them know who they came from. Used to stick them in their letter-boxes. Got hold of the addresses from her brother. Secretly from his notes. But she seems to have given a few Nazis the papers quite openly now. Anyway, the last number. She won't admit it, but how else could she have got them back?"

Hilde. She had done that before—but no one had told me anything about it. Franz must have known about it too.

"We can't give her any more for the time being. That would only end badly!"

"I wanted your agreement to that," Teichert says. "In any case, we've got to detach her from work for a while. She is absolutely broken up."

He thinks for a second.

" I'll let Käthe know. They can meet now and again. They know each other from the commercial school—that's a good enough explanation."

He mentioned that Hilde had told him her brother runs around with an embittered expression the last few days. He does not talk politics at home any more. Although he used to make long propagandist speeches. He had only remarked once that his Stormleader wanted to get a job for him. As prison warden. He had refused. Had answered that he was a locksmith and nothing else. Hilde believed that her brother was also beginning to lose faith in the Nazi movement. When she complained about the exorbitant deductions from her wages, or her mother grumbled about the rise in prices, he did not defend the Government as in the old days. All this must have made Hilde become less careful.

I am very surprised. Felix, the Troop leader!

I remain to arrange the technical details for the next paper, which I take over as usual. Teichert promises to attend to the leading article.

It is late when I leave the house. Our street seems deserted. The infrequent gas-lamps cast a dim light on the few solitary humped one- and two-storey cottages. They've stood here for more than a century. The moss-covered, weather-beaten tiled roofs seem about to slip down from the walls.

The dull, tireless hum of the machines in the Power Works.

. . . .

One of the Rote Hilfe functionaries which organises aid for our imprisoned comrades gave me a few thin typewritten sheets of paper to-day. The report of a high legal officer on the Ahé trial, which sentenced Richard Hüttig to death. This report is to be passed on to the foreign Press.

" With remarkable skill Richard Hüttig succeeded in revealing the truth, although he was quite aware what awaited him for doing so. He asked for private proceedings in order to be able to mention the true facts in his evidence. He described the mistreatment meted out to him and his comrades during the cross-examination, which was conducted as follows:

"Hüttig and one of the other accused sat in front of the presiding police commissioner.

"The latter first asked Hüttig: 'Did you do any shooting?'

"Hüttig: 'No.'

"Then the other accused, including the eighteen-year-old Herbert Carius, were brutally flogged by the guards with *sjamboks*[101] in Hüttig's and the commissioner's presence.

"The commissioner again put the question: 'Did Hüttig do the shooting?'

"Answer: 'Yes.'

"Then Hüttig was asked: 'Did you do the shooting?'

"Hüttig: 'No!'

"Commissioner, to other accused: 'Is Hüttig lying?'

"Answer: 'Yes.'

"Commissioner: 'Take the whip and hit him for telling barefaced lies.'

"Hüttig emphasised that the accused cross-examined in this way always repudiated their evidence when it came to this point, and refused to hit him. It was only after Voss and Drescher had been murdered and the floggings had been continued for weeks on end that the police succeeded in obtaining the incriminating evidence they desired. Hüttig further told the court how the S.A. men thrashed the people in the Columbiahaus. The prisoner lay on the ground, usually incapable of moving. Two S.A. men stood on each side and flogged his back with the *sjamboks* so that the blows formed a V-shaped weal. Voss, who refused to incriminate the others, was literally flogged to death. He died about an hour after one of these cross-examinations.

"'When I had been beaten half dead, I tore my shirt

off and called out to the S.A. team, " Here, shoot me dead, but leave my comrades alone ! "

" ' The S.A. men had been so impressed by this that they relaxed the tortures a little,' Hüttig told the court.

" He then added that as a result of his experiences in the Columbiahaus he was determined to remain a Communist until the end of his life.

" The Public Prosecutor's only remark to Hüttig's shattering collection of evidence was that it was possibly true that the accused were not treated too gently ! "

Paul Voss. Flogged to death—because he would not incriminate Hüttig. " Baker Voss," we had always called him. He had shown me the scars from the S.A. stabs in 1932, after he came out of the hospital. He had always wanted to join my group on Sundays, help us with the propaganda for our paper. " You've got such a loud voice, Jan," he used to say; " one can hear you two blocks off. You can easily take one more along." His broad, pale face with the long black hair rises up quite clearly in front of me. How he used to swing his arms when he walked. He walked slightly bent, the legs a bit knock-kneed. This came from the long hours at the baking-trough. Baker Voss—Richard Hüttig. We're not all Dimitroffs. We can't all speak like him. But thousands of unknown Dimitroffs are fighting all over Germany.

They want to get the reports into the foreign papers. Perhaps Richard Hüttig can still be saved !

I walk through the streets for hours, the same thought revolving in my brain. Exhausted, with an aching head, I return to our street, when I suddenly realise that a man has been walking behind me the last two streets. He turns into our street with me. I stand in a dark doorway for a second, then peep out. The man passes on, disappears over the way behind the bend in the street. Must have been a chance late-comer. It's already half past one in the morning.

I undress quietly, bury my head in the pillows.

. . . . . .

I jump up in bed. Someone is knocking at the door of my room. There it is again ! I have a buzzing feeling in my head. It aches so. My pyjama jacket sticks wetly to my back. I press my hands to my temples, force myself to wake—stand up. The alarm clock shows it is only four o'clock—and knocking ! House search—police ! I am paralysed with fright. My hands tremble; I can't hold them still. I've still got the report here—the report ! Anything else ? No. The report is well hidden ! I go slowly to the door, open it. My landlady is standing in the corridor outside. She has pulled a dressing-gown on over her nightgown; the plait of thin, white hair hangs over her shoulder.

" For the dear Lord's sake, Herr Petersen, what's wrong ? You've been shouting so loudly ! " she says worriedly.

" With me ? Nothing. I'm sorry I disturbed you ! " I force myself to say.

The old woman goes back to her room, shaking her head. But I stand staring out of the window.

The street is veiled in a dim greyness.

This has been going on for weeks. At night, in my sleep, the Browns chase me; during the day I listen to each step on the stairs, to every ring of the bell. My nerves. I must relax for a while soon. What had I been shouting about ? I don't remember very clearly; must have been something about Baker Voss. Does the landlady often hear my shouting during these nightmares ? I might even betray myself to her by this.

I stare at the rumpled sheets, at the eiderdown on the floor, for a long time. I shiver; my teeth chatter; the jacket sticks clammily to my body.

. . . .

X, the S.A. reserve man, reported to Ernst Schwiebus two days ago. At his job, in the perfumery. X, who had told me about Kurgel's torture in the Maikowski Barracks. (Kurgel was only arrested by the Thirty-threes because they wanted to know where Franz Zander was. Franz is dead—but Kurgel is still in the Oranienburg Concentration Camp.)

X is now sitting in front of me, drawing at his cigarette,

without saying a word. I don't urge him, yet the thought comes: He used to belong to one of our mass organisations, has remained the same, has known me for years, and yet finds it so difficult to unburden himself.

" Altogether a hundred and twenty S.A. men have been arrested from the Charlottenburg Storms. For grumbling and lack of discipline. They are in the Charlottenburg police barracks, in the Königin Elizabethstrasse. They are treated as ' privileged prisoners ' ! Are allowed to talk to each other, play cards, smoke. But they get their heads screwed on for them all right a couple of hours in the day. Have to exercise in the yard."

" Hundred and twenty. Are you sure ? "

" Yes ! I even heard from a few what for."

X extinguishes his cigarette-end.

" One of the ' old guard.' Had taken an active part in founding his Storm. The Storm had found work for him. He had been unemployed for years. At the end of the second week he kicked up a row in his factory—one only earned a dog's wage. And the slavery was worse than ever ! "

(Teichert had told me about a similar incident at his factory, too.)

" And another one. It was the other way round with him. He had a good job; joined the S.A. in March 1933 because he didn't want to lose it. The continual marches got on his nerves. His girl left him because he never had any time for her Sundays. He just didn't turn up any more. Got two doses of eight-days' arrest for that. Alexanderplatz, police headquarters. Then he shirked duty again. They're supposed to be treating him as one of the ' March converts ' in the police barracks now."

X crosses his legs; his fingers tap at his heavy trench-boot.

" But they arrested the majority because they were conducting propaganda for the second revolution."

" We've heard about that. Do you know any details ? "

" Only what they say among themselves: ' The S.A. snatched the chestnuts out of the fire all right but we've been deceived. The bosses have our Socialism; they've climbed into all the soft jobs on our backs, that's all they've changed in Germany,' and such talk."

He takes a piece of paper from the table, tears it into narrow slips.

" Did you have a share in that ? "

" Perhaps. I don't know anything about it," I answer noncommittally.

X twists the strip of paper about in his hand. Keeps his gaze fixed on it.

" Hm ! Well, yes. I heard the following tale too. One of the men they afterwards arrested came into the Storm premises with a cyclostyled paper in his hand. ' The Red S.A. Man.' Someone had stuck it into his letter-box. He read a few extracts. An article on the ' leaders' ' swell way of living. Names were mentioned. The Reds had also said a number of good things in the old days too, he had remarked. ' But that was not their reason for suppressing the Communists. Oh, no, not because of that ! ' "

(Of course I know the paper. It is published by S.A. men who already sympathise with us.)

He is silent for a long time.

" Do you know Director Thomas ? " is his sudden question.

" No. Why ? "

" His case caused a lot of excitement in the S.A. A few of the ' old guard ' are in the police barracks because of that too ! " He plays with the paper again. What a time it takes until he says anything !

" Director Thomas was a Nazi commissioner. Appointed on the Berlin Transport Co. He disappeared suddenly. A few days later the papers printed the announcement that Director Thomas had been drowned in the Havel. It soon came out that he had inserted the notice in the papers himself. The police arrested him. In a sea-port. He had the benevolent funds of the Berlin Transport Co. on him; only a couple of hundred thousand marks. . . ."

" And the S.A. men, why were they arrested ? "

" They were tram conductors. A notice appeared in their plant station that Director Thomas had died, the funeral was on such and such a date, but none of the workers were allowed to go. And of course this surprised them. The Nazi bosses usually have such swell funerals...."

"Well! Carry on."

"It's coming. The embezzlement tale soon got round. The S.A. talked about it at work; they even went to their Nazi superiors and asked for an explanation. They considered it their duty, as old S.A. men—— And then they had their mouths closed. ' Rotten grumblers '; off with them to the police barracks..."

X's opinion was that it was these arrests which had been the cause of making the incidents the topic of conversation among the S.A. There were whole groups which were dissatisfied, and could only be held together under severe compulsion. The Nazi leaders knew that too.

I asked X whether he wouldn't try and talk to these opposition S.A. men about our ideas now and again. It is our job to make the most of this dissatisfaction. We must direct it along our channels. He should at least tell us the names of the S.A. grumblers. We would send them papers, might even try to get into touch with them ourselves later on. X refused. It was too risky for him; he had a family to consider. He would be sure to hear more details and would then pass them on. But we could not expect more from him. I told him how important these reports about the feeling among the S.A. were for us. (Preuss had also told me that there were S.A. prisoners in the Brandenburg Concentration Camp and in the field police barracks in General Papestrasse. Comrades from other districts report the same.)

X is our group's contact with the S.A. This was the first time that we heard details about the disintegration among the Charlottenburg S.A. The comrade in charge of our district committee told me that they also had other connections with the Charlottenburg S.A.

We must induce X to speak more openly with disillusioned S.A. men in the future, and see that he later introduces them to us.

. . . .

Frau Zander closed the door of her flat. Her neighbour was standing in her doorway. She went up to the old woman, laid her arm on her shoulder.

"Now, now! You're surely not wanting to go down, when you've only been up for a few days? You've still got to take care of yourself, you know," she said reproachfully.

She supported Frau Zander, who seemed to have shrunk since her illness. The months in bed had told on her. Her cheeks were sunken.

"You're all so kind to me—I only want to buy something," she answered.

"But Käthe can do that when she comes home. And if you need it at once I can go," the kindly neighbour protested.

Frau Zander shook her head.

"It's time I started again; must get accustomed to things again. What would Franz say if he saw me like this?"

"Franz, always Franz," thought Frau Schulze. "We've kept it from her for weeks that Franz is dead. All the tenants in the house. But what'll happen when the old woman gets to know things in the end?"

"You were the last one to see him. What did Franz say? When did he want to come again?" Frau Zander asked.

"He said he'd be back soon," she answered hesitatingly. "Yes, quite soon."

"Soon, soon," Frau Zander repeated; "but it's such a long time ago."

She went to the banisters, supported herself heavily against the railing.

"But you shouldn't go out, you really shouldn't!" the neighbour repeated.

"But I want to—and I must."

The neighbour looked after her, shaking her head disapprovingly. The old woman took one step at a time, her hand slipping down from rail to rail.

There was only one other woman with a market-bag on her arm in the dairy. She was talking to the shop woman, who was cutting thin slices of cheese. As the door opened the latter quickly put the knife down and ran round the counter.

"Frau Zander, you here!" she said, astonished. "But you're getting up much too soon, really!"

She supported the old woman, pulled a chair out for her.

"Now do sit down, just rest yourself, do."

Frau Zander sat down.

"I've got to start again, you know." She was breathing heavily.

The dairy woman started cutting her cheese again; the customer went up to the old woman.

"So you're Frau Zander?" she said thoughtfully. And then pityingly: "Then Franz was your son?"

"Yes. Do you know him, my Franz?" Frau Zander asked.

"I knew him well. I often used to see him. I remember him quite well," the woman replied.

"Frau Meier! Frau Meier! Do you want anything else?" the woman interrupted from the counter. Frau Meier turned round. She wondered why the dairy woman was shouting so. The latter was standing behind the glass case in which different kinds of food were displayed, and nodding across, shaking her head, and holding her finger warningly to her mouth. But Frau Meier did not understand the signs. The dairy woman kept on nodding across, tapping her finger against her mouth.

"What's the matter?" Frau Meier asked at last. "Yes, let me have a quarter of salami, and a quarter of tongue sausage!"

She pointed to the glass case.

"You know him?" Frau Zander asked her softly.

"Yes, I knew him. He was a good sort. It's a great pity," Frau Meier said.

At that the dairy woman called out again, "Frau Meier! Frau Meier!"

The latter was beginning to get angry.

"Yes, of course that's right—that one there!" she said, vexed. The dairy woman continued making signs, but her customer did not bother herself with them any more.

"He hasn't been here for ages—and yet he wanted to

come back soon," Frau Zander confided. She smiled secretly to herself.

"Who?" asked the other woman doubtfully.

"Why, Franz, my son," answered the old woman quietly, as if she were talking to herself.

Frau Meier then walked right up to the old woman and looked her straight in the eyes. She took no notice of the dairy woman hammering away on the counter with the handle of her knife.

"Your Franz?" she said quickly. "He can't come any more. Why, we buried him six weeks ago!"

Dead silence in the shop. The dairy woman stood with her mouth open and drooping shoulders; the knife had slipped out of her hand. Frau Zander made a convulsive movement at her heart; her fingers plucked at her blouse. She sat like that for long seconds. Stiffly, with staring eyes. (In these few seconds she must have understood a lot that had happened during the last weeks; the neighbours ever ready to help, the compassionate faces of the other tenants, Käthe's nervous manner, the reason for her being so pale and sad.)

All of a sudden the old woman jumped up from her chair. Her face became distorted; she shrieked at the top of her voice. The other customer ran off to fetch help. But Frau Zander was still shrieking when they carried her out of the shop. In the yard, on the stairs. Then the whole house became quiet.

With sullen faces, with their lips pressed together, the people stood at their doors and windows.

· · · · · · · ·

I stand in front of the advertisement pillar. It is an advertisement pillar like all the others. A huge poster is pasted on the upper half. A woman is depicted; the body is formed by a cigarette. "The Berlinerin," "The big round Juno," is written in large letters underneath. And near it the bright cinema posters, *Love and Kisses, Veronika, Annemarie, the Bride of the Company.*

I read and read that. I can't keep on reading the yellow poster in the centre. I can't do that.

"PUBLIC NOTICE!

"The judicial Press service announces that Richard Hüttig, of Berlin, born on March 18th, 1908, in Bottendorf, was sentenced to death by the legal verdict of the special court of the Berlin Tribunal on February 16th, 1934. The death-sentence was executed this morning in the courtyard of the penal prison at Plötzensee.

"Berlin, June 14th, 1934."

I do not know how long I have been standing in front of the notice, but I cannot stay here any longer.

Left foot, right foot, left foot, right foot, the movement is mechanical, independent of my will. The people rush past; the traffic noises seem to come from a long way off.

I slowly return to our street.

Born March 1908—executed in Plötzensee this morning— twenty-six years old. The sun is shining brightly. Its rays are reflected in the gleaming rows of windows. Long rows of cars roll past; the traffic Schupo at the corner waves his arms; pedestrians hurry along. Everything as usual!

. . . .

I was in the city. The poster has not been pasted up anywhere there. Only here in Charlottenburg, among us. Intended to intimidate us. I go through our street in the afternoon again. They walked along with me here; we had often stood here. I stop at the Berlinerstrasse corner, look up to the blue and white street sign.

MAIKOWSKISTRASSE

This street will one day be named:

RICHARD HÜTTIGSTRASSE

Although he had not lived in our street. But he had fought here with us.

I walk on slowly.

His rough barking voice, the fair disordered hair, the thick eyebrows. They had sent the clergyman into Hüttig's cell last night. He had refused him. Had also refused to send a petition for pardon to Goering. I go back to the advertisement pillar. Draw a small slip of paper from my pocket and moisten it quickly. Stick it diagonally across the words " Public Notice." The following words are stamped on it with a child's toy printing set:

The dead also can speak to us !
Our fight goes on !
We will avenge !

. . . .

The next day. Ede brings me the news. Richard Hüttig's last wish was that his coffin should be driven through his street.

The Brown Shirts want to fulfil it. Why not? Quite a number of funeral cars drive daily through Berlin's busy streets.

But we have heard of it !

Our summons is passed from mouth to mouth to the comrades in our street. Be there !

The appointed hour approaches. In twos and threes we go to the little working-class street in which Richard Hüttig had lived. It is a quarter of an hour distant.

Ede and Emil Schmidt are walking ahead of me. The other comrades in our group are at work. They don't know anything about it. I had to argue with Heinz Preuss for some time until he agreed that he, fresh from the concentration camp, dare not be present. We walk in silence. Hate and sorrow are printed on all the faces. We all feel that Richard Hüttig is taking leave of us to-day. Almost as if he is issuing his last command to his Buildings Defence Groups and us: " Line up for the last time."

We all know that each step can bring us closer to the lurking brown police. But we are ready to face that as he was ready, his life long.

Bands of police walk up and down the narrow street. Small groups of S.A. stand at the corners. But they had not counted on us getting to know anything about the funeral. The uniforms look up to the windows of the houses with strained expressions. They are closed. But people are standing outside the houses. Women holding market-bags, a number clasping their children's hands. The men stand motionless near them. Their hands in their trouser pockets. The street is short and narrow. We are not the first ones to come along. " Pedestrians " walk up and down in scattered groups. More keep on coming from the side-streets. Ede and Emil Schmidt now cross to the other side of the street. I had told them what to do in case one of us is arrested here. The people pace the pavements in groups well separated from each other. Their caps pulled down over their faces, their hands tucked in the ragged clothes. " Pedestrians." Hundreds of them. We nod to each other imperceptibly, exchange silent glances. A number of comrades with whom I had lost touch are present. I know them from the " legal " days. Otto, Albert, Willi, they're all still here, all still here !

Hundreds are walking up and down—yet it is dead quiet in the street. Ominously quiet. Two boys roll a hoop along the asphalt. They call to each other in shrill young voices. A brewery's man throws barrels of beer on to the straw sacks on the pavement. The thud resounds each time.

The two broad-shouldered men ? Gestapo agents ! Light hats, perfect summer suits; everyone here recognises them at a glance ! The younger one has a short beard. The other one clean-shaven. The bloated face, the bull neck—a regular thug's face. They are also pacing up and down. Glance sharply at the faces as they pass. On the right, the cobbler ! His shop door is wide open. He has moved " his work nearer the light." Scrapes assiduously at a boot badly in need of repair. The fruiterer ! He has suddenly discovered that his fruit-baskets, his display windows, require " touching up." There is continual movement in the street. For all that, it seems to me that time is standing still. As if we are all holding our breaths. My nerves are on edge. The minutes drag like hours. Now! To the left, at the end of the street, uniforms appear! Blue police uniforms, with a few brown ones among them. The hearse. Two S.A. men hold the horses' reins. The crowds on the pavement seem to turn to stone. All heads are turned towards the road. The people stand closely packed together in the gutter. They come out of the doors, join the others. All of a sudden the windows overlooking the street fly open, as if an alarm bell had warned the tenants.

In front, on the left, they are raising their caps. The movement ripples along the rows. Silence. Breathless silence. The horses' hoofs clatter. The hearse—the uniforms—approach slowly. Behind me a woman sobs loudly. Now the hearse is at our level. My eyes widen. I swallow hard. And then a bunch of red flowers flies through the air, rebounds against the hearse, falls on the asphalt. I jerk my head round. From the windows above us—there, another one!

"You've died for us, Comrade Hüttig! We'll avenge you!" a woman cries shrilly from another window. We are all of a sudden no longer here as so many individuals. We have in an instant become one body, one mouth. Hundreds of voices cry as one voice:

"Revenge! Revenge! Red Front!"

The S.A. pull at the horses' reins. The hearse stops with a jerk, stands deserted in the middle of the road. The uniforms run towards the pavements. They lash out at the crowd, knock people down on to the ground.

THE END

NOTES

NOTES

1. Stahlhelm: reactionary ex-servicemen's organisation.
2. S.A. (Sturmabteilung—storming detachment): Para-military organisation of the National-Socialist Party which paved the way for the Hitler Government by means of terror.
3. Nazi: Abbreviation for National-Socialist.
4. Schupo: Abbreviation for Schutzpolizei. Expression equivalent to Bobby.
5. Social-Democrat: Term applied to Socialists organised in the German Sozialdemokratische Partei affiliated to the Second International.
6. Karl Liebknecht: Son of Wilhelm Liebknecht, pre-war Social-Democratic member of the Reichstag. Karl Liebknecht was the leader of Left Wing of the German Social-Democratic Party before the war. Voted *against* the war credits when the war broke out. During the war he rallied the revolutionary opposition and founded the Spartakusbund (Spartacus League), the forerunner of the German Communist Party. Organised a huge anti-war demonstration in the centre of Berlin in 1916 and openly spoke against the war at the meeting. He was arrested as a result and sentenced to a term of penal servitude, even though a member of the Reichstag, and only released when the Revolution broke out in 1918. Under his leadership the Spartacus League attempted to retain and expand the revolutionary achievements. The Ebert-Scheidemann Government (Soc.-Dem.) suppressed the Spartacus rebellion with the aid of reactionary troops in January 1919. Karl Liebknecht was arrested and later murdered, on January 15th, 1919, by reactionary officers.
7. Bülowplatz: A square in the centre of Berlin. The Karl Liebknecht House, the offices of the Central Committee of the German Communist Party, are in the Bülowplatz. The Karl Liebknecht House was renamed the Horst Wessel House after Hitler seized power.
8. Braunhemd: Brown shirt. The brown shirt is part of the S.A. uniform. The Fascist leaders use the word as a title of honour for their terrorist groups.
9. "Internationale": Revolutionary marching song of the international workers.
10. *Smash the Reds up,*
    Clear the streets for the marching S.A.
    Provocative song of the National-Socialist terrorist groups
11. Three arrows: Socialist badge.
12. Stormtroop: S.A. division.
13 and 14. Text from the songs sung by Spartacus fighters in January 1919:
    In January at midnight, a Spartacist stood at his post. . . .
    . . . *and the artillery booms thunderingly, Spartacus has but infantry.* . . .
15–18. Text from the Russian pilots' songs, very popular among the German workers.
    . . . *we circle watchful over the Soviet State, the first Red Air Army in the world.* . . .
16. ". . . *and higher, and higher, and higher, we rise despite hate and scorn.* . . ."
17. ". . . *and every propeller sings songfully* . . ."

18. "... we're guarding the Soviet union ..."
19. Revolutionary workers' slogan opposed to the S.A.: "The S.A. have golden braid, and the people empty bellies."
20. Popular workers' song: "Brother to the Sun, to Liberty."
21. Thälmann: Leader of the German Communist Party. Arrested in Berlin in March 1933 by the National-Socialists. Still in prison to-day, without ever having being tried or any verdict having been passed. The trial has often been announced by the Goebbels Propaganda Ministry, but has never taken place.
22. Schröder: Leading German banker who had already been financing the Hitler movement before Hitler came to power.
23. *Angriff*: Berlin National-Socialist newspaper founded by Goebbels.
24. von Papen: Reichs Chancellor before Hitler. Very much disliked by the National-Socialists, yet arranged for Hitler to take over office after negotiations with the latter to this effect. Hitler promised him the Vice-Chancellorship for his pains, but he was later passed on to an unimportant post.
25. Aschinger: Popular restaurant with many branches.
26. Reichswehr: Official army of the German Reich.
27. *Clear accounts with the oppressor,*
Army of slaves awake.
27 and 28. Text from the "Internationale" (see 9).
28. *Fight for human rights.*
29. Rote Hilfe: International non-party organisation for aiding political prisoners and their dependants.
30. Internationale Arbeiter Hilfe: I.A.H. International non-party organisation for aiding political prisoners and their dependants. Organises political solidarity among the workers.
31 and 32. Braunschweig and Altona: The National-Socialist terrorist organisations, the S.A. and S.S., marched on the workers' districts in both towns on one occasion and attempted to "conquer" them. They used their pistols, and knocked the defenceless workers down with their steel bludgeons. The workers offered resistance, a veritable fight in the streets developing, the result being that the Fascists had to flee. These encounters occurred long before Hitler came to power. After the Nazi Government was formed the National-Socialists revenged themselves with great brutality for their one-time defeat. The workers who had taken part in the encounters were arrested, sentenced to death, and executed. Even workers who had taken no part in the struggle, but were known to be Communist functionaries, suffered the same fate. In this connection Edgar Andre, the plucky leader of the Hamburg Communists, met his death on the block, although he had taken no part in the Altona encounters. Edgar Andre was executed five years after these conflicts took place, but the Nazi court simply construed "intellectual connections."
33 and 34. See 6 and 41.
35. 1923: Inflation and famine resulting in revolutionary turbulence throughout Germany. Revolutionary barricade fights in Hamburg.
36. Text from the Horst Wessel song. Is to-day the official German National Anthem. See 37.
Clear the streets for the brown battalions,
Clear the streets for the storm detachment man.

37. Horst Wessel: The son of a lower middle-class family completely unsuccessful in all branches of practical life. Attended the university but did not finish his studies. Then tried all kinds of occupations, never staying long at one, finally living with a prostitute who kept him. The degenerate student considered his unsettled life very " revolutionary " and " anti-bourgeois." He joined the S.A., the Nat.-Soc. terrorist organisation, long before Hitler seized power. The Landsknecht *milieu* of the S.A., made up of the romanticism of the nocturnal military marches, and hazy national and social ideals, combined with the brawling fights at political meetings, was a fitting complement to Horst Wessel's irregular mode of life. He was promoted to the position of S.A. Stormleader, but did not relinquish his relations with the prostitute. This girl naturally had relations with other men as well. Horst Wessel was shot while quarrelling with one of these other men. Dr. Goebbels, to-day the Reichs Propaganda Minister, but at that time only the district leader of the Berlin Nazis, used Horst Wessel's death as an opportunity for gigantic propaganda. He represented Horst Wessel as being the victim of a " Communist murder," declaring him to be " a hero and martyr of National Germany," describing him as the " blood sacrifice of the movement." This propaganda was repeated year after year, with a never-varying sameness. The Horst Wessel song became the National-Socialist song; the text was supposed to have been written by the shot Stormleader. After Hitler came to power the Horst Wessel song was declared to be the new National Anthem.

38. Reichstag: Originally Parliament of the people's representatives democratically elected by popular vote. Composed of Nazis only after Hitler seized power, and thus degraded to the status of a sham Parliament.

39. Deutsch Nationale Partei: German National Party. Reactionary Junker Party with monarchist aims.

40. Hugenberg: Leader of the Deutsch Nationale Partei. He assisted Hitler in becoming Chancellor, was made Reichsminister in Hitler's Cabinet for doing so, but soon replaced by a National-Socialist. His party dissolved.

41. In January 1919 the lie that the Spartacus League had shot fifty imprisoned detectives was propagated by the Government and reactionary troops in order to defame the fighting revolutionary workers.

42. Volkswehren: People's Forces, formed by the Government in 1919 to oppose the Spartacus League. The name was misleading, as the forces were composed of enemies of the people.

43. *Die Rote Fahne*: *The Red Flag.* Official organ of the German Communist Party. Many thousand copies are still illegally published and distributed in Germany to-day.

44. R.F.B.: Abbreviation for Rote Frontkämpfer Bund—Red ex-servicemen's League. Revolutionary workers' mass military organisation. Most effective counterweight to the S.A. Prohibited in 1929 by Severing, the Innenminister of the Weimar Republic.

45. Volksgenossen: Comrades of the People. Demagogic form of address adopted by the Nazi leaders toward the people.

46. " *Margarine is getting dearer, and butter more so; People, take to arms.*"

47. Gleichschaltung: Compulsory placing in line of all the German associations and societies with the National-Socialist organisations.

48. " Little bird, eat or die." A German expression meaning that there is no alternative.

49. " The Blessings and Benefits of Employment."

50. "... We are the Thirty-threes...." Text from the song of the S.A. Storm 33.
51. "... Comrades ... who have been shot. ..." Text from the Horst Wessel song. See 36, 37.
52.   Here fell on January 30th, 1933,
          On the day of the National Rising,
        The Stormleader of the S.A. Storm 33,
          HANS EBERHARD MAIKOWSKI
             He fell for Germany.
53. Auslandsdeutschen: Association for Germans Living Abroad. Compulsory National-Socialist organisation for all Germans living abroad. Exists in practically all countries. Starting-point for National-Socialist propaganda in the respective host countries. At the same time a breeding-ground for the National-Socialist Secret Service and the Gestapo. The latter spies on the political emigrants. See 56.
54. Hitlerjugend: Compulsory organisation to which the German youth must belong.
55. Jungvolk: Compulsory children's organisation.
56. Gestapo. Abbreviation for Geheime Staatspolizei, Secret State Police Organisation responsible for the persecution of the anti-Fascists. Responsible for the torture and murders in the concentration camps, prisons, and penitentiaries.
57. Arbeitsbeschaffung: Providing Employment. See 58.
58. Arbeitsdienst: Work Service. Unpaid compulsory work for young men and women up to the age of twenty-five. It aims at the artificial reduction of unemployment statistics.
59. S.A.J.: Sozialistische Arbeiter Jugend. Socialist Working Youth. Youth section of the German Social-Democrat Party corresponding to the Labour League of Youth.
60. Türkisches Zelt: Turkish Tent. Café where the Charlottenburg revolutionary workers held their meetings.
61.   *We do not want to be a Nation with Inferior Rights.*
       For Honour and Liberty! Vote Yes on November 12th!
          The wounded Ex-servicemen vote Yes!
62. Every German a Rotter, who does not demand what an Englishman offers him.
Vote Yes!
63. With Hitler for the Peace of the World!
64. The Fatherland's gratitude.
65. On the field of honour. ...
66.   *Never again will we bear arms;*
      Let the bosses fight their own quarrels out.
67. Rosa Luxemburg: Helped to found the Spartacus League; Karl Liebknecht's closest political comrade (see 6). She was arrested with Karl Liebknecht and murdered with him on January 15th, 1919. The most prominent woman leader of the revolutionary workers' movement in Germany.
68. Beware! Seifahrt, who murders workers, lives here now!
69. Murderous " red " attack.
70. Communist murderers.

OUR STREET   285

71. Storm of Honour, the " old guard " Storm. "Alter Kämpfer ": old fighters. Title of honour for members of the National-Social Party who joined *before* Hitler came to power.

72. By touching the Maikowski blood flag.

73. The swastika flag carried during Hitler's *Putsch* attempt in Munich on November 9th, 1923. On the previous evening Hitler had declared in the Hofbraue Haus, Munich, " To-morrow either sees the victory of the National Revolution or my death ! " The Reichswehr shot at the Putschists the next day, killing sixteen people. Hitler immediately fled in a car.

74. *Volksempfängern*: People's sets.

75. Winterhilfswerk: Winter Help organised by the Nationalsozialistische Volkswohlfahrt, (N.S.V.) National-Socialist People's Welfare.

76. *Pflichtgroschen*: Duty coppers.

77. *Pfundspenden*: Pound contributions. The small shopkeepers had to contribute goods by weight for the Winterhilfe.

78. Eintopfgericht: One-course meal, all parts of which have to be served in one pot, one Sunday a month, by law enforced.

79.   *When on a Sunday morning the Reichskanzler speaks,*
    One-course meal, one-course meal, cabbage,
    And fat Goering pulls a wry face,
    One-course meal, one-course meal, cabbage.

80. Arbeitsfront: Compulsory State union. Suppresses discontent among the workers and aims at getting them to collaborate with the employers.

81.   *Come, Herr Hitler, and be our guest,*
    And fulfil the half
    Of what you promised us.

82. Law " Zum Schutz von Volk und Staat ": For the Protection of the State and the People. Demagogic wording of a law passed the day after the Reichstag fire, February 28th, 1933, which annulled all democratic rights as well as the liberty of the individual, permitting boundless Nazi terror in their place.

83. The Bavarian Soviet Republic was declared on April 7th, 1919, in Munich, and a Red Army was formed with the aim of guarding the revolutionary achievements of 1918. The Social-Democrat Reichswehr Minister, Noske, had already rallied Fascist troops in North Germany in order to suppress the revolution in Bavaria. The Bavarian Soviet Government was composed of Left-Wing Socialists and anarchists. The anarchist writer Erich Mühsam was also a member. The Communists had at first refrained from participating in this vague Soviet Government, only later taking over leadership in the fight against the advancing white army. They were unable to prevent Munich being defeated by the whites and the heroic leader of the Munich Communists, Eugen Leviné, being sentenced to death and shot by a court martial of the Fascist troops.

84. The white troops advancing on Munich shot all the " red " soldiers they captured. Twelve Fascists who had been preparing a Fascist *Putsch* were arrested in Munich. They were all members of the reactionary " Thule-Association." These Fascists were shot on April 30th, 1919, in response to the continual shooting of " red " soldiers. But this had been a spontaneous gesture on the part of a single Red Army division and was not instructed by any responsible quarter. Apart from this, Erich Mühsam had been captured by the white troops long before the hostages were shot, viz. on April 13th,

286 OUR STREET

1919. He was later sentenced to five years' penal servitude for participating in the Munich Soviet Republic. Erich Mühsam was murdered in 1934, in a Concentration camp. The Nazis, of course, maintained that he had hanged himself.

85. *Völkischer Beobachter*: Official National-Socialist organ.

86. Landhilfe: Helping on the Land. Conditions similar to Arbeitsdienst. See 58.

87. Ernst Röhm: Founder, organiser, and Chief of Staff of the S.A. (See 2.) Hitler ordered him and many other S.A. leaders to be shot on June 30th, 1934. He had also been Reichsminister.

88. Heinrich Himmler: Director of the Geheime Staatspolizei. See 56.

89. Fascist military associations, partly supported by the Reichswehr and its generals, began the so-called Kapp Putsch to restore the monarchy. The Fascists occupied the Berlin government buildings and prepared to seize power all over Germany. The Social-Democrat Ebert-Noske Government fled to the South of Germany. The German workers declared a General Strike against the Fascist Putschists and spontaneously conducted an armed struggle against the Fascists in all parts of Germany. In the Ruhr district, Germany's largest industrial area, the workers formed a Red Army within a few days. The Red Army on the Ruhr chased the Fascists off the Rhenish Westphalian industrial area, although the regular troops and police forces had joined the Putschists. The Kapp Putsch failed. The workers had saved the Weimar Republic. But the revolutionary fighters on the Ruhr would not lay down their arms immediately after the victory. They stipulated that the Social-Democrat Ebert-Noske Government they had saved should first fulfil their demands: viz. the final dissolution of the Fascist military organisations, severe punishment for the Putschist generals, and the establishment and recognition of the revolutionary achievements that they had restored with such heroic sacrifice. The Social-Democrat Minister, Severing, ordered the Red Army on the Ruhr to lay down arms at once, and during the negotiations promised to fulfil their demands—and then had the army and the recently dispersed Fascist military organisations march against the workers. The Red Army on the Ruhr, deluded by the negotiations and promises, was already partially disbanded. The white troops took dreadful revenge, mass shooting and torture becoming the order of the day. The Red Army on the Ruhr was defeated by treachery and superior forces. The fight on the Ruhr was the greatest and most heroic armed rising in the history of the German workers.

90. See 35.

91. Horst Wessel song. The text is supposed to have been written by Horst Wessel. See 36, 37.

92. Armed revolt of the revolutionary Austrian workers against Austrian Fascism, February 1934.

93. Heimwehr: Home Forces. Reactionary Austrian military organisation.

94. Volksgemeinschaft: People's Community. Demagogic phrase used by the National-Socialist leaders to describe a Community of United Germans, intended to camouflage the social differences.

95. *Rassenforscher*: Racial investigator (ethnologist).

96. Luftschutzbund: Anti-Aircraft Association.

97. Pioneer books: Fiction and educational books for the children's (Pioneer) organisations attached to the revolutionary workers' movement in Germany.

98. Politische Polizei: Political police.
99. Geheime Staatspolizei: Gestapo: Secret State police. See 56.
100. John Scheer: Became the leader of the *illegal* German Communist Party after Thälmann was arrested. He was caught while engaged on illegal political activities, and mercilessly tortured to make him divulge organisational secrets. He remained firm, suffering terribly yet not betraying a thing. Murdered with three other prominent leaders of the Party in 1934.
101. *Sjamboks*: whips made of rhinoceros hide.